THE EARTH, ITS WONDERS, ITS SECRETS

SECRETS OF THE SEA

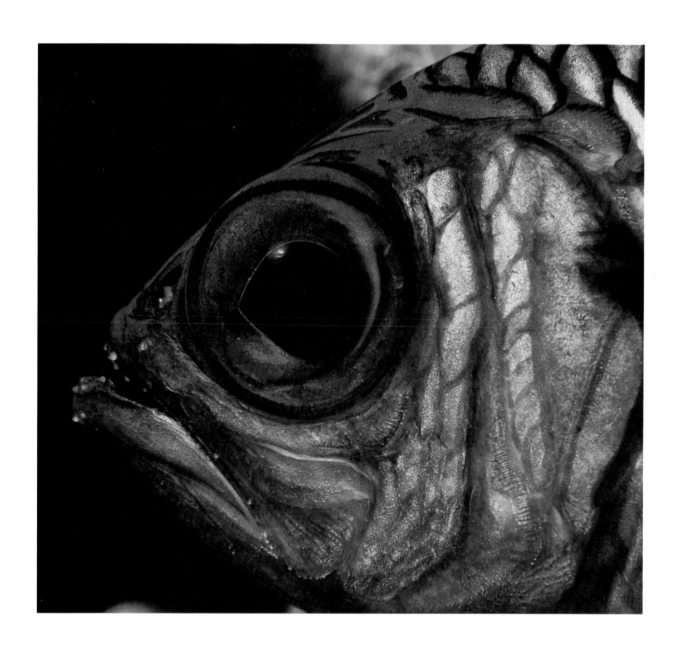

PUBLISHED BY

THE READER'S DIGEST ASSOCIATION LIMITED

LONDON NEW YORK MONTREAL SYDNEY CAPE TOWN

SECRETS OF THE SEA
Edited and designed by Toucan Books Limited
with Bradbury and Williams
Written by Linda Gamlin

Printing and binding: Printer Industria Gráfica S.A., Barcelona
Separations: David Bruce Graphics Limited, London, England
Paper: Perigord-Condat, France

ISBN 0 276 42167 1

FRONT COVER *A coral polyp releases its eggs into the sea. Inset: A
clownfish living in the shelter of a sea anemone.*

BACK COVER *Sunlight streams through the waters of a coral reef. The
reef provides a haven for a rich variety of plant and animal-life.*

PAGE 3 *Large eyes equip the soldierfish for night-time feeding. There are
about 70 species of soldierfish, also known as squirrelfish, living in the
world's coral reefs.*

Contents

MYSTERIES OF THE DEEP

Owing to the immensity of the sea, the elusiveness of its inhabitants and the difficulties of exploration, much about life in the deep remains a mystery. Modern exploration techniques, however, are gradually revealing its secrets.

Today there are no longer any blank spaces left on the maps of the continents. The voids of human knowledge have been meticulously filled in, with every corner of the planet studied, charted and explored. The innate human longing to find untrodden ways, to feel the exhilaration and fear of entering true wilderness, can no longer be satisfied on land.

Only the sea retains its essential mystery. Much of it is still a defiantly unknown realm. The immense pressure that is generated by the weight of the water excludes human beings, unless they are specially equipped for the conditions, from all but the surface and top few yards of the oceans. Below that, in the twilight depths that plunge eventually into an absolute darkness, we can descend only in specially armoured submersibles designed to withstand the pressure. While this advanced technology offers unprecedented access to the 'abyssal zone' – the ocean's farthest depths – a manned submersible

DEEP SECRETS *Manned submersibles (left) have revealed the bizarre life that clusters around hot-water vents in the deep ocean (below).*

JACK-IN-THE-BOX *A moray eel*
darts from its burrow, but
can retreat just as rapidly.

with its massively thick walls actually allows less direct contact with the deep-sea environment than an astronaut on a Moon walk has with the surface of the Moon.

HOT LIFE IN THE COLD DEPTHS

Nevertheless these submersibles, manned or unmanned, have made sensational discoveries about the oceanic depths. As recently as 1977 they revealed the astonishing existence of rich oases of life in the dark, depopulated abyss: dense clusters of animals whose very life depends on super-heated water jetting up from the Earth's fiery core, laden with minerals. These small, close communities of blind animals huddled around their hot fountains are all dependent for their sustenance on bacteria living in the water. The bacteria, in turn, feed on the rich mineral broth that comes from the very heart of our planet.

The discovery of such bizarre oases of life in the chilly depths underlines, once more, the sea's capacity to astonish us with its secrets. Even near the surface, animal life is often surprisingly elusive. Fish dart away at speed; moray eels and octopuses vanish like ghosts into impenetrable crevices, and sand eels withdraw into their burrows in the blinking of an eye, leaving

no sign behind them of ever having disturbed the smooth seabed. The complex dimensions of this habitat, and the superior swimming abilities of its inhabitants, their sinuous grace, stealth and speed, often leave the human explorer with little more than tantalising glimpses.

THE VANISHING GIANT

Even the largest of all fish, the whale shark, has evaded divers and scientists so skilfully that we still have no idea how many there may be worldwide. We do not know where they spend most of their time or how deep they can dive.

This harmless grey or brown spotted creature – so sluggish and such a slow swimmer that it has even been known to collide with ships – usually measures around 30 ft (9 m) from nose to tail, although some individuals have reportedly attained twice that length. Sometimes, whale sharks loom silently out of nowhere, startling divers with

HUGE BUT ELUSIVE *A diver*
is dwarfed by the colossal
body of a whale shark.

their slow-moving immensity. They come in search of food, including thousand-strong shoals of anchovies, or even tinier creatures such as surface-dwelling shrimp-like animals called krill.

Paradoxically, these, the tiniest creatures of the sea, sustain both whale sharks and the largest of the whales, including the blue whale. The whale shark and the blue whale are entirely unrelated to each other – one is a fish, the other a mammal – but evolution has shaped them in remarkably similar ways, thereby producing two filter-feeding goliaths. Both strain out the krill and other tiny nutritious morsels from huge mouthfuls of sea water.

While their feeding habits are known, the procreation of the whale shark remains an enigma. Does the female give birth to live young, in common with many other sharks? Or does she lay eggs and allow these to hatch undefended on some part of the ocean floor? Such questions will probably remain unanswered as long as the location of the whale sharks' breeding grounds are unknown.

Tracking the whale sharks to these breeding grounds has proved impossible. Indeed, even following them for a short while is difficult. Despite the slow swimming pace of the whale shark, the strongest human swimmers cannot keep up for long, and if an attempt is made to 'hitch a

pounding, as we dived, spun, twisted, surfaced for air and dived again, never letting up our antics for fear of losing the dolphins' attention.'

UNBOUNDED SPACE

This sense of the ocean's wildlife as fleeting and inaccessible is, in some ways, a uniquely human perspective, that of an outsider whose body is poorly suited to swimming. From the viewpoint of its true inhabitants, the open ocean is a perilous, unbounded space with few hiding places. This is particularly true of the well-lit upper waters, whose limpid blue tints and shimmering lattices of light are no paradise for those animals that must forage there. Predators are ever present: swift, agile and cunning.

There is safety, of a relative kind, in numbers. When a fast-moving shoal of silvery bodies swerves as one in a twisting, darting dance – a miracle of coordinated movement – the complex, ever-changing patterns of light that they reflect can confuse a predator in its pursuit. Some of the shoal may fall prey, but far more will escape. Many types of fish owe their survival to these tactics, and the small, silvery-skinned squid that inhabit the surface waters also swim in shoals for safety.

Other animals find protection in being transparent, so that their form is scarcely noticeable even at a short distance. A variety of animals survive in this way, from

OCEAN WANDERER *Green turtles seem to disappear during a crucial part of their life cycle.*

ride', by holding on to the shark's dorsal fin, the reclusive whale shark responds by power-diving for the depths, forcing the diver to let go.

SECRET WATERS

There are other large species that seemingly vanish into the baffling immensity of the oceans. A vital stage in the life cycle of the turtle, for example, is played out in secrecy in some so far undiscovered waters. The young turtles, newly hatched and at sea for the first time, make their way to floating rafts of sargassum weed, where they live as carnivores, feeding on shrimps and small jellyfish. Then the youngsters disappear and are not seen again until they have quadrupled in size and measure at least 10 in (25 cm) across.

By then they are herbivores, grazing on eelgrass meadows in shallow tropical bays. Where they live in the meantime, and how they feed, is one of nature's greatest

puzzles. Since turtles are descended from land-living, tortoise-like ancestors, and must breathe air at the surface (unlike the whale sharks), they cannot be concealing themselves in the ocean's depths. It is both remarkable and heartening to realise that there is still some part of the ocean's surface that is so rarely visited that it allows the location of these turtle nurseries to remain a secret.

With so many creatures proving elusive and unknowable, those rare moments when the giants of the sea voluntarily approach a human diver, in a spirit, it seems, of friendly curiosity, inspire awe and delight. One such diver, Martha Holmes, in her book *Sea Trek*, describes swimming with wild dolphins: 'All my senses were alert and my body was pushed to its limits, lungs straining and heart

SHOALING FOR SAFETY
Silverside fish swirl about in a dizzying swarm, as they evade a tarpon.

colourless jellyfish and comb jellies to see-through shrimps and larval fish.

When captured and photographed with perfect lighting against a dark background, these insubstantial animals are transformed into exquisite works of art, sculptures in glass of bewitching delicacy. But in a sense this is a deceptive view, for all its beauty. In the sea they are pallid and unimpressive: their survival depends on being ignored, not admired.

THE UNSEEN FORESTS

The sunny upper waters of the ocean are the most dangerous, not only because they are illuminated, but also because food is concentrated there. In its quest for food, most marine life is crowded into the top few yards. The primary source of that food is, in fact, invisible. A mass of microscopic plants make up the ocean's unseen 'forests', generating food with the help of sunlight. This food is consumed by tiny animals, scarcely large enough for the naked eye to see.

Known as plankton – the term refers to both plants (phytoplankton) and animals (zooplankton) – many of these microscopic creatures display extraordinary, intricately sculpted surfaces that larger living forms cannot rival. Yet for all their complex splendour they are generated and disposed of at profligate speed, hatched in their millions and then giving birth themselves at a frantic pace, only to be harvested within weeks, or even days, by the larger creatures of the ocean realm.

This frenetic activity (which is revealed to our eyes with the help of microscopes and regular plankton sampling) generates the food that nourishes the giant whales, the sharks, the marlin and tuna. Indeed, almost all the life of the ocean depends on the plant plankton, save only those oases in the depths whose food comes from the Earth's core.

RETREAT INTO DARKNESS

So hazardous yet so bountiful are the upper waters, that many animals venture there only by night. In the relative safety of the dark hours, small predators graze on the microscopic creatures of the plankton,

retreating into the lower twilight zones long before daybreak. The migrations performed by these predators are truly staggering. Some small crustaceans known as copepods, no larger than a speck of dust, make a round trip of more than half-a-mile (800 m) every day. Scaled up into human terms, that is equivalent to swimming over 50 miles (80 km) each day.

For many animals, their evolutionary path has taken them away from both the challenge of life in the sunlit waters and the strenuous migrations that are involved in visiting the surface by night. These dwellers in the permanent darkness of the depths rely on what falls down to them from the upper waters: the droppings and

FLOATING BY Jellyfish live among the microscopic plankton and benefit from the abundant food.

the dead, the detritus of life above. In a cold, dark, half-alive world of rare meals and little activity, animals such as the gulper eels and deep-sea anglerfish simply watch and wait.

Many are equipped with cavernous mouths that can swallow prey as large as, or even larger than, themselves. In the case of gulper eels, the elastic, boneless body attached to the jaws expands like a balloon to engulf the meal. There must be rare moments of drama – although these have never been witnessed by human eyes – when one such creature encounters another, and either could become the predator, either the prey.

This contest, in which the stakes are so high, is undoubtedly played out in slow motion because these emaciated, cold-blooded animals are geared to conserving energy at all times. A grim, slow, silent, lethargic battle must ensue, in which one loses its life, while the other obtains sufficient nourishment to sustain it for as long as six months. The evidence that such battles occur comes from fish hauled up in trawl nets: the victors of such contests have bodies that are grotesquely distended with the prey.

With access to the deep ocean restricted by the frailty of the human form and the extremely high cost of submersible exploration, much of our knowledge relies on drawing marine animals up from their habitat to inspect them at close quarters on the surface. Species such as the megamouth shark and the giant squid, both animals of colossal size, are known only from dead or dying specimens.

The maximum size of the giant squid is still hotly disputed. The largest specimen ever reliably measured was 47 ft (14 m) in length, but there is evidence to suggest that squid up to twice this size may lurk in the ocean's darkest depths. Such gigantic molluscs, outsized relations of the humble garden slug, were once thought to be entirely mythical, but the evidence for them is now incontrovertible.

That evidence consists of many fragments that fit together like a jigsaw puzzle: there are, for instance, decomposing carcases of astonishing size washed ashore in Newfoundland; giant sucker marks found on the heads of sperm whales, and huge squid beaks recovered from sperm whales' stomachs. They add up to a creature that measures at least 70 ft (21 m) in length, although much of this is accounted for by its two longest tentacles.

Many fishermen who know the waters around the Caribbean believe that the giant octopus is as real as the giant squid, but its status among scientists still remains questionable. In the Bahamas it is part of local mythology: a long-armed sea monster called Lusca seizes men and boats, dragging them down into the depths. Some of the stories about Lusca probably describe the effects of the strange blue holes of the Bahamas, underwater caves that connect up with the caverns below the land, and which suck in sea water with alarming force at times, regurgitating it at others. The suction from a blue hole can indeed swallow up a small boat.

Other Lusca stories do not fit in with this explanation. They tell of quite large crab-fishing boats being towed along by unseen creatures that have seized the crab-containing trap. From the speed at which the boat is towed, it seems that these are creatures of outstanding strength and stamina. Some claim to have seen the animal briefly, but there is still no solid evidence that it is indeed a giant octopus.

INEXPLICABLE SHAPES

The unsolved puzzles of the ocean are innumerable. Why does the larva of the pearl fish possess a whip-like dorsal fin, as long as its slender, eel-like body, and why does that fin have bizarre, leaf-like extensions growing from it?

These are unlikely to be lures for prey, since they are far larger than the fish's head and would attract the wrong size of animal. The suggestion made by some biologists that the fin helps the fish to orient towards the current seems equally implausible, since thousands of other ocean species manage to sense the currents without encumbering themselves in this way. Perhaps the fin and its attachments are there to distract predators from the fish

TRANSPARENT PLOY *The jellyfish's transparency acts as a camouflage, making it difficult to see from a distance.*

HALFWAY HOUSE *This bonnethead has a less extreme shape than other hammerhead sharks and may reveal how their bizarre skulls evolved.*

itself, the fin being shed in an emergency for a quick escape. Certainly, if the larvae of pearl fish are caught and then brought to the surface, their extraordinary fin has almost always snapped off, suggesting that the attachment is very brittle.

Far larger, but no less bizarre, are the hammerhead sharks, peculiar animals with long, plank-like heads set at right angles to the body. In one hammerhead species, the head takes up half the length of the body. Biologists are at a loss to explain this T-shaped monstrosity, although speculation abounds. The farthest tips of the head each carry a single eye, while the nostrils are located on the front edge, much farther apart than in most sharks. It seems logical to assume that widely spaced eyes or nostrils might confer some advantage on the shark. But what?

Perhaps nostrils located at a distance from each other make it easier for the shark to pin down the exact location of a scent that is wafting towards it on meandering currents. By turning its head this way and that it might be able to get a

better 'fix' on the exact direction from which the scent is coming. Since scent – especially a minute trace of blood in the water – is the vital food-finding clue for many sharks, nostrils 'on stalks' might be beneficial.

Hammerheads, like other sharks, also have organs that can detect minute electrical impulses and thus help them to find buried prey. The electrical sensors are spread out along the underside of the head, covering a far larger, flatter surface than in other sharks. From the barbed spines found embedded in their jaws, hammerheads are known to feed heavily on stingrays, fish that conceal themselves in the sediments on the ocean floor. Other circumstantial evidence comes from observation of hammerheads swimming close to the seabed, swinging their heads from side to side like metal-detectors. Are they scanning for electrical output from their prey?

This seems a plausible explanation, yet it is hard to see how the food-finding advantages of the expanded head would outweigh the extra growth required, or the complex re-arrangements of its internal structures that must have occurred over evolutionary time. And manifold disadvantages seem likely. The flattened edges of the head would be an easy target to seize and injure in a fight between a hammerhead and another species

of large, aggressive shark, such as a tiger shark or a great white.

With eyes widely separated, the hammerhead must also have an area directly ahead that is not well covered by either eye – a huge 'blind spot' where one would expect the shark to need maximum vision when swimming forwards. Perhaps science will eventually be able to explain these paradoxical creatures. The key may come from studying the smallest species of hammerhead, called the bonnethead, where the development of the head is far less extreme; it is simply flattened and rounded to give a head like a shovel. Perhaps this species is a halfway house, a relic of the evolutionary path followed by the larger hammerheads, and a clue to the advantage of their outlandish shape.

SEX IN THE SEA

'Living creatures press up against all barriers; they fill every possible niche all the world over . . . We see life persistent and intrusive – spreading everywhere, insinuating itself, adapting itself, resisting everything, defying everything, surviving everything!' This is how the early 20th-century Scottish naturalist, Sir John Arthur Thomson, described the living world.

Thomson's description is apt, but in the ocean one can find points where life

FRAGILE LIFE *The colours and rich diversity of coral reefs are vulnerable treasures, easily destroyed by human activity.*

begins to lose the battle, where the hostile physical world becomes overwhelming. This can be seen in the deepest parts of the ocean – those trenches that plunge to as much as 7 miles (11 km) below sea level – where life is scarce and unflamboyant, oppressed by the colossal pressures and intense cold.

A nadir of another kind is reached under the polar pack ice where the glacial cold and greenish gloom of perpetual winter repel all but the most resilient and stoic species. Life is almost defeated again by the excessive quantities of salt in the Dead Sea, but even here there is life of a

sort: bacteria survive, pitting their resilient outer coats against the chemical affronts of the water around them.

By contrast, some parts of the ocean are so rich in life that species swarm over one another, and riotous life insinuates itself everywhere, as Thomson observed. The ebullience of life is best seen on a coral reef, particularly on those nights when the corals spawn. Synchronised, through some mysterious sensory powers, by the phase of the moon, they release eggs and sperm into the water in fantastic, uncountable numbers.

The effect is like a blizzard in the sea, except that the 'snowflakes' float upwards, and they are pretty shades of pink or pale orange. Swarms of worms – strands of scarlet or emerald green squirming and wriggling about in their millions – appear

soon afterwards, either to spawn or to feed on the coral eggs. The nutrients squandered during spawning serve as fertiliser for the plant plankton that blooms in the next few days, attracting plankton-eaters such as minke whales, whale sharks and giant manta rays.

This abundant and flamboyant carnival of life is a testament to the bounty of the ocean. How alarming, then, to see what humankind can do to such rich environments. The coral reefs of Florida are dying, and many of those elsewhere show the deadly effects of silt from deforestation on land, chemical pollution, tourist pressure, spear-fishing, coral-collecting and changing world temperatures. The wonders and mysteries of the sea are delicate and extremely vulnerable living wonders, at risk from human activities.

THE WORLD'S SEAS AND OCEANS

1

SEA SLUG *The waters off the Maldive Islands are home to this brightly coloured sea slug.*

THE OCEANS COVER 70 PER CENT OF THE EARTH'S SURFACE. EARTH IS ALONE AMONG THE PLANETS OF THE SOLAR SYSTEM IN HAVING SURFACE WATER, AND IT WAS HERE, IN THE OCEANS, THAT LIFE BEGAN NEARLY 400 MILLION YEARS AGO. THE SEAS AND OCEANS STILL PROVIDE HABITATS FOR AN ASTONISHING RANGE OF PLANT AND ANIMAL LIFE, FROM MICROSCOPIC PHYTOPLANKTON TO HUGE BLUE WHALES, FROM ARCHAIC SURVIVORS SUCH AS THE STRANGE-LOOKING COELACANTH TO MORE FAMILIAR CREATURES SUCH AS SEALS. THE OCEANS ARE ALSO THE SETTING FOR SOME EXTRAORDINARY FEATS OF MIGRATION, INCLUDING THE FOUR-YEAR TRANSATLANTIC PASSAGE OF THE EUROPEAN EEL, DURING WHICH IT IS TRANSFORMED FROM LARVA TO ELVER.

LAVA ISLE *Seabed volcanoes formed many Pacific islands.*

THE CRADLE OF LIFE

From the surge of crashing waves to the rise and fall of tides, the constant movement of water in the oceans creates a variety of habitats for marine life. Ocean currents link distant parts of the planet and affect the climate everywhere.

The sea runs in our blood. It was from the sea that our most distant ancestors originated, almost 400 million years ago. The tissue fluid that surrounds the cells inside our bodies is a legacy of that remote past, and contains concentrations of salts in proportions that are similar to those of sea water. We might no longer be able to quench our thirst by drinking from the sea, but occasionally we hunger for salty foods to maintain that delicate balance of essential chemicals.

Meanwhile, the oceans still provide us with food, energy, minerals and medicines. They have shaped not only human life on Earth, but the life of all the planet's other plants and animals, the weather and climate, even the rocks and continents.

Humankind has grown to fear and respect the power of the oceans. They have been a source of myth and intrigue, curiosity, inspiration and terror. Stories of vengeful sea monsters, engulfing whirlpools, storms, tidal waves, sunken cities, treasure and mermaids have stirred the imagination of generations. With the aid of technology, humans have ventured

HOW THE OCEAN FLOOR WAS FORMED

SEABED VIOLENCE *Hot currents in Earth's core drive the drama of the ocean floor. Magma, a mixture of molten rocks and gases, forces its way to the surface, creating ocean ridges and volcanoes that form sea mounts.*

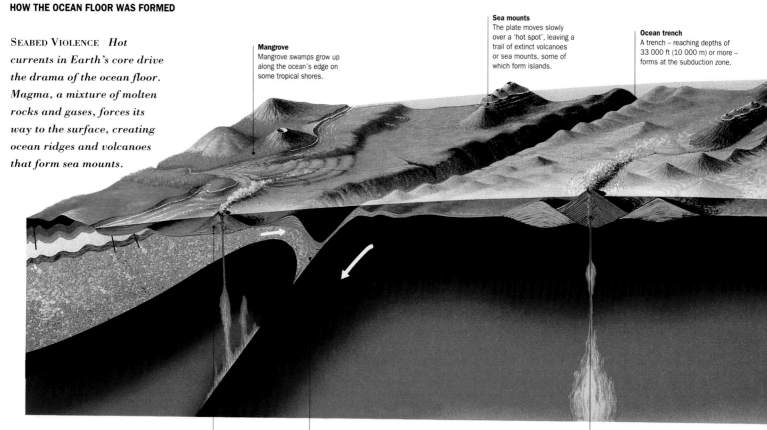

Mangrove
Mangrove swamps grow up along the ocean's edge on some tropical shores.

Sea mounts
The plate moves slowly over a 'hot spot', leaving a trail of extinct volcanoes or sea mounts, some of which form islands.

Ocean trench
A trench – reaching depths of 33 000 ft (10 000 m) or more – forms at the subduction zone.

Stratovolcano
The buckled crust around a subduction zone allows magma to force its way to the surface in highly explosive stratovolcanoes.

Subduction zone
Two plates meet, one being forced underneath the other.

Shield volcano
Molten basalt forces its way to the surface over a 'hot spot', creating a broad-based shield volcano.

HAWAIIAN ERUPTION *Steam from volcanoes and geysers formed the first oceans.*

deeper and deeper into the hidden depths to uncover the secrets of the sea. And yet, even now, while we are exploring space, much of the ocean remains an enigma.

Earth is unique among the planets of our Solar System in having surface water, an essential ingredient for the emergence of life. Our neighbouring planets are either so hot that water would boil away instantly as steam, or so cold that it would freeze as supercooled ice. But the Earth is at just the right distance from the Sun. As the seething young Earth began to cool, water was expelled from volcanic vents, hot springs and geysers. The steamy vapour condensed, falling as rain to form vast ocean sheets. Minerals from the Earth's crust dissolved in the waters, so that they became a rich broth of sodium, chloride, calcium, magnesium,

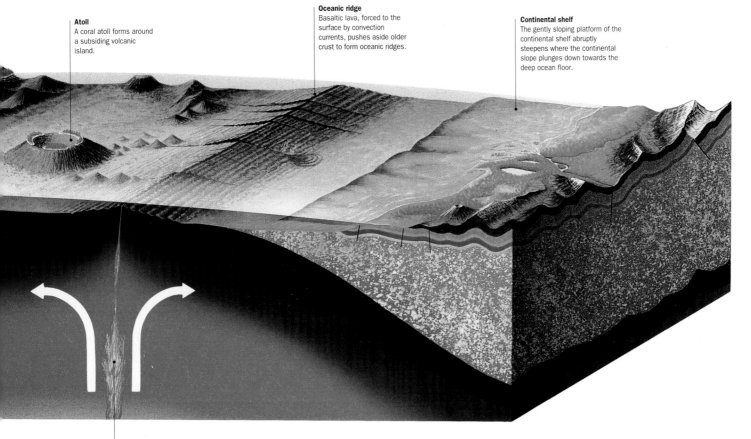

Atoll
A coral atoll forms around a subsiding volcanic island.

Oceanic ridge
Basaltic lava, forced to the surface by convection currents, pushes aside older crust to form oceanic ridges.

Continental shelf
The gently sloping platform of the continental shelf abruptly steepens where the continental slope plunges down towards the deep ocean floor.

Moving heat
Convection currents moving through the Earth's mantle rise towards the surface.

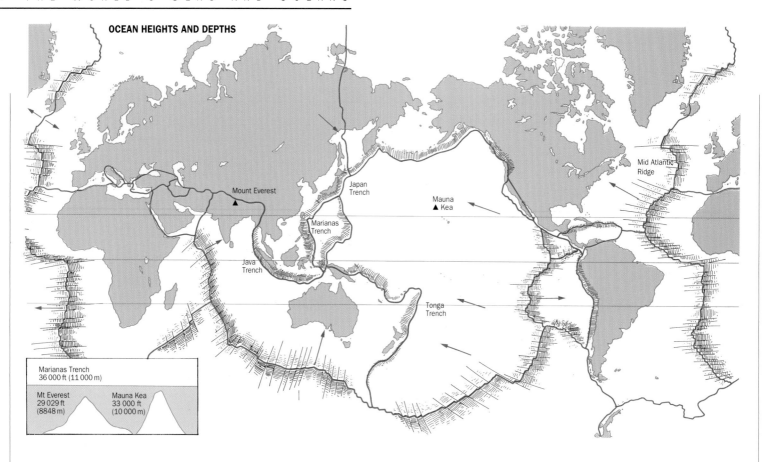

OCEAN HEIGHTS AND DEPTHS

Marianas Trench
36 000 ft (11 000 m)

Mt Everest
29 029 ft
(8848 m)

Mauna Kea
33 000 ft
(10 000 m)

RECORD BREAKERS *The Hawaiian volcano Mauna Kea rises 33 000 ft (10 000 m) from the seabed, dwarfing Mount Everest. Either would fit inside the Marianas Trench, which plummets nearly 7 miles (11 km) beneath the surface of the Pacific.*

potassium and many other substances. It was in this watery mixture of nutrients that the first forms of life took shape, over 3500 million years ago.

The true vastness of the oceans is best conveyed in terms of their volume. At least 1000 times more living space is provided by the undersea realm than by the terrestrial one. Animals live throughout this enormous depth, yet the inhabitants of the ocean's uppermost layers are entirely different from those of its abyss, as dissimilar as the wildlife of the Amazon is from that of the Antarctic.

At increasing depths from the surface, the conditions for life change. Initially the light fades. The orange and red light in the spectrum is the first to be filtered out. To divers, red objects appear black and blood looks an alarming shade of green. Deeper still, the only light is blue. The absolute limit to blue light is at about 3250 ft (1000 m)

down, below which everything is engulfed in blackness. The temperature drops to 50°C (122°F) and pressure steadily builds up to a level that the human body cannot withstand. At an average of $2^{1}/_{2}$ miles (4 km) below the surface is the seabed, coated by deep, oozing sediments. Meteoric dust, ash from volcanoes, mud from river estuaries and the skeletons of millions of minute sea animals, all find their way into the steadily accumulating debris.

THE ACTIVE OCEAN FLOOR

Scientists know that the Earth was formed some 4600 million years ago. But sediment samples that have been drilled from the depths of the sea show that none of the rock or sediment found at the bottom of the oceans is older than 200 million years or so – in other words, it is less than a twentieth of the Earth's age. This curious discrepancy is explained by the constant activity in the Earth's crust – the pushing up of fresh rock and the swallowing of old – that has recycled the seabed throughout the millennia since the Earth began.

But the seabed is not just an uninterrupted plain across the ocean basins. It is gashed with ravines and trenches, pimpled with hillocks and divided by several long, mountainous ridges. There is an almost

MOVING PLATES *The Earth's crust consists of six large tectonic plates and many smaller ones.*

continuous range of mid-ocean ridges that wind their way around the world for a distance of some 36 000 miles (58 000 km). At one end is the Reykjanes Ridge, which protrudes through the surface as Iceland. This merges into the Mid Atlantic Ridge as it snakes south and curves around Africa to meet the ridges of the Indian Ocean.

The South-East Indian Ridge curls between Australia and Antarctica to meet the East Pacific Rise, which terminates in the Gulf of California. Altogether, ridges cover about a third of the ocean floor, and rise to $2^{1}/_{2}$ miles (4 km) above the seabed. The deepest sections of the ocean are the narrow, plummeting trenches: the Marianas Trench of the Pacific descends to nearly 7 miles (11 km) below the surface.

To create such a landscape requires the work of some monstrous force. The same force is responsible for moulding the shape of the continents and the mountain ranges on land. It is provided by a ferocious heat generated in the very centre of the Earth, where the iron core blazes at unimaginable temperatures of some 5000°C (9000°F).

RESTLESS FORCES *Rising gas indicates activity on the seabed.*

hauled apart, the sea floor spreads. Molten rock gushes up in pulses through extensive fissures, spews outwards, then cools and solidifies. This is the beginning of a new oceanic ridge, which is built up by further upwelling. Deep sea trenches mark sites where the floor is engulfed once more; plates are forced together until the edge of one rides up over the rim of another. The vanquished plate is forced downwards and gradually succumbs to the furnace temperatures below, melting back into the semi-fluid rock of the mantle. Thus geological forces ensure that great tracts of rock – seemingly so permanent and stable – are melted and remade over hundreds of millions of years.

The seabed and continents are both part of the Earth's crust – a relatively thin layer of solid rock, about 20 miles (30 km) deep, that floats on a semi-molten mantle within. It is now known that the crust is divided into a series of about 12 separate slabs or plates, like giant pieces of a spherical jigsaw puzzle. Plates may be composed entirely of seabed or support continents as well. Heat and pressure differences generate currents in the semi-molten mantle that drag the plates in different directions as they jostle in slow motion for position.

Wherever the plates are laboriously

CATASTROPHE AND CREATION

Most of these movements of the seabed go unnoticed by us on land. Nevertheless, there are times when the moving plates create major disturbances. Where two plates are grating past one another, for instance, they may temporarily lock, until the pressure behind them is so great that they are jarred into motion once more, setting off a series of shock waves as they wrench free. The result may be a catastrophic earthquake, and if this occurs underwater it can trigger *tsunamis* or 'tidal waves' – vast walls

BUBBLING UNDER *Molten rock erupting from seabed fissures may bubble to the surface.*

of water with enormous power that travel one after another at speeds of up to 500 mph (800 km/h) in deep water. They rear up in shallow coastal areas to inundate the land, destroying all in their path.

Undersea volcanoes occasionally burst through the surface water in explosive plumes to create whole new islands. In 1963, the island of Surtsey, lying to the south of Iceland, erupted from a fissure in the Mid Atlantic Ridge. Other volcanic islands occur where a plate is moving over a stationary 'hot spot' – a concentrated plume of magma rising straight upwards from a point deep in the mantle. As the plate is pulled onwards, a younger volcanic island is created behind the first, until there is a curious line of them protruding from the sea – like the islands of the Hawaiian chain.

Peaks emanating from the seabed often dominate those on land in size and grandeur, for they have not been worn down by the relentless abrasion of wind and rain. The largest of all, Mauna Kea on Hawaii, measures 33 000 ft (10 000 m) from its base on the sea floor to its peak. That is about 4000 ft (1200 m) taller than Everest, yet only 40 per cent of this height is visible above sea level.

As a result of the constant activity in the Earth's mantle, the very shape and layout of the continents have undergone

LITTLE SURTSEY *An island created by a volcano in 1963.*

The Birth and Death of Seas

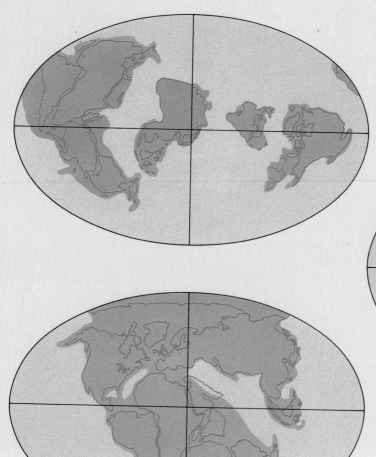

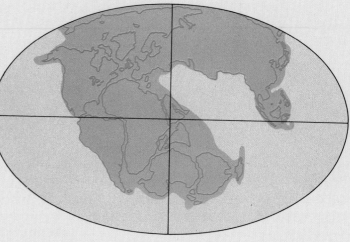

The theory of plate tectonics, which gained scientific respectability only 30 years ago, gives us a dynamic vision of our planet, in which the Earth's surface is a constantly moving jigsaw of crustal plates. As these plates slowly journey across the globe, they drag their continental passengers along with them. Between the moving continents, some oceans become crushed and obliterated, whereas others appear, or expand, as the landmasses are torn asunder.

About 200 million years ago, the world was bathed by Panthalassa, a predecessor of the Pacific Ocean. It was much larger than the ocean we know today, for Pangaea, Earth's single supercontinent, had only just split apart, and the newborn continents were still clustered together on the far side of the globe as the two great landmasses of Laurasia and Gondwanaland.

The Tethys Sea filled the breach between these two. Later, as rifts split the southern landmass of Gondwanaland apart, the Indian, Atlantic and Antarctic oceans came to be born. These comparatively young oceans are still growing at the expense of the Pacific.

Today, remnants of the seabed from the ancient Tethys Sea can be found on the very top of the Himalayas. As the Indo-Australian Plate moved inexorably northwards about 45 million years ago, it collided with the Eurasian Plate. The Tethys Ocean's floor was propelled upwards and crumpled into the dramatic folds of the Himalayas. Other parts of the Tethys are still preserved between moving continents. The western Mediterranean and the Black Sea are two remnants of this once great ocean. The Caspian Sea, a completely landlocked fragment of the ancient Tethys, became trapped when what is now India, Saudi Arabia and Iran collided with Asia.

The Caspian Sea is divided between Iran and the former Soviet Union. Stretching for 144 000 sq miles (372 900 km^2), it is the largest of all inland seas, but the demands made on it by humans have taken a great toll. Drainage and the damming of tributaries for hydroelectric power have led to its shrinkage over the past 50 years. Similarly fated by the demands of humans, the Aral Sea has been reduced in volume by two-thirds since 1960, as water from its tributaries has been diverted in order to irrigate cotton crops. Fish have disappeared, marshes, oases and forests died; and former ports now languish 50 miles (80 km) from its shore. The doomed Aral Sea may completely disappear in the next 20 years.

Most famous of all moribund seas is the Dead Sea – whose intensely salty waters are eerily devoid of the larger forms of life. A few specialised bacteria are the only creatures that thrive in such conditions. Lying between Israel and Jordan, the Dead Sea of today is all that remains of a much larger inland sea, about 190 miles (300 km) long, that once filled the whole Jordan Valley. Over the years, in this desert-like climate, sun-warmed water has evaporated, leaving its burden of salty minerals behind. Dead Sea water has a salt content of 30 per cent, ten times higher than that of normal ocean water. Fish from the River Jordan die on entering it, and the extreme saltiness gives an unusual buoyancy, so that a person can 'sit' afloat with no effort.

Although they are so salty, landlocked seas are officially classified by geographers as a type of lake. They tend to occur in regions with hot climates and at sites where incoming fresh river water has no possible outlet to the sea. Most are getting saltier, as the rate of evaporation is faster than the inflow of fresh water.

No other lake or inland sea lies farther below sea level than the Dead Sea. Its surface is 1292 ft (394 m) below normal sea level. The steep-sided basin is part of a great chasm, or rift, in the Earth's crust known as the Great Rift Valley. The rift marks a point where the African plate is moving away from the smaller Arabian plate and the Somalian subplate. In all, it stretches 4200 miles (6700 km) from Turkey to southern Africa.

After passing through Syria, Israel and Jordan, where the Dead Sea lies, it stretches on to Eilat, where the ocean has invaded and the valley is filled with the waters of the Red Sea. Between the Arabian peninsula and the Horn of Africa, the valley swings eastwards and divides into two. One half passes along the Gulf of Aden into the Indian Ocean, while the other continues through Africa, where it cradles the deep East African lakes.

A rift valley begins life when plumes of semi-molten magma push upwards and then spread in diverging currents under the Earth's crust. Tension splits the crust apart in long fissures, known as faults. Between them, a narrow wedge of land subsides into a chasm to produce a valley with cliff-like walls along the fault lines. If the sea level rises, the valley may well become flooded. As the rift continues to widen, a new sea grows.

CRYSTAL ISLANDS *These intriguing Dead Sea isles are made of salt crystals.*

The Red Sea, which floods part of the Great Rift Valley, is one of Earth's youngest oceans. Its growth continues but at a slow pace, widening by 3 ft (1 m) or so every 100 years. None the less, millions of years hence, it may rival the Atlantic. Another new ocean may arise from the Rift Valley in East Africa. Meanwhile, the aging Pacific may disappear, following the fate of countless unknown oceans in the distant history of the Earth.

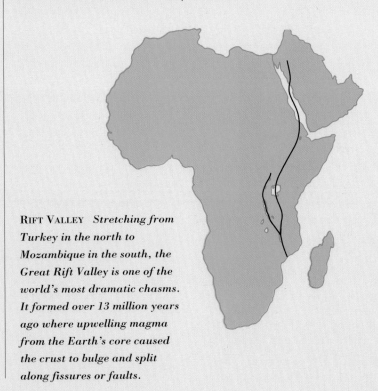

RIFT VALLEY *Stretching from Turkey in the north to Mozambique in the south, the Great Rift Valley is one of the world's most dramatic chasms. It formed over 13 million years ago where upwelling magma from the Earth's core caused the crust to bulge and split along fissures or faults.*

THE FORMING OF THE RIFT VALLEY AND INLAND SEAS

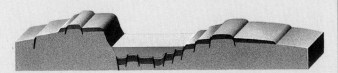

THE BEGINNINGS *As cracks form in the Earth's crust, blocks of land between them may subside or slump.*

DEVELOPMENT *The resulting valley floods, and further cracks appear causing more slippage.*

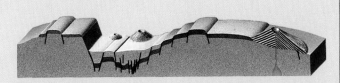

FILLING IN *In some places lava seeps up from the cracks, filling in parts of the valley.*

FOOD AND MINERALS: THE RICHES OF THE OCEANS

The oceans have supplied human populations with food for thousands of years, and fish are still the principal source of animal protein for coastal communities in Africa, Asia and the Pacific. But worldwide, the sea now provides less than 1 per cent of human food intake. Nevertheless, fish stocks are at risk from over-exploitation due to more effective fishing methods. It has been suggested that humans could exploit the abundant shrimp-like krill as a major alternative to fish, but problems arise with processing krill into a palatable food and with the high fluoride content of the catch.

The oceans are a vast storehouse

DEEP-SEA RESOURCES *An oil platform off Alaska.*

of mineral wealth. Sea water contains over 70 elements, but most of these are more available to the animals and plants of the sea than they are to humankind – despite the best efforts of modern technology. There are a few exceptions. Sea salt has been extracted from sea water for over 4000 years by solar evaporation. And offshore mining for aggregates (sand and gravel) has long been important for the construction industry. Now technological advances are allowing the extraction of offshore petroleum and gas; nearly half of the Earth's oil and gas resources lie hidden beneath the rock of the continental shelves. There are also large deposits deep below the seabed, which are currently inaccessible.

Under the right conditions, some of the rarer minerals are deposited in solid form in rocks, which makes extraction possible. Deposits of gold have been discovered on Alaskan beaches; tin in Malaysia and Indonesia; and titanium sands in India, Australia, Brazil and Sri Lanka. Silver, copper and zinc are contained in the muds of the Red Sea. In the 1960s, excitement was roused by the wealth of riches waiting to be plucked from the oceans. Finds of manganese nodules on the seabed, nodules which also contain silver, copper, nickel and cobalt, promised high rewards. Eventually, however, both

MINERAL WEALTH *Manganese nodules take millions of years to grow to this size.*

HERRING HARVEST *Fishermen from New Brunswick in Canada haul in their catch.*

businessmen and scientists had to agree that most of this fantastic, newly discovered undersea wealth could not be exploited without prohibitively expensive technology. Much of it still remains untouched.

In the future, the production of energy from the sea may become an economically viable option. Tidal energy, wave energy, and, in some regions, thermal energy, are all possibilities. The production of fresh water from sea water is another attractive proposition for densely populated, dry coastal regions. But desalination is a costly venture, and one that is unlikely ever to be practical on a large scale, except in the Middle East, in Saudi Arabia.

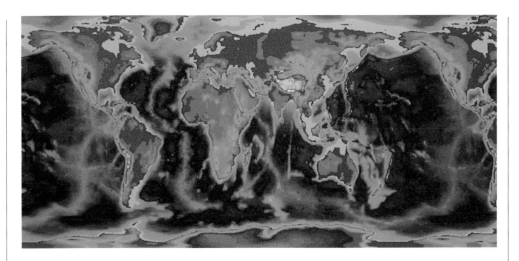

SEA VIEW *In this computer-generated map, oceanic ridges appear blue, trenches pink.*

dramatic changes. A clue to what has happened is seen in the almost jigsaw-like fit of the coastlines of Africa and South America, something that intrigued early geographers, although the obvious explanation defied belief. The suggestion, made in the 1920s by the German meteorologist, Alfred Wegener, that they had once been joined together was ridiculed for many years. It was not fully accepted until the 1960s, when a series of discoveries proved that the Earth's crust was not a solid unit, but a series of individual plates. Continental drift was at last recognised as an indisputable fact, while the revolutionary theory of plate tectonics provided an explanation for the slow, meandering journeys of the continents.

As a wealth of evidence now shows, landmasses have travelled about the globe since the very beginning. The world that is so familiar to us from maps and atlases has been in existence for about 30 million years – a relatively short time compared with the 3500 million years since the Earth's creation. Going back 500 million years, the Earth consisted of three large and separate landmasses, none of which corresponds directly to today's continents. Gradually these three were pushed together by the movements of the underlying plates, and coalesced into a single supercontinent we now call Pangaea – a Greek name meaning 'all land'. That was 250 million years ago, when a single ocean encircled the globe.

By 180 million years ago, the supercontinent had split up again. As the plates forged past one another, the landmasses were torn apart. Into the rifts that opened up between them, sea water and rivers poured in, and so new oceans were born.

OCEANS IN MOTION

Continental drift continues today. It is predicted that in the next 50 million years Australia will move north and collide with Indonesia. North and South America will drift apart, and the Americas will continue to travel westward, causing the Atlantic to expand at the expense of the Pacific. The Pacific is the world's largest and oldest ocean: it is nearly five times the size of the African continent, and dates back about 600 million years. However, in the changing scheme of things it may be superseded by a younger ocean many millions of years hence, when the world will be a very different place.

Like the rocks of the sea floor, the water of the oceans is constantly in motion. Because the oceans are all connected, they behave as a single dynamic 'organism', linked by currents and pulled by the tides. Every molecule of water is tugged along within the larger cycles of waves, tides and currents, which are driven by the heat of the Sun, the gravitational pull of the Moon and the spin of the Earth.

As part of an even larger cycle, the Sun evaporates about a million million tons of water from the sea every day. These water molecules return to the Earth as rain or snow, and may reach the sea after passage

SATELLITE EYE *The warm waters of the Gulf Stream show complex eddies while the cool coastal waters are calm.*

OCEAN CURRENTS

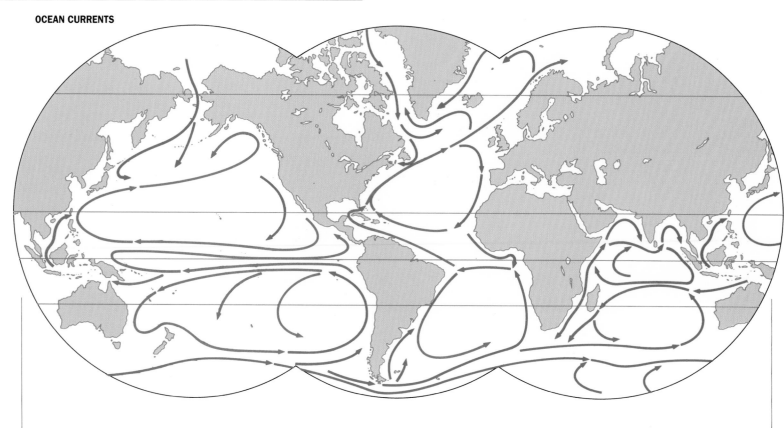

HOT AND COLD *Global wind patterns drive surface currents that redistribute* *cold and warm water between the North and South Poles and the Equator.*

Warm currents ⟶

Cold currents ⟶

through soil and rivers or storage in glaciers. The endlessly circulating currents of the oceans, and the restless flow of wind and water vapour in the atmosphere are closely interdependent: between them they determine climatic patterns all over the world.

In any one ocean basin, there are many layered water currents at different depths, each of them travelling at differing speeds and in different directions. Surface currents are generated by the winds that sweep over the ocean. Because of the spin of the Earth, the circulating currents flow clockwise around the ocean basins in the Northern Hemisphere and they flow anti-clockwise in the Southern Hemisphere. They meander and sometimes break off into swirling eddies.

Deep down in the ocean are much slower and larger currents. These are caused by dense streams of water descending from the surface and flowing along the ocean floor. Water density changes with temperature and saltiness: where water is particularly cold or laden with salt, it sinks. The saltiness of sea water varies, in its turn, with the addition or

removal of fresh water; it is increased by evaporation, and it is reduced by rivers, rainfall, melting icebergs and glaciers meeting the sea.

VAST GLOBAL NETWORK

The currents act as an enormous global transport network, channelling heat and a great variety of nutrients from one part of the oceans to another, rather like the ancient trade routes along which silk, gold and spices were transported slowly from place to place. Like those trade routes, the effects of the currents may be far-reaching. The exchange of warm and cold currents between the Poles and the Equator evens out the extremes of temperature experienced by the planet, making it more hospitable to life.

Currents can also have a more specific effect on the climate of a particular area. An example is the Gulf Stream, a warm surface current in the North Atlantic that travels from the Florida Straits at 140 miles (225 km) per day on a north-easterly path. Off Newfoundland, some of the water swings eastwards, then circles south, and some flows on in a north-easterly direction

as the broad North Atlantic current. It is this water that bathes the shores of north-west Europe in near-subtropical warmth. Without the Gulf Stream, the temperate countries of north-western Europe would be far colder in winter.

As it is, the coasts that benefit most from the Gulf Stream, such as the west of Ireland, which lies on the same line of latitude as Winnipeg, are warm enough to be virtually frost free, allowing exotic subtropical gardens to be planted. Even seeds are carried by the Gulf Stream and are washed ashore, where they may germinate and grow as alien plants from a distant continent. Occasionally animals from warmer shores stray onto western British coastlines. Rare finds might include violet sea snails on their rafts of bubbles, or a stranded turtle.

The interplay of the currents has biological consequences. Where two currents converge head on, warm surface water is forced downwards. Conversely, where currents diverge, cold upwelling water from the deep ocean fills the gap; rich in nutrients, it fertilises the surface waters and fosters an abundance of marine life.

TIDAL FLOW *As the Earth spins, the gravitational pull of the Moon on the seas produces the ebb and flow of the tides. The highest tides happen when the Moon and Sun are in a straight line (A and C), with the Sun's pull assisting the Moon's. The lowest tides happen when the pull of the Moon and Sun are acting at right angles (B and D).*

THE MOON AND TIDAL FORCES

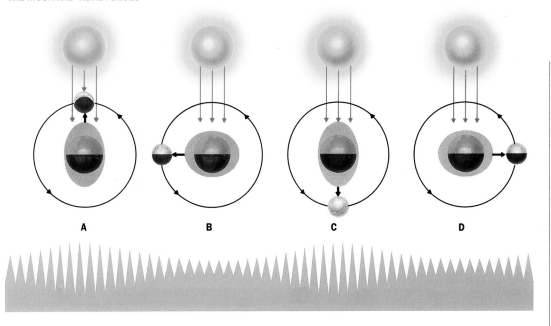

A   B   C   D

Where offshore winds drag surface waters away from coastlines, the same phenomenon occurs, and nutritious water wells up to replace the departing flow. Such areas are rich pastures for fish and birds; South America's west coast, for example, is particularly abundant.

FREAK CONDITIONS

Sometimes such ocean pastures turn suddenly into barren seas. When upwelling ceases, because of a change in atmospheric conditions, there can be catastrophic ecological repercussions – such as those experienced off Peru during El Niño years.

The notorious Niño is a periodic breakdown of normal weather patterns over the Pacific Ocean. Changes in barometric pressure over eastern and western parts of the Pacific produce unusual westerly winds. These cause surface currents to reverse and warm water to surge towards the coasts of South America, repressing the normal upwelling of cold, nutrient-rich water. Fish die, marine mammals and birds starve, and the fishing industry suffers severely – to the point of collapse if there has been over-fishing before El Niño. In 1972 the slump in catches of anchovies off Peru was so serious that it ruined the livelihoods of thousands of people. These disasters occur about twice every decade, around Christmas time, hence the name: El Niño means 'the child' and refers to the birth of Christ.

El Niño triggers chaos far across the globe: it can cause a chain reaction of unseasonal weather conditions or exaggerate the normal changes, so that there are droughts and heatwaves in Africa, southern Asia and Australia, at the same time as torrential rains, mud slides and floods hit South America, and hurricanes sweep the North. The mechanism causing these events is being unravelled by research scientists, who have traced the origin of El Niño back to the western Pacific.

The surface of the sea is rarely still. Waves, like the surface currents, are usually generated by the wind – the exceptions being those caused by earthquakes and earth tremors, and internal waves between layers of deep water. The wave that we see is actually a pulse of energy supplied by the wind. It sweeps through the water, scooping water particles around in a vertical, circular movement as it passes. The size of a wave depends not only upon the strength of the wind, but also the distance over which the wind has been blowing (called the 'fetch'), and the time that it has stayed in that direction.

At any one place there may be a mixture of waves of different heights and directions and these interact, giving the sea a 'choppy' appearance. The terrifying monster waves of mariners' tales really do occur on occasion – where local and distant waves combine in force, perhaps meeting a strong current head-on. The east coast of South Africa is infamous for its freak waves, but the greatest reliable recording is of a 112 ft (34 m) high wave in

KNOCK-ON EFFECT *Massive turbulence occurs under water when a wave hits a coral reef.*

SEA SCULPTURE *Over thousands of years, the relentless beating of waves has shaped this Oregon headland.*

the North Pacific, recorded in 1933 by a passing ship on its way to Manila.

Where the sea meets the land, the powerful waves of the open are translated into crashing breakers that pound against rocks or explode into foamy surf upon the beach. This happens because the repeated, circular motion of the water particles is interrupted in shallow water. Unable to cycle normally, the wave crests rise higher and higher, until they curl over and finally break, venting their pent-up energy as they pound against the shore.

TIME AND TIDE

Superimposed upon all its other movements, the sea rises and falls in a recurrent series of tides. Unlike the waves and the currents, the ebb and flow of the tide is due to the gravitational pull of the Moon, and to a lesser degree, the Sun.

The relative positions of the Sun, Moon and Earth in Space affect the strength of this pull: when the Sun and Moon are in line, the pull is at its strongest, and we experience the greatest extremes of high and low tide on the shoreline. These are the confusingly named 'spring tides', yet they occur throughout the year, twice a month, around the time of a new moon or a full moon. During 'neap' tides, the water level fluctuates much less. The Sun and Moon are exerting forces at right angles to each other, and so their effect on the ocean is not so powerful.

basins amplify or dampen the effects of the tides. Some regions have very exaggerated tidal ranges. Probably the most spectacular example is in the Bay of Fundy, on the east coast of Canada, where tides rise and fall by nearly 50 ft (15 m). In contrast, enclosed seas such as the Mediterranean and the Baltic have very weak tides.

Sometimes, where the tide flows into a sharply tapering estuary, surging walls of water called 'tidal bores' develop. These are caused by the incoming tide riding against the outflowing river water during spring high tides. On the River Severn in England, waves of 10 ft (3 m) high may travel up to 20 miles (32 km) inland. Other famous bores include those on the River Hooghly in India and on the River Chang Chiang (Yangtze) in China.

Where the waves beat the shore with the rise and fall of the tides, they sculpt the coastline. Continual pounding at rocky coasts weakens the rock along its existing fault lines and crumbles away loosened pieces, rolling them eventually into smooth, rounded pebbles. Abrasive sand and tiny pebbles, propelled by the waves, may scour away at cliff bases. In other places, sediments and gravel are deposited as beaches

LOW TIDE *Mud and silt are laid down in this estuary, as the river forces its way to the sea.*

and spits, so that the land extends into the sea. On these margins, tides are the major factor controlling animal and plant life, which undergoes inundation by the sea and exposure to the air twice daily. Only highly mobile sea creatures such as crabs can keep pace with the tides. Most living things must adapt to either a marine or a terrestrial lifestyle.

It is on shallow coasts that the sea is most productive. The water is rich with nutrients washed down from the land and churned up from the shallow sea floor by the currents. Estuaries, algal beds, mangrove swamps, coral reefs and salt marshes all throng with different forms of life. To many of us the oceans still start and finish at the shore; even boats, snorkels and diving equipment only really allow us to 'scratch' at their surface. We perceive their vast expanses as barriers. But landmasses can be seen as the true barriers that divide the much more interconnected, global sea.

Most coastlines experience two low tides and two high tides daily. At any one place, high tide can be expected to arrive 50 minutes later than it did on the previous day. This is because it takes 24 hours and 50 minutes for the Moon's cycle to coincide once more with the same meridian (an imaginary line around the globe that passes through both poles) on the Earth's surface.

If the Earth were completely covered with water, the tides would be similar throughout the world. In reality, however, the unevenly shaped landmasses and ocean

LIFE IN THE OCEANS

The ocean is a strange world, a natural laboratory for experiments in evolution, and a museum of life forms that have survived from the dawn of time. Almost all life here depends on microscopic plants, invisible to the human eye.

Between 1838 and 1843, Sir Joseph Hooker, an eminent botanist and Charles Darwin's closest friend, was engaged on a gruelling journey that took him to the waters of Antarctica, where he collected samples of sea water and examined them under the microscope on board his research ship. Hooker was amazed at the high numbers of diatoms – tiny, single-celled organisms shaped like pillboxes – in the water. He had never seen these microscopic life forms in such profusion before.

Puzzling over this observation, and marvelling also at the richness of animal life in these icy seas, Hooker suddenly realised that the two were connected: the diatoms, tiny floating plants at the surface of the sea, must be the ultimate source of food for the fish, whales, seals and penguins that thrived in the Antarctic Ocean. Hooker described the diatoms and other microscopic plants as the 'ocean pastures': the mainstay of life

FOOD OF LIFE *Each diatom species is uniquely patterned.*

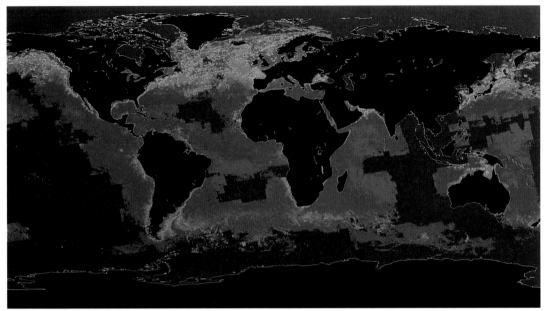

NORTHERN SPRING
*Red indicates where
planktonic plants are
most abundant.*

sufficient fish to keep a hump-back whale alive.

The various plants of the plankton, like land plants, need light to manufacture food. Strong sunlight only reaches as far as the uppermost layers of the ocean, which is why they must float at the surface. They are made buoyant by delicate hair-like or spiny projections, or by drops of lightweight oil within their bodies.

Some of these microscopic plants, called the 'dinoflagellates', even have a lashing, whip-like appendage that propels them through the water. These organisms are covered by protective, transparent, armour-like plates that cause them to sink if they are inactive. They use their power of movement both to stay afloat and to swim towards the light. The larger ones can move at speeds of up to 65 ft (20 m) per day, but they are still 'plankton', essentially passive wanderers whose movements are dictated by current, wind and wave.

In addition to light, plants need various

VULNERABLE WANDERER *Even
though it can swim using a
whip-like 'oar', this microscopic
dinoflagellate is still at the
mercy of the currents.*

in the sea, just as grass and leafy plants are the mainstay of life on land. It was a dramatic and accurate insight.

Diatoms and other minute, single-celled plants had been observed in sea water since the invention of microscopes in the 17th century, but no one had realised their overwhelming importance in the economy

OIL SLICK WITH A DIFFERENCE

Surprising though it may seem, oil slicks sometimes have a natural cause. In 1971, a US coastguard ship on duty in the North Pacific found itself surrounded by a mysterious red slick of oil that stretched as far as the eye could see. Samples were analysed by scientists and found to contain 82 per cent wax. More detailed analysis showed that the slick had a biological cause: it was produced by millions of dead copepods. These planktonic animals store wax as an energy reserve, in the same way that humans store fat.

of the sea. Many centuries before that, seagoing fishermen had noticed that a sudden change in the colour of the sea (called a 'bloom') was often followed by a period of exceptionally large catches. But they were unaware that tiny plants, too small to be seen with the naked eye, were responsible for the change in colour. With Joseph Hooker's flash of insight, the mystery was explained.

Further research followed, and the

British Royal Navy ship, HMS *Challenger*, on a round-the-world voyage in the 1870s, made a systematic search for the invisible plants of the surface waters. The discovery that they existed throughout the world, but were most abundant in rich fishing waters, confirmed their importance.

In 1892, the term 'plankton', from the Greek word meaning 'wanderers', was coined for the floating life forms, both animal and plant, of the oceans' uppermost layers. The name reflects the fact that these creatures are carried passively by the waves and currents, rather than being in control of their movements. Diatoms and their kind are known as 'phytoplankton', which means 'wandering plants'.

There are about a thousand different species of these simple, unobtrusive plants. Modern research has shown that the animals of the sea are almost entirely reliant on them for food: the contribution made by much larger plants, such as seaweeds and eelgrass, is negligible compared with that of the phytoplankton. Without them the ocean would be a truly sterile and barren realm.

To sustain such a wealth of life requires astronomical numbers of phytoplankton and, consequently, very fast reproduction. Scientists estimate, for example, that a basic supply of 200-400 billion diatoms per hour is needed to provide sustenance for

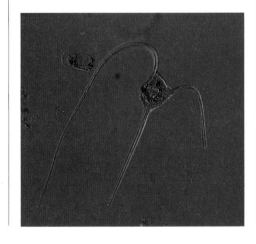

essential chemical nutrients – similar to those supplied in garden fertilisers. These come from weathered rocks, via river sediments, and are usually extremely plentiful in coastal waters. Nutrients are also recycled when the bodies of dead animals, or their faecal pellets, decay.

FAVOURABLE CONDITIONS

Gravity is a problem for the phytoplankton: the decaying particles that supply it with essential nutrients tend to sink to the ocean floor, and the limited quantities in the surface water are rapidly used up. The phytoplankton must usually survive in a nutrient-starved upper layer, out of reach of the life-giving sediment on the seabed below. Growth can only continue if nutrients are brought up to the brightly lit layers by a strong stirring motion, caused by temperature changes, by the wind, or by upwelling currents, such as those off the coast of Peru and California in the Pacific, off West Africa in the Atlantic, and off Arabia in the Indian Ocean.

The sort of conditions that combine the mix of nutrients and plentiful light only occur at certain times of the year. At high latitudes, this is limited to a short period in the summer. In intermediate latitudes, it occurs in spring and again in

autumn. When conditions are favourable, the phytoplankton proliferate massively in an explosion of life: at best they can increase threefold in a single day, creating a plankton bloom.

Where a bloom occurs, it provides a feast for millions of grazing planktonic animals, known as zooplankton. Commonest are the tiny, one-eyed crustaceans (relatives of the crabs and shrimps) known as cope-

PRECIOUS DROP   A wealth of zooplankton species are to be found in just a single drop of sea water.

pods, which are thought to be the most numerous multicellular animals in the world. They row through the water and scoop up the plant cells. The larvae of fish, barnacles, crabs, sea anemones and many other animals also graze on the phytoplankton and, for a time during their growth, form a major component of the zooplankton. Herring-like fish and mid-water shrimps join the zooplankton in their banquet.

The plant-eaters are extremely thorough in their eating habits; whole blooms of phytoplankton are almost entirely devoured during their most prolific phase. It is as if the rapid flowering of the desert after rain was instantly stripped bare by a devastating plague of locusts.

On land, trees and shrubs live for several years and thus have a chance to recover from grazing damage. They have

RED TIDES THAT SPELL DISASTER

A reddish scum on the surface of the sea may signal the arrival of a toxic 'red tide'. The culprits are billions of one-celled plants called dinoflagellates, which multiply so rapidly that they turn the water red or brown with their pigment. Incidents are commonly reported off India, Japan, south-west Africa, Peru, California, Texas and Florida. They generally occur in warm, shallow water with high levels of nitrogen and phosphorous.

Red tides can be disastrous for other marine life. The presence of so many dinoflagellates uses up the

oxygen required by other animals. Some species, notably *Gymnodinium brevis*, become toxic as they get older. Their poison, ten times as effective as cyanide, kills shoals of fish. It may also accumulate in the

TOXIC BLOOM   One-celled dinoflagellates create a poisonous 'tide'.

digestive tracts of shellfish and produce food-poisoning outbreaks in humans. Florida manatees have sometimes died from eating sea squirts that had consumed the dinoflagellates of a red tide.

Red tides sometimes produce so much hydrogen sulphide gas that white houses in coastal cities have turned black, and people living in the area have developed respiratory complaints.

OCEANBOUND *It would be impossible for many marine body forms to survive on land. This sea cucumber, camouflaged with flaps and frills, needs the supportive medium of water.*

hard, woody parts that are unpalatable, so that even if they are stripped bare of leaves, they are still able to recover. Grasses and other small plants have underground roots or tubers that can survive grazing. And seeds can survive intact inside the stomach of an animal or bird. Not so for the seas' single-celled plants – if eaten, the whole plant dies.

Despite the severe 'boom and bust' cycles of the phytoplankton, the amount produced in a 'boom' period is usually enough to sustain the whole marine food chain through slacker times. When one type of phytoplankton becomes very scarce, the grazers switch to another type, so that a few plant cells are always left – enough to begin the cycle again when nutrients become available.

Just as the phytoplankton are consumed by zooplankton, so it is the fate of most animals in the sea to become food for others. The plant-eating zooplankton are swallowed up by slightly larger animals and these small predators in turn provide food for larger fish, whales and seals. Thus the zooplankton are the first link in the chain that connects the phytoplankton to whales, dolphins, sharks and other large predators, including humankind.

THE OCEANS: AN EVOLUTIONARY HOTHOUSE

From our thoroughly terrestrial viewpoint, the ocean seems an inhospitable and alien world. In fact, it is an environment far more congenial to life than the air. The tumbling waves and thrashing surface of the sea, seen from a boat, belie what is generally a steady and equable habitat below. Temperatures in the ocean fluctuate only gently, compared with those on land. While the deep sea might indeed be very cold, it is uniformly and permanently cold. Gravity is of less importance than it is on land, because of the buoyancy provided by the water.

This allows the existence of the floating plankton, organisms that have virtually no equivalent in the air. Animals of the sea do not necessarily need skeletons or well-developed muscles because their bodies are buoyed up by water. And what is more, many are able to spend their life sitting still, waiting for the currents to deliver their food.

Marine animals can attain sizes that would be inconceivable on land; the giant squid may be as much as 70 ft (21 m) in

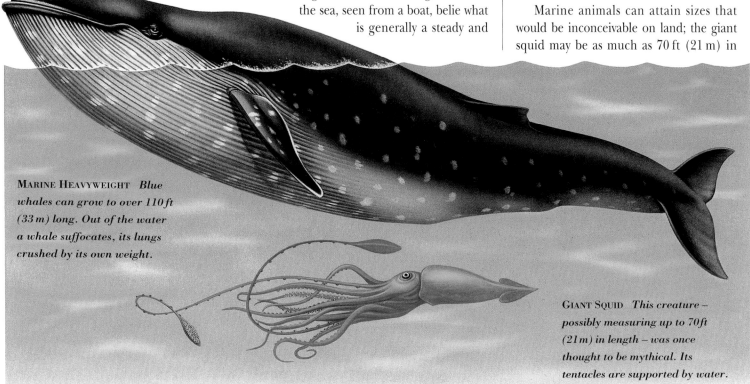

MARINE HEAVYWEIGHT *Blue whales can grow to over 110 ft (33 m) long. Out of the water a whale suffocates, its lungs crushed by its own weight.*

GIANT SQUID *This creature – possibly measuring up to 70 ft (21 m) in length – was once thought to be mythical. Its tentacles are supported by water.*

FOSSIL REMAINS: LIFE FROZEN IN STONE

Fossils are snapshots of another era. They are a rather random record of animals and plants that inhabited the Earth in previous ages, sandwiched in historical order between the compressed layers of sedimentary rock, as flowers are pressed between the pages of a book. Until the true nature of fossils was established, people invented fantastic and mystical explanations for their existence. The incongruous presence of seashells on mountain tops presented particular problems of interpretation. One idea was that 'spores' of animals and plants were carried from the sea as water evaporated, then deposited by raindrops on the mountains, where they infiltrated the rocks and grew into stony versions of their true forms. Others believed that fossils generated spontaneously from the earth, that they were unsuccessful attempts at creation, or the remains of creatures drowned in the great Biblical flood.

The truth is that fossils are impressions or remains of animals and plants, buried after death in fine mud or sand and compacted into sedimentary rocks. Sometimes plant and animal bodies are chemically altered, molecule by molecule, and replaced by minerals that harden into perfect replicas, exact in every detail. The formation of fossils is not common: only a minute fraction of the billions of organisms that have inhabited the Earth become fossilised. Fewer still are discovered by humans. Often it is only the hard parts of animals that are preserved, such as bones and shells. Despite many gaps, however, the fossil record has helped biologists to piece together the path of evolution over the millennia.

TINY REMNANTS *This shoal of fish was fossilised millions of years ago in the soft sediment of a seabed.*

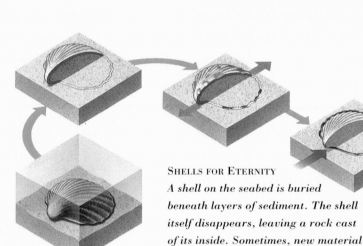

SHELLS FOR ETERNITY
A shell on the seabed is buried beneath layers of sediment. The shell itself disappears, leaving a rock cast of its inside. Sometimes, new material such as silica replaces the shell.

length, while the blue whale weighs the equivalent of 25 full-grown elephants. Delicate feathery structures, gelatinous bodies and long, soft tentacles have all evolved in this supportive environment. The resulting body forms appear at the same time both beautiful and bizarre to our land-adjusted eyes.

The oceans have been a natural laboratory for experiments in evolution since life began 3.5 billion years ago, and many groups of animals are found here that exist nowhere else on Earth. Biologists classify animals into large groups called 'phyla'; members of one phylum have a broadly similar body plan and are thought to share a common evolutionary origin. Of the 33 animal phyla recognised by biologists, 15 are not found at all on land.

For all the diversity of their body plans, the 33 phyla sprang from a single ancestral group: this much is shown by the shared chemistry of their most basic life processes and the common genetic code that translates the hereditary information in their DNA. The fossil record suggests that the ancestral life form was a very simple, bacteria-like, one-celled organism. About

SLOW MOTION *Jellyfish move by repeatedly contracting their gelatinous bodies.*

1500 million years ago, a more complicated type of cell developed, when certain bacteria-like cells became absorbed by others, or perhaps invaded them. In the larger and more complex cells that were produced, the skills of the inmates complemented those of the host cells. From these combined cells, one-celled plants (called algae) and one-celled animals (called protozoa) evolved.

THE EARLIEST ANIMALS

The very first fossil evidence of animals with many cells comes from around 600 million years ago in the Precambrian era. During the Cambrian period that followed, there was an explosion of evolution and diversification in the oceans. Up to 90 per cent of these experiments in evolutionary design became extinct, but the others became the ancestors of today's animal groups.

Even though the fossil record has not preserved many of the early soft-bodied animals, there is still enough variety of living forms in the sea today for us to speculate about how evolution might have progressed. It is possible to imagine, for example, that a single-celled animal living side by side with others in a colony was less likely to be devoured by tiny predators than a similar one on its own. What scientists call 'multicellularity' had its advantages, and evolution was quick to work on them.

The most simple of today's

STARK SIMPLICITY
*Sponges (right) are
the simplest of all
multicellular animals.
Corals and sea anemones
(below) are only a little
more complex.*

ARMOURED ANCIENTS

Some animals have remained virtually unchanged since their now-fossilised ancestors roamed the seas millions of years ago. These creatures from a bygone age appear curiously alien and antiquated to us. But they are not obsolete: their early features still serve them well in the ocean's environment. Quite why their form has remained unchanged while other groups have evolved, and even become extinct, over similar time periods remains a mystery.

In Delaware Bay, on the New Jersey coast, millions of horseshoe (or king) crabs clamber over one another onto the beach to spawn each May. They have a tough, curved shell and a spine-like tail, and, despite their name, are really not crabs at all. They are classified in a group called the Xiphosura, meaning 'sword tail', and their nearest living relatives are the spiders, ticks and scorpions. But the horseshoe crabs have survived on Earth for a very long time: their curious body structure is remarkably similar to that of fossils found in rocks that are at least 300 million years old.

Deep in the waters of the tropical Indo-Pacific are a few surviving species of *Nautilus*, which are related to the squid and octopus but have a large, coiled shell and many more tentacles. Animals such as these once dominated the oceans. In the era before bony fish evolved, the nautiloids were the first large, swimming carnivores –

CURIOUS REMNANT
The Nautilus has survived hundreds of millions of years.

the early forms had a straight shell and were up to 13 ft (4 m) long. Coiled-shell nautiloids evolved by gradual steps from these straight-shelled forms, and the modern *Nautilus* is very similar to fossils found in rocks dating back as far as 230 million years. The nautiloids' success came from their ability to control their buoyancy, which they achieved by holding buoyant gas in the chambers of their shell.

ANCIENT FORM *Horseshoe crabs are little changed from 300-million-year-old ancestors.*

LAZY EATERS
A feather star clings to coral. Both remain in one place for life, feeding on passing particles.

multicellular animals are probably the sponges, jellyfish and corals. Sponges are collections of animal cells that form soft, stationary masses perforated with volcano-shaped pores. Seen under the microscope, the individual cells look like spiky baskets. Amazingly, if a live sponge is broken apart and passed through a fine sieve, the constituent cells reassemble themselves into a sponge body, each finding its place within the whole. But sponges have no nervous system and no muscle fibres; these more sophisticated adaptations only appear with the jellyfish and their relatives.

The group of animals that are known as cnidarians have simple bodies made of just two layers of cells. They are also armed with stinging cells that help them to catch food and defend themselves. Some float, others sit on the bottom.

From the same basic body plan come animals as diverse and beautiful as the flower-like sea anemones, the medusoid jellyfish with their trailing tentacles, and the extraordinary, sculpted corals of the tropical reefs.

Such simple animals may have made no obvious biological 'advances' for millions of years, but they have, none the less, survived. Success does not necessarily come from having more complicated body forms. Of the more complex body types evolved from the uncomplicated ones, many died out eventually – evolutionary curiosities that could not sustain their initial success once their environment changed.

More complex than simple sea anemones and jellyfish are the members of the echinoderm phylum. They include: spidery, ten-armed feather stars; sea urchins that lever themselves on rotating spines; and starfish with their hundreds of synchronised tube feet. Then there are wriggling worms that, despite superficial similarities, belong to several different phyla.

More complex still are the crustaceans: wraith-like shrimps, scuttling crabs and ponderous

FATAL ATTRACTION *The flower-like 'petals' of these sea anemones are in fact predatory tentacles, covered with stinging cells that can maim or kill smaller prey.*

STONE CRABS
Crabs belong to the
highly successful
biological group
known as crustaceans.

bottom; its larval form has a simple forerunner of the spinal cord and a primitive brain. Scientists believe that the vertebrates probably evolved from this larva by a process called neoteny, where the larva never turns into an adult, but becomes sexually mature and can breed successfully while still in its juvenile form. This is a way in which evolution can make a sudden and radical change, the adult stage (the dull, sedentary sea squirt) being lost altogether and the free-swimming larva becoming the raw material for an entirely new life form.

SUIT OF ARMOUR *Crustaceans,*
such as the spotted lobster,
are encased in armour, which
they shed at intervals to grow
a new and larger suit.

To complete the evolutionary picture, there are animals such as the turtles, sea snakes, whales, dolphins, seals and sea cows. All of them are creatures that have

lobsters, with protective shells and hinged legs. And everywhere in the sea there are molluscs, soft-bodied creatures ranging from the lethargic mussels and limpets to the brightly coloured sea slugs and jet-propelled cuttlefish, squid and octopus.

Gliding through the shallows, skimming the surface and propelling themselves through the deep are the fish, streamlined swimming machines supremely well adapted to life in the oceans. The unlikely ancestor of the fish, and indeed of all animals with backbones, is a creature resembling the flaccid sea squirt, an insubstantial, translucent, tubular animal that lives on the sea

COMING OUT *Sea slugs are*
molluscs that have lost their
shells in the course of evolution.

found their way back to the sea from land-living roots, and that are now fully adapted to a marine lifestyle.

Despite the fact that life evolved in the oceans and that almost half of all phyla are found nowhere else, only 160 000 of the million or so animal species identified by zoologists are marine creatures. Of these, no more than about 2 per cent live in the open water. All the others live on the ocean floor, buried in its sediments or crawling over the bottom.

Part of the reason for this extraordinarily low figure is that the ocean is more interconnected and less compartmentalised than a forest or a mountainside. Thus it offers fewer opportunities for speciation (the formation of new species) than the land, where populations are more discreetly separated from others. The other reason is the sheer inaccessibility of the deep-sea realm to scientists. The sea holds on to its secrets, and there is still much that we do not know. It is estimated, for example, that there may still be up to a million undescribed species on the deep sea floor.

REMARKABLE DISCOVERIES

Although it is exciting to find a new species, it is more remarkable to find a new family or class of animals. To find a whole new phylum is a truly rare event. This century, only three new phyla have been described.

The beard worms (*Pogonophora*) were first found as a result of deep-sea dredging in 1914. The *Gnathostomulids* (meaning 'jaw mouth') also evaded detection for a long time – until 1956. They are microscopic worms that live in deep, black muddy habitats smelling of hydrogen sulphide.

The third of the new phyla was not chanced upon until 1983 in France. The tiny animals, known as loriciferans, were discovered by accident when a sample of sand was not washed in salt water – the normal procedure in laboratories – but was rinsed in fresh water, which loosened these tenacious creatures from the sediment.

No one can know how many secrets remain concealed in the sea. But while there is still the promise of living fossils and new phyla to be discovered, the oceans of the world will remain a challenge to modern science and to the inquisitive human mind.

COELACANTH — THE LIVING FOSSIL

In 1938, the crew of a South African fishing trawler hauled in a mysterious 5 ft (1.5 m) long fish, the like of which they had never seen before. It was covered with heavy scales, had large eyes, powerful jaws, stout fins and a finned, stumpy tail. The specimen was taken to the curator of the local museum, who instantly detected something unusual and contacted Professor J.L.B. Smith, an authority on African fish. He recognised the animal as a coelacanth – and caused a sensation. It was an unprecedented discovery.

Remains of coelacanths had been identified in rocks dating back nearly 400 million years, but geologists believed them to have died out about 70 million years ago. Smith calculated that coelacanths must have survived, almost unchanged, for 30 million generations. The coelacanths and the lungfish are the closest living relatives of the type of fish that, 375 million years ago, made the important evolutionary move from water onto land.

Fourteen years after the first discovery, a second specimen was found in the Comoro Islands of the Indian Ocean. It became apparent that the local fishermen were familiar with the fish, which they had been catching occasionally, and unintentionally, for years. It was not good to eat, but the scales were used as sandpaper and for rubbing down bicycle inner-tubes prior to patching them. Far from being extinct, the prehistoric fish would appear to have been flourishing in the hidden depths.

We can only speculate about how many other living fossils remain to be discovered. In 1898 a bizarre shark was caught in Japan – a prehistoric-looking creature with a sharp protuberance on its forehead. It was a rare goblin shark (*Mitsukurina*), thought to have been extinct for 100 million years.

THE LIVING DEAD *A fossil coelacanth from 200 million years ago (top), and its living relative (below).*

WAYFARERS OF THE SEA

Epic migrations are made across the oceans by animals

pursuing prey, in search of more congenial waters or intent

on breeding. Scientists are finally beginning to understand

the special senses that allow them to steer their course.

The seabed is of such importance to shipping that it must be mapped, and areas of dangerously shallow water, where a ship might run aground, carefully recorded. For centuries maps were drawn from hard experience, each treacherous bank or shoal inked in was a record of tragedy, sunken cargoes and lost lives.

Then, during the First World War, came sonar, a device similar to radar, that could map the bottom by emitting sound waves and recording their echoes. It seemed that the seabed was at last directly visible, with all its mysterious contours precisely revealed. The sonar pulse would be like a bright beam of light shining into the mysterious darkness of the ocean.

In fact the seabed became more puzzling than before. Passing through waters that were supposedly several miles deep, a ship would suddenly record an echo from a few hundred feet below the surface. The risk of running aground would be too great for the ship to investigate further, so the captain would steer away from the potential hazard, but make an official report of his finding. In this way, the deep-water areas on nautical charts came to be peppered with records of

NIGHTLY MIGRATION *Shoals of hatchet fish rise to the surface waters after dark to feed.*

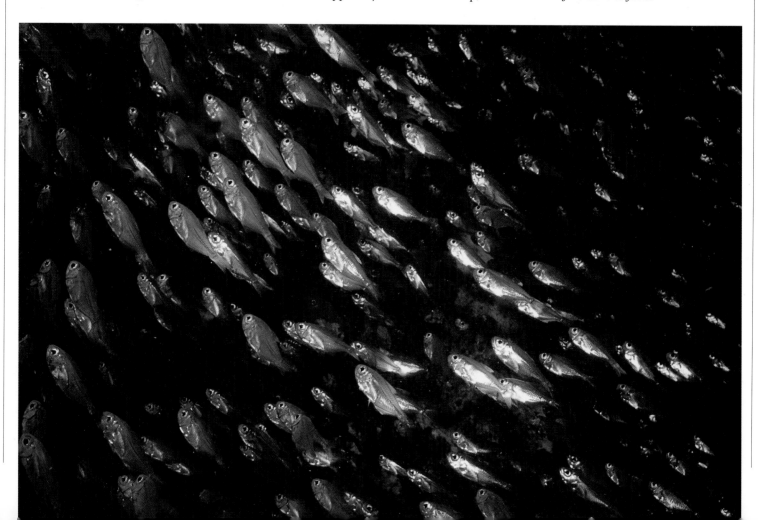

GOOSE MYTH *In the Middle Ages, legend held that barnacle geese (below) developed from goose barnacles (left).*

bodies are invisible to echo-location devices. The zooplankton themselves make twice-daily migrations of many thousand feet to obtain food and to avoid daytime predation. In the day they sink into the deeper, darker layers, returning at night to the surface to feed on the plant plankton. This is a vast journey in relation to their body size; it can roughly be compared with a human walking a 50 mile (84 km) round trip daily to obtain food.

These daily movements are just one

shallow-water shoals, each labelled 'ED', meaning 'Existence Doubtful'. Another ship might later sail through the same waters and find nothing but deep ocean.

ECHOLOCATION

The puzzle began to be solved during the Second World War, when US scientists were trying to find ways of locating submarines by using more refined sonar techniques. In the open ocean, above areas of water that were thought to be several thousand feet deep, there would some-times be an echo from no more than about 700-900 ft (210-270 m). The most bizarre aspect of findings like these was that the echo disappeared at night.

Clearly this could not happen, and further research showed that a faint echo of the true bottom could usually be detec-ted below the one at 700-900 ft – proving that this was indeed a 'phantom bottom'. By taking a series of soundings through the twilight hours and into the night, scientists found that the phantom bottom, far from sinking downwards, was in fact rising upwards after sunset, coming close to the surface and then dispersing. At first it was thought that some physical property of the

water – a change in temperature at dif-ferent layers, perhaps – might produce these strange readings. But the answer proved to be a biological one.

The phantom layers detected by the echo sounders were in fact congregations of animal bodies – those of predators such as lantern fish (*Notoscopelus elongatus*) – lin-gering in deeper water by day, then swimming upwards to feed near the surface under the com-parative safety of darkness. Lantern fish are small, silvery or dark-bodied carnivores, and measure 1-6 in (2.5-15 cm) long. They owe their name to the luminous organs scattered over their undersides. In their night-ly journey, they are joined by plant-eating shrimps and car-nivorous squid.

Predators come to the sur-face to feed on swarms of ani-mal plankton, whose delicate

AGILE BREED *Their ability to slither over mud and damp grass makes eels more mobile than most other fish.*

THE EEL'S LIFE JOURNEY

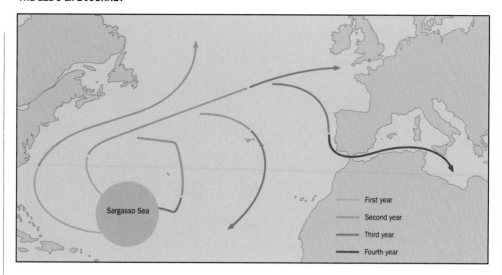

First year
Second year
Third year
Fourth year

Sargasso Sea

BEYOND THE SARGASSO *Eel larvae embark on astonishing migrations from their spawning grounds.*

example of the immense voyages undertaken by ocean animals. Throughout the oceans, at the surface and far below, enormous processions of animals achieve astonishing feats of navigation and endurance. Some are passive riders on the powerful ocean currents; others propel themselves with compulsive zeal towards a precise goal thousands of miles away. From the largest to the smallest, the drive to travel is often fuelled by the need to feed or to reproduce.

Why animals travel so far and how they achieve such feats of navigation has presented biologists with an enormous puzzle. Even today, many of the mysteries of migration remain to be unravelled.

MIGRATION MYTHS

In historical times, the regular appearance and disappearance of animals was a mystery bordering on the supernatural. In an attempt to explain the peculiarity, naturalists suggested a range of bizarre and misleading solutions. It was suggested,

for example, that one species mysteriously changed into another with the seasons.

One of the most implausible but popular myths involved small, immobile sea creatures growing into birds and flying away. This myth was a solution to the puzzle of the barnacle goose. They had never been seen to lay eggs in Europe, so in medieval times people were convinced that the geese developed from a type of long-stalked barnacle. These barnacles are found attached to rocks and driftwood on the shoreline, and as a result of the legend they became known as goose barnacles – a name that is still used today. It was believed that the stalk of the barnacle represented the neck of the bird, while the petal-shaped shells developed into its body; the modified feet, or 'cirri', do indeed look convincingly feather-like.

Although there was no sign of a head or a beak, medieval illustrations showed the miniature birds clinging on with their beaks until they were fully formed and could fly away. The myth persisted stubbornly for many years after sailors found barnacle-goose nests on their voyages.

Even the ancient Greek philosopher,

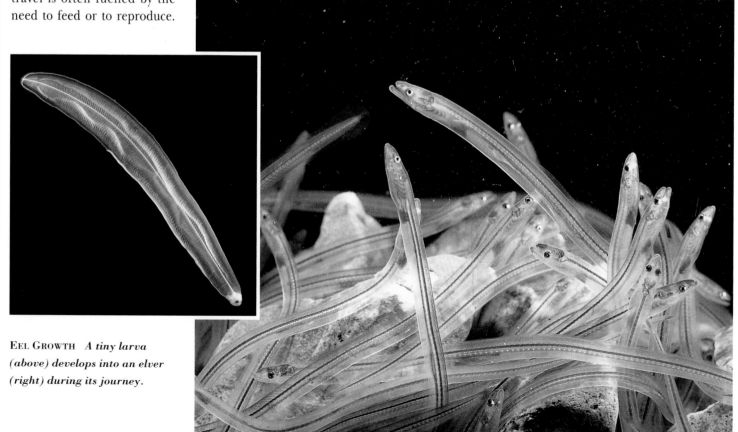

EEL GROWTH *A tiny larva (above) develops into an elver (right) during its journey.*

LIFE IS A JOURNEY FOR THE SALMON

Atlantic salmon (*Salmo salar*) spend most of their lives in the open ocean, but when the time comes to produce young, they return to the freshwater streams where they themselves were spawned. Each female can produce several thousand eggs. She lays them in a shallow gravel hollow on the river bed, and covers the makeshift nest with sand to prevent the eggs being swept away downstream. They are abandoned there, relatively safe over the winter until the young fry hatch in the spring. After feeding for a few weeks on their yolk sacs, the young salmon travel downriver, where they feed and grow for one to five years until they reach 4 in (10 cm) long. At this stage they develop a silvery marine camouflage, and migrate downstream, tumbling over waterfalls and rapids until they reach calmer waters and, finally, the sea.

RIVER-BRED *Salmon eggs and fry in clear river water.*

The salmon remain at sea for one to four years.

As the time to spawn approaches, mature salmon assemble in shoals and return – almost miraculously – to the river of their birth. They may be using the water currents, the Sun, or a magnetic sense to guide them, but they ultimately trace their birthplace by recognising its unique 'smell' of chemicals. This has been proved in that fish with their nostrils plugged cannot find their way. The scent signature, derived from the mud and the animals and plants that live up-stream, is learned by the fish when they are young. As they approach, the scent gets stronger and stronger. To reach its source they battle through the opposing current, thrash up rapids and leap clear of obstacles, not stopping to feed.

On reaching their ancestral

YOUNG SALMON
The youngsters travel downstream to the sea.

tributary, the exhausted salmon eventually spawn. After spawning the death rate is very high. Only about a quarter of the fish return to the ocean to live another year and repeat their arduous voyage. Pacific salmon (*Oncorhynchus* species), whose lifestyle is otherwise similar, all die after spawning, spent and diseased.

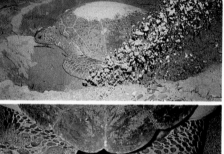

TIME-HONOURED TRADITION
*A green turtle hauls herself
up onto a breeding beach
on Ascension Island (left).
Once ashore, she digs a
hole for her eggs (below).*

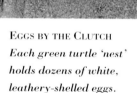

EGGS BY THE CLUTCH
*Each green turtle 'nest'
holds dozens of white,
leathery-shelled eggs.*

Aristotle (384-322 BC) was deceived by the migration enigma. Freshwater eels, like barnacle geese, were common in Europe, but were never known to produce eggs or young. Aristotle concluded that they sprang, fully formed, from the 'entrails of the earth'. On the other hand, the Roman naturalist Pliny (AD 23-79) decided that young eels grew from fragments of the adults' skin, which the eels generated by scraping themselves against rocks.

EPIC JOURNEY

It was not until the end of the 19th century that scientists managed to track down the elusive breeding ground where European eels lay their eggs. It then emerged that American eels used exactly the same place, deep in the Sargasso Sea, south-east of Bermuda. Here the eels spawn, and from the eggs hatch translucent, leaf-shaped larvae. These had been found before, but

NAVIGATION AND THE GREEN TURTLE

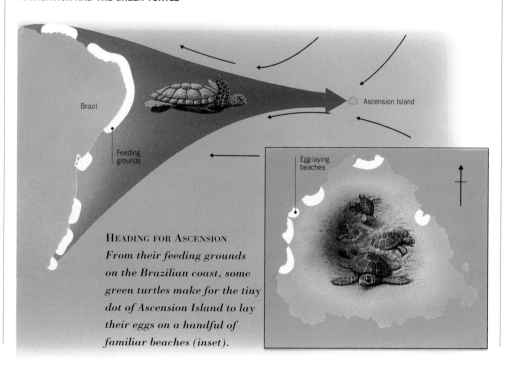

Brazil

Feeding grounds

Ascension Island

Egg-laying beaches

HEADING FOR ASCENSION
*From their feeding grounds
on the Brazilian coast, some
green turtles make for the tiny
dot of Ascension Island to lay
their eggs on a handful of
familiar beaches (inset).*

they had previously been classified as a species of fish in their own right, since they look nothing like eels.

The larvae are carried all the way to the shores of both Europe and North America by the warm, meandering Gulf Stream. During the journey, which takes up to four years for European eels (who have farther to travel across the Atlantic), the larvae mature into transparent, wriggling 'elvers', exchanging their leaf-shaped form for something far more eel-like.

On their arrival, the elvers swim into rivers, where they become pigmented and continue to grow. After 5 to 15 years, they transform into a final, silver, marine stage and head back to the Sargasso Sea. The mammoth journey from Europe takes between four and seven months, during which the eels do not appear to eat. In the Sargasso, they mate, spawn and die, the cycle complete.

Salmon migration is virtually a mirror image of the eel cycle. After hatching in fresh water, young salmon travel downriver as far as the open sea, where they grow and mature. Many years later the adult salmon return to the river of their birth to spawn.

It is still not known exactly why these fish travel such tremendous distances to breed. The case of the eels is particularly surprising, since they are known to be very inefficient swimmers. Eels need warm water – about 20°C (68°F) – to reproduce, and the Sargasso Sea is perhaps one of the few places that offers such temperatures at suitable depth – about 1700 ft (500 m). Some scientists believe that the movements between sea and river protect the young from parasites. Any marine parasites, which are adapted to a saltwater life, would be killed by the transfer to fresh water.

An alternative theory is that the eels' behaviour is an accident of history, a bizarre relic of continental drift. Their migrations may have begun more than 50 million years ago, at the time when Europe and North America were only beginning to part company and were separated by no more than a narrow, seaweed-filled channel.

As the continents moved slowly apart, the eels' habit of returning to the sea to breed gradually involved them in a slightly longer journey with each passing year. As one generation of eels succeeded another, the inherited migration instinct directed them back to the same spot, while natural selection favoured those with the stamina to get there. If this theory is correct, the present epic journey of the European eels is a living reminder of how far the continents have drifted across the globe over the millennia.

In the 1970s, scientists proposed that continental drift might also be responsible for the strenuous migration undertaken by green turtles (*Chelonia mydas*), some of which feed along the coast of Brazil, but journey halfway across the Atlantic to mate and lay their eggs on the beaches of Ascension Island.

LEARNED HOMING INSTINCT

It was suggested that some 70 million years ago, when South America was breaking away from Africa, the turtles nested on volcanic islands close to the coast. As the ocean floor spread, the distance between shore and islands indiscernibly increased, fraction by fraction, so that, millions of years later, the turtles were travelling a good 1250 miles (2000 km) by an outdated homing instinct.

More recent genetic evidence has discredited this theory. Adult turtles feeding off the African coast were probably diverted to Ascension Island by accident in relatively recent times, on currents that flow from east to west. Rather than returning to their feeding grounds in Africa they then probably wandered farther west, helped by the same current, and adopted feeding grounds off

NEW ROUTES FOR THE ATLANTIC COD

Most Atlantic cod (*Gadus morhua*) return to the area where they themselves hatched in order to spawn. It may be anything between 5 and 15 years before they make this first return journey. There are separate cod spawning groups, each with its own migration circuit. A year before they spawn for the first time, immature cod make a complete practice migration with the adults of their group to learn about the route. Scientists once thought that patterns of fish migration learned in this way remained fixed generation after generation. They now know that fish are more adaptable than that, exploring and taking up new opportunities as they arise.

There has been a general warming of the northern oceans in the 20th century, and fish such as the Atlantic cod have altered their migration routes to benefit from the change. One group of cod, for example, has travelled for years between spawning grounds in Iceland and feeding grounds off south-west Greenland. Earlier in the 20th century, a group of immature cod broke away from the traditional migration circuit and set up a new one off the west coast of Greenland, formerly too cold. Cod and tuna are both prized fish: understanding their migrations has become an important part of exploiting them.

HARDY VOYAGER *The Atlantic cod undertakes long migratory journeys.*

BEACHED SEALS *Northern fur seals spread out on a Pacific beach. Fur seals gather together when they are breeding.*

Brazil. Ever since, their young have returned to Ascension Island because they have an instinct to breed at the beach of their birth: the suitability of this breeding beach is vouched for by their own survival.

Their homing instinct (which applies only to the breeding ground) seems to rely on learned rather than inherited information. This means that it is adaptable and may allow for the colonisation of entirely new sites if a female gets lost or a previous nesting beach becomes unsuitable.

CHANCE ARRIVALS?

Accidental migrations have undoubtedly been important in the colonisation of islands and continents over the millennia. Before species were deliberately or inadvertently transported by humans, many of the plants and animals of oceanic islands were originally brought there by wind or by water, some just blown off their usual course, others never intending to travel at all. Ships have often sighted natural rafts of logs and matted vegetation drifting in ocean currents. Each can carry an assortment of passengers, from seeds and spores to wood-boring insects, snails, lizards and tortoises.

Although most of such animals adrift in a hostile ocean die, some occasionally arrive, washed up by chance on a distant island shore. If there are a few of the same species, or a female already carrying eggs or young, they may start a new colony.

For some animals, drifting in the currents is no accident. A floating, larval stage is an important part of the life cycle of many marine animals, such as barnacles, sea anemones and shellfish. Such life cycles allow these invertebrates, with limited powers of locomotion, to colonise new areas, sometimes thousands of miles away.

Experiments show that the transparent, spider-like larvae of the Australian rock lobster (*Panulirus longipes cygnus*) have been carried west across the Indian Ocean, round the tip of Madagascar and as far as the east coast of Africa, 3750 miles (6000 km) away.

SUMMER AND WINTER *Grey whales migrate annually between summer feeding grounds in the north and warmer seas in the south for calving.*

WHEN THE GREY WHALE MIGRATES

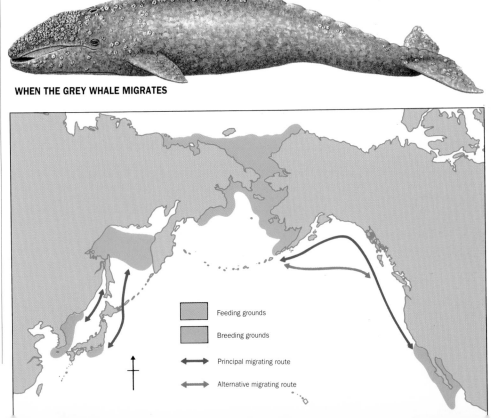

Feeding grounds

Breeding grounds

Principal migrating route

Alternative migrating route

THE LONG TREK *Spiny lobsters migrate in single file from their summer home into deeper water.*

forced by the encroaching pack ice and the needs of their expected calves, which will be sensitive to the cold when newborn. Not until the calves have developed a thick insulating layer of blubber can mother and young return to the Antarctic.

RESOURCEFUL WHALES

Some whales travel an astonishing distance of 12 000 miles (20 000 km) each year, in order to be in the best places for either feeding or breeding. However, life must always be a compromise. In the warm, tropical waters that are suitable for calving, adult whales find themselves short of food. Zooplankton density may be only 1 per cent of that in the polar waters, so the animals must rely on the energy stored in their fatty blubber to survive and to produce milk for their young.

The blubber, built up over the summer feeding bonanza, can be up to 12 in (30 cm) thick in some species. Fed by their mothers' milk, the young are not affected by the temporary food shortage. In effect, the adult whale has brought the abundance of the cold polar waters with her, stored in her own body.

The grey whales (*Eschrictius gibbosus*) travel farther than any of the other whales and dolphins. Californian stocks of grey whales undertake an epic journey from their summer feeding grounds in the Bering Sea, in the North Pacific, south-west of Alaska, to calving sites in the sheltered lagoons of Baja California in Mexico. The orderly southward procession is headed by heavily pregnant females, who have been carrying their young for nearly a year, followed by a remarkably orderly procession of recently impregnated females, immature females, adult males, and finally the young males. On the return journey, the mothers and their new calves bring up

This emphasises just how much planktonic larvae are at the mercy of the tides and currents. Some float for months before arriving at a suitable place to settle; others are eaten before finding such a site.

Chance factors always play an important part in extending the range of a species. But some animals deliberately explore beyond their familiar surroundings in search of new areas to live. These exploratory migrations are usually undertaken by inquisitive, immature animals before they settle down to mate and breed. If their ventures are successful, this younger generation may adopt new feeding or breeding grounds. Young fish use exploratory migrations to seek out food-rich waters – and some populations of the Atlantic cod and bluefin tuna have adopted new migration circuits as a result.

YOUNG EXPLORERS

Exploratory migration is common among juvenile seals and sea lions, which, as adults, normally remain faithful to a single breeding site. Females of the northern fur seal (*Callorhinus ursinus*) may travel 1700 miles (2800 km) from their breeding grounds to feed, but they return each year to islands just outside the pack ice in the northern Pacific. Until 1966, the species only bred on Robben Island in the Sea of Okhotsk, in the North Pacific to the north of Japan, and on the Commander and Pribilof Islands in the Bering Sea. Recently, some young, exploratory individuals adopted a completely new breeding site on San Miguel Island off California. Such a move probably offers improved living conditions, and a respite from overcrowding, parasites and diseases.

Large-scale migrations are widespread among the marine mammals. Although

---

EATING FOR TWO

While feeding her baby, the female southern right whale (*Eubalaena australis*) loses at least 8 tons in weight. She prepares herself for the business of calving by gorging herself with food in the krill-laden waters of the Antarctic, and then migrates northwards to the warm calving waters of the Great Australian Bight where she gives birth. Once there, the mother's usual diet of Antarctic krill is unavailable, and so she has to fast for a period of several months. During this time her calf consumes about 350 pints (200 litres) of milk a day.

---

their journeys may be even longer than those of the green turtle, it is easier to see the advantages of such migrations. The greatest mammalian travellers of all are the 'baleen' whales. These air-breathing giants sustain themselves on a diet of animal plankton such as the shrimp-like krill, which they sift from the water. Krill is most abundant in the icy, nutrient-rich waters of the Antarctic. But during the winter months, the whales move away to warmer seas,

BLACK SURF PERCH *The lateral line, which senses vibrations, can be seen on the right side of the fish.*

65 animals, they march determinedly in single file. Captive spiny lobsters have been observed to 'migrate' in line around their enclosure, both day and night for two weeks. Travelling together in lines is thought to make the dynamics of movement easier, but it may also aid in orientation and defence.

The purpose of the lobsters' march remains a mystery. It could be a behavioural relic from a past Ice Age, when seasonal movements were essential to escape cold winter currents. An alternative explanation is that the lobsters are moving to deep water to avoid the buffeting of winter storms and to seek out colder conditions. If food is short in winter, the cold helps to slow the metabolic rate and the crabs use less energy to stay alive (this is why some land animals hibernate in winter).

It is the network of the ocean realms that

the rear, as they meander along the time-honoured route, to reach their summer haunt in the Arctic after about 90 days.

LOBSTER ROUTE MARCH

Not all animals migrate in order to breed or to feed. Some may be motivated by other factors, such as the avoidance of predators or harsh conditions. In the case of the adult spiny lobster (*Panulirus argus*) of Florida, the reasons are still obscure, yet 100 000 of them make a mass exodus from the coral reefs as autumn approaches. The trigger is normally diminishing light combined with the first squall of winter.

One by one the lobsters line up, each touching the tail of the animal in front with one of its antennae. In formations of up to

WHEN OPPORTUNITY KNOCKS FOR THE CHUB

Although salmon and eels can adapt from fresh water to salt water and back again, most fish are confined to one or the other. The majority of freshwater fish cannot tolerate the ocean brine, so for them it is a barrier to migration.

A handful of freshwater fish from British Columbia in Canada have achieved the seemingly impossible: they have managed to cross the prohibitively salty Straits of Georgia and reached the rivers of Vancouver Island, 30 miles (48 km) away. They include the peamouth chub (*Mylocheilus caurinus*) which is usually killed by much shorter journeys in salt water.

Scientists have discovered that fresh water gushing from the Fraser River on the mainland creates a nearly salt-free surface channel across part of the Straits of Georgia.

Normally this passage extends only a short way towards Vancouver Island, but in years of exceptionally fast snowmelt, the fresh water is propelled right across to the opposite bank. The researchers suggested that, in these conditions, peamouth chub could escape the confines of their usual range and colonise a new area. But such opportunities would be extremely rare – there would have been only 50 days over the past 30 years in which the chub could safely have crossed the Straits.

Given the rarity of the critical conditions, scientists had to engineer an elaborate laboratory experiment to check their hunch that the journey was possible. Using a water tunnel in which the current strength and saltiness of the water were

controlled, fish were subjected to a simulated voyage, similar to the one they might experience between mainland Canada and Vancouver

STRAITS OF GEORGIA *Rare occasions of fast snowmelt make a corridor of fresh water.*

Island. Nine out of the ten fish swam for long enough – 100 hours – to have arrived at their destination, proving to sceptics that the voyage was possible.

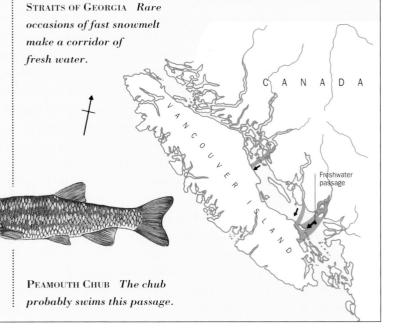

PEAMOUTH CHUB *The chub probably swims this passage.*

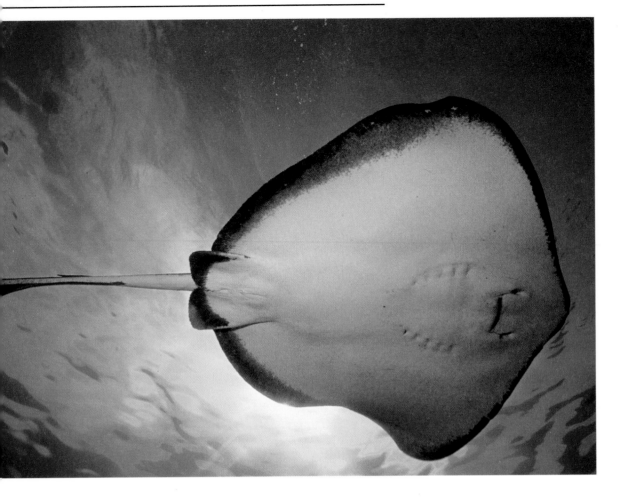

may see different parts of the light spectrum, hear frequencies of sound that do not register in our ears, and detect stimuli of which we are completely unaware. A small fish, seeming to glide silently by, is actually making a murmur of sound that can attract a passing shark. A shark's eyes are ten times more sensitive to light than our own, and its sense of smell so acute that it can detect blood in the water 1/3 mile (roughly 0.5 km) away. Furthermore, sharks can sense tiny pulses of electricity given off by the muscle movements of other animals.

MIND-MAPPING

Almost all fish can detect underwater vibrations, or pressure waves. They register these using an organ called the lateral line, which runs along both sides of their body. When swimming, the vibrations they create bounce off nearby objects. Fish register the returning vibrations and from them they can build up a mental picture of their surroundings or of their position within a moving shoal.

Marine animals draw on a whole combination of senses in order to gather information about the immediate world around them. Many young animals also build up a mental map of their local area

SCENT DETECTORS *The nostrils of this stingray can be seen close to its mouth. Different water 'scents', which vary from place to place, may aid navigation.*

makes it possible for animals to migrate over such enormous distances. Yet how then, in such an apparently uniform environment, and one where visibility is poor, do animals manage to navigate with such pinpoint accuracy?

To imagine that stretches of water are featureless deserts is a human viewpoint. Humans rely mostly on visual stimuli to find their way. Anyone who has used a snorkel will know how disorientating the sea can be using vision alone, even in shallow water. When you glance above the surface, the shore is often not where you had expected it to be. The prospect of swimming through a deep blue void in a fixed direction, without the aid of a compass, is a daunting one.

But the watery depths, undifferentiated and characterless to our eyes, hold all manner of gradients, barriers and guides that are essential to a marine animal.

Currents signal direction, and layers are defined by light intensity, temperature, pressure and saltiness. Chemicals from sediments and rocks, from decaying animals and plants, from dissolved gases, and even from man-made pollutants, give different waters their own characteristic flavours. The landscape of the seabed has many memorable ridges and trenches, cliffs, hills and valleys. Even the turbidity, or cloudiness, of the water and the type of material lying on the bottom can be usefully 'map-read' by a migrating animal.

Most mysterious to us is animals' 'sixth sense', an uncanny and seemingly supernatural power beyond the experience of human beings. In fact, there is not just one 'sixth sense', but a whole array of them: many animal senses are quite different from our own. Animals

EAGLE-EYED *A lemon shark looking for prey. Many species of shark have eyes ten times more light-sensitive than ours.*

by exploration. But the question of navigation over long distances remains. How does a green turtle know in which direction to travel to locate the tiny mass of Ascension Island in a vast ocean? How do animals hold a certain direction with no apparent reference to landmarks at all? And is the behaviour inherited or learned? Such questions are still awaiting answer by research scientists. One of the most important breakthroughs of the past 20 years is the realisation that many animals are sensitive to the Earth's magnetic field, and can use it to determine direction in much the same way that we use a compass.

Just as there are currents in the ocean, so there is a constant, powerful flow of molten rock in the Earth's outer core. These hot currents of liquid rock contain enough metals to generate electricity by their motion, which in turn creates the Earth's magnetic field. The field extends in the shape of a giant teardrop over the Earth and out into space. For those creatures that can detect magnetism, it presents a three-dimensional reference map for navigation. Yet it is a map that may suddenly prove to be obsolete, or at least inaccurate, as the dynamic processes that create the magnetic field – the violent currents deep beneath the seabed – undergo their own mysterious changes.

MAGNETIC RESPONSE

The first living things to reveal their magnetic responses to science were bacteria living in sediments. They were found to contain tiny crystals of a substance called magnetite, which invariably lines up with the magnetic poles. Yet magnetite was not a new discovery in itself. Larger crystals of the same material were used by early sailors and navigators as a forerunner to the modern compass. Crystals of magnetite have now been found in the bodies of tuna fish and turtles, as well as in many birds and insects – all of them creatures that have a strong sense of direction. No doubt there is a magnetic sense in many other oceanic animals.

Scientists suspect that fish use the magnetic field, in combination with an electric sense, for direction-finding. When an object such as a fish's body moves across the magnetic field, tiny electric currents are generated. Fish such as sharks, rays and skates can detect this electricity through small pits in their snouts. Bony fish may also have this ability, though it is not yet proven.

Over the millennia, changes in the currents of the Earth's core have completely reversed the Earth's magnetic field, not just once or twice, but at least 170 times in the last 76 million years. Rocks formed by sea-floor spreading acquire a

MASS STRANDINGS — WHALES ON THE SHORE

Large groups of healthy whales occasionally swim up onto the shore and become stranded. With their great bulk unsupported by water, they are helpless and unable to return to the sea. But would they go back even if they could? The answer seems obvious, yet if they are towed out to deep water, the whales sometimes turn about and came ashore again, to the distress of their rescuers. Mass strandings such as these occur on all kinds of coastline. Incidences are highest in whales that migrate long distances, and strandings of pilot whales (*Globicephala* species) are particularly common.

The reason for this determined, and apparently suicidal behaviour, has been a mystery for centuries. Recent research has shed light on a possible cause. Stranding sites were plotted on contour maps showing variations in the intensity of the Earth's magnetic field. Intriguingly, all the stranding sites coincided with 'magnetic valleys' – areas of low magnetism that ran directly from the sea onto the shore. It seems that the whales were following 'magnetic maps', which would function well in deep water, but would betray them if they wandered into unfamiliar, shallower areas, for the maps could not distinguish between land and sea. The dates of strandings coincided with times when there had been recorded disruptions to the normal patterns of Earth's magnetic field, which may have confused the whales' navigation system.

WASHED UP *Longfin pilot whales stranded on an Australian beach.*

magnetic polarity as they cool. Over the different eras rocks have been polarised in opposite directions, so that there are now stripes of polarity in the rocks of the sea-bed – a giant geological 'bar code' that is characteristic of a particular area.

Stripes that have the same orientation as the present magnetic field enhance its strength, while stripes with a reverse polarity weaken its effect. Whales seem to follow these 'high' and 'low' magnetic contours to navigate.

TURTLES ON COURSE

Much research has recently addressed the secrets of navigation in young sea turtles. As soon as they emerge from the sand where they hatch, the tiny, determined turtles instinctively set off towards the sea. Although it is night, they are guided by the quality of the light reflected from the ocean surface. Once in the water, they somehow know how to strike a course to the open ocean.

Experiments have shown that their navigational sense is partly magnetic. Young loggerhead turtles (*Caretta caretta*) from Florida's Atlantic coast, removed from their beach as eggs and hatched in a laboratory, swam in a north-easterly course once they emerged, which in the wild would have taken them out to the Gulf Stream. Changing the magnetic field around the turtles, by use of powerful electromagnets, changed their preferred direction. Further study showed that turtles in the sea are also guided by the waves. Close to the shore, they swam directly into the waves, apparently allowing this cue to override any magnetic instinct. It is thought that the magnetic sense might be used in deeper water where wave direction is a less reliable guide.

The behaviour of adult turtles is more complicated and far more difficult to study. The tiny hatchlings need only hold the correct directional course to head out to sea, but adults must have more than a simple compass sense to find the nesting beach of their birth. They require some awareness of where they are in relation to their goal: in effect, a 'map sense'. Turtles, like whales, may use the magnetic stripes

of the ocean floor as some kind of map. Their orientation cues could include the direction of the waves and swell, or the chemical 'taste' of their nesting beach, as in salmon. Unlike birds, turtles are probably unable to orientate themselves by the stars, since they are very short-sighted above water.

It is still not known for sure whether humans possess a weak, undeveloped magnetic sense. Experiments indicate that we do have an innate sense of direction, which is disrupted if a magnet is placed against the head. Certainly, some people

HAWKSBILL TURTLES *The hatchlings head for the sea.*

are able to navigate without the aid of compass and map. Polynesian sailors in the south Pacific have been able to navigate for centuries using the stars, the pattern of the swell and the taste of the water. Other early navigators sought the help of animals' senses to find their way: they released birds and followed them to find land, or used natural populations of fish, birds and plants as indicators of land, ice or open water.

ON THE OCEAN'S EDGE

2

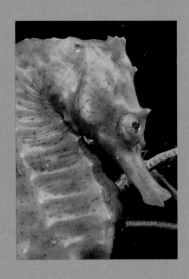

LEAFY DISGUISE *The head of a sea dragon, a frilly relative of the sea horse.*

FROM THE ICY BUT NUTRIENT-RICH WATERS OF THE ARCTIC AND ANTARCTIC TO THE BUZZING ACTIVITY OF TROPICAL MANGROVE SWAMPS, LIFE ALONG THE OCEAN'S EDGE IS NEVER LESS THAN VARIED. PENGUINS, SEALS AND BALEEN WHALES SCOOP UP TINY, SHRIMP-LIKE KRILL IN THE ANTARCTIC; KILLER WHALES, WALRUSES AND POLAR BEARS PROWL THE SEA AND ICE OF THE ARCTIC. IN MORE TEMPERATE CLIMES, RAZORSHELLS BURROW THEIR WAY INTO SANDY SHORES; WHELKS, MUSSELS, LIMPETS AND SEA ANEMONES CLING TO ROCKIER COASTS. TURTLES, SHELLFISH, COUNTLESS SPECIES OF FISH AND BIRDS, AND RARER CREATURES SUCH AS DUGONGS AND MANATEES FIND REFUGE IN THE RICH GRAZING GROUNDS OF KELP FORESTS AND EELGRASS MEADOWS.

IN THE FOREST *Strands of giant kelp off California.*

KELP FORESTS AND EELGRASS MEADOWS

For creatures such as sea snails and sea cows, the oceans' beds of giant seaweeds and flowering plants are like the fields and forests for land animals. They support an abundance of life, providing homes, hiding places and feeding grounds.

Imagine a forest where animals such as wolves and foxes fly among the trees, swooping down from the leafy canopy to the forest floor in pursuit of their prey. It is a forest with such violent winds that the tops of the trees are torn to shreds and must regrow at rates of 18 in (46 cm) a day to compensate. Stranger still, in this forest there is no rich brown layer of rotting leaves lying on the ground, but instead its debris is dispersed all around – the air is thick with particles of food, and many animals drink in their meals as easily as they breathe. The trees, too, can soak up any minerals they need from the air around them.

This is the extraordinary world of an underwater forest, where seaweeds that are known as giant kelps (*Macrocystis* and *Nereocystis*) grow to a staggering 140 ft (42 m) in length, as tall as many trees in rain forests. The wolves and foxes are actually sea lions and sea otters, furry warm-blooded animals like their woodland relatives that swim between the trunk-like stems of giant kelps in graceful sweeping glides. The sea lions are in search of fish, while the otters have a preference for sea urchins, mussels, abalone and other shellfish.

LIFE SOURCE

The kelps must grow upwards to the surface and expose themselves to sunlight – something that is essential for the growth of any plant. Air-filled floats help to buoy the fleshy stems up towards the Sun. But the surface is also a destructive place, where storm waves can rip their fronds apart, leaving innumerable fragments of kelp in the water.

This apparent destruction is, however, a source of life, and without it there would be few animals in the kelp forests. The fragments are decomposed by bacteria in the water, turning the sea into a nutritious broth on which immobile creatures such as mussels, sponges and

LIGHT SEEKING *Kelp forests grow from the ocean floor towards the light, buoyed up by air-filled floats.*

THE ANIMALS THAT LIVE IN A KELP FOREST

In a kelp forest, even the holdfasts – the part of a plant that fastens to something else – hide varied kingdoms of tiny animals. A holdfast of the relatively small British kelp (*Laminaria*) may contain more than 1000 individuals. The outer rootlets support crusts of filter-feeding animals, such as sponges and tube worms. Within the whorls there may be miniature snails, shrimp-like crustaceans, bristle worms and crabs.

Between the clusters of holdfasts, the bare rock is colonised by a garden of smaller shade-loving seaweeds. The feathery foliage and water that is thick with appetising detritus attract a multitude of hungry worms, shrimps, crabs, anemones, starfish, sea urchins and sea hares. On the sea floor are shellfish such as clams, mussels and abalone. Hundreds of fish are tempted by the bounty of potential food and by the excellent hiding places in the mane of kelp fronds. In their wake come fish-feeding birds, plunging through the surface in deadly accurate dives. Moray eels may lurk on the bottom, and barracudas roam in search of a meal.

1. Seal
2. Opal eyes
3. Giant kelp fish
4. Garibaldi
5. Sea lion
6. Blacksmiths
7. Otter
8. Black rockfish
9. Sheepshead
10. Greenling
11. Norris snail
12. Brittle starfish
13. Spiny lobster
14. Yellow fringehead
15. Starfish

THE SEA OTTER'S MEALTIME ANTICS

As a human might prise an oyster from a rock with a knife, so the sea otter sometimes carries a stone to chisel away at firmly lodged prey during a dive. Otters often keep the same stone for the duration of several dives; it is tucked into a flap of skin under the armpit while swimming.

Returning to the surface, the animal floats on its back to consume its meal. On its chest the otter may use a large flat stone as a portable anvil. Clams or abalones are repeatedly beaten with both paws against the stone until their shells shatter. The stone then functions as a 'table top' for its meal.

In fact, sea otters are thought to be the only mammals, outside the primate group (man, apes and monkeys), that use tools to tackle their food. Young otters learn this

behaviour by watching their parents and through experimental play.

MEALS AFLOAT *An otter makes short work of a clam.*

reason, there is not enough drift kelp available for them – for instance, after a violent storm – then their behaviour changes: they move out of their crevices and start to feed directly off the live plants. Their most destructive habit is to chew through kelp stems, leaving whole giant kelps simply to drift away on the tide and to be washed up in pungent heaps on the beach.

From the coasts of Alaska as far south as California, sea otters are unusual among predators in that they can overcome the urchins' spines, crack the thin shell that lies beneath the spines and eat the soft-bodied animal within. They do this by first wrapping the urchin in a severed kelp frond, which is thick enough to smother the spines completely and to make the urchin easy to handle. Few other marine animals would have either the dexterity or the intelligence to carry out this feat, and it is just one example of the otters' tool-using behaviour.

DISAPPEARING KELP

Although they are now protected by law, sea otters were hunted almost to extinction in the 19th century for their thick fur, more dense than that of any other living mammal. It used to be widely assumed that the recent increase in the numbers of sea urchins and the gradual disappearance of the kelp beds were linked to the disappearance of the sea otter.

Certainly, it was found that islands in the Aleutian chain – spread across the northern Pacific between Alaska and Russia – that had large otter populations had both low urchin densities and a dense growth of kelp, whereas places with few otters had more urchins and less kelp. But as more pieces of the jigsaw were added, the facts did not quite fit. Although predators play some part in controlling the sea

anemones can feed. They, in turn, nourish larger animals such as starfish, octopuses and sea slugs.

Unlike the leaves of trees, giant kelps cannot easily be grazed by plant-eating animals – their thick, rubbery, gelatinous fronds are so heavily defended against wave and tooth alike that few animals are rash enough to attempt to bite into them. Only about one-tenth of the kelp is directly eaten from the living fronds. Indeed, without the pulverising action of storm waves and the decomposing bacteria in the water, kelp forests would be dull and deserted – as it is, they teem with animals, some of them visible and spectacular, others secretive and unseen, hidden in the sinuous folds of the kelp.

Among the few animals that can graze on giant kelp are certain sea snails, which rasp relentlessly at the fronds with hundreds of tiny teeth embedded on a structure known as a 'radula', which resembles a

miniature wood plane. Far more damaging, however, are sea urchins – creatures that look like nothing more than a ball of prickles but which have a powerful set of jaws set in the underside. Exceptionally, whole areas

PRECIOUS RESOURCE

The prolific growth of a single kelp plant may support more than 500 000 small animals. Such a wealth of life and productivity means that the seabed's giant kelp forests are potentially very valuable: 1 sq mile (2.5 km²) of *Macrocystis* kelp is estimated to be worth about $1 million a year. Fish and shellfish are just some of its products. The kelp itself yields alginates, used in the production of paper, textiles, pharmaceuticals, food and cosmetics. One use for food is in ice cream – the alginate is added before freezing to prevent the ice cream from crystallising.

of the seabed may be stripped completely bare of plants by vast armies of urchins.

In normal circumstances, sea urchins live in cracks, moving little and feeding on a few loose pieces of drift kelp. If, for some urchins and the kelp plants, many other complex factors are involved. The interplay of the currents, water temperature, nutrient levels and freak storms – in addition to the feeding behaviour of sea urchins – all these factors influence the health and vigour of the kelp.

Giant kelp forests are found all along the North American coast as far north as Alaska. Off the coast of British Columbia, Amerindian fishermen once used the filament from the stalk of the tough, leathery kelp to make their fishing lines. Similar kelp forests are scattered throughout the Southern Hemisphere, particularly on the western coasts of South America and South Africa, in areas that receive nutritious upwelling currents from the deep ocean.

Although these seaweeds are as tall as trees, they are, in fact, very simple plants. Most seaweeds lack the specialised parts of land plants such as leaves, flowers, fruits, roots, woody branches and trunks – parts that each do a different job and have a different internal structure. Instead, the whole plant is made of much the same type of material. Like all seaweeds, kelps are more closely related to the invisible one-celled plants of the plankton than to trees and flowers. Along with the phytoplankton, seaweeds belong to the plant group known as algae, the most primitive plants on the evolutionary scale.

The fact that seaweeds soak up minerals directly from the soupy water around them makes specialised roots unnecessary. Although there is a rootlike structure at the base of each kelp, it is not a true root at all.

Known as a 'holdfast', it is nothing more than a leathery claw, the kelp's anchor, which keeps a firm grip and withstands the strongest of storm surges. It cannot absorb water and minerals as do the roots of a tree.

In most seaweeds there are no sap arteries in the stems either, although the kelps are exceptional in having channels within the stems that take nourishing sap down to the holdfast. This is needed because the holdfast is so far beneath the sunlit surface that it can make little food for itself.

Most strikingly, the giant kelps have no need of strong woody trunks and branches because the water buoys them up and

MOTHER AND CHILD *A mother otter and her young one rest in a bed of kelp on the shore.*

FIRM GRIP *The massive kelp frond is anchored against the ocean surges with a 'holdfast' like a leathery claw.*

Eventually, over many, many generations, they came to survive total submersion. The shifting and muddy sandbanks of temperate coastal estuaries are home to underwater fields of eelgrass (*Zostera* species).

EELGRASS UNDER THREAT

Stretches of eelgrass were once abundant on both sides of the Atlantic and these eelgrass beds were home to creatures such as the common cuttlefish, prawns, tiny shrimps, snails, sea anemones and small jellyfish. There were scavenging dogwhelks and fleshy sea hares carrying their tangled pink threads of spawn.

Ducks, geese and swans all came to feed – until a mysterious disease wiped out large areas of the eelgrass meadows in the 1930s. There was no common agreement among experts about what caused this disease, though more recent research has shown that a strain of the organism *Labyrinthula* causes the same symptoms. In Europe, the decline of eelgrass actually caused changes in the coastline: without the stabilising effect of the offshore eelgrass, that previously trapped sediment and helped to reduce erosion, the level of beaches fell. Populations of eelgrasses, along with the animals they support, have only recovered very gradually from the devastation.

The tropics have their own variety of rippling seagrass meadows that are found from the coast of Australia through the Pacific, Asia, Africa and the American tropics. Dense waving 'turfs' establish themselves on the shallow sea floor inside coral

supports their fronds. If the sea level were suddenly to fall, exposing the kelp forests, they would collapse dramatically, as the rubbery stems and fronds experienced the full force of gravity for the first time.

MEADOWS OF THE SEA

Many areas of the shallow sea bottom are covered by a lush growth of green marine grasses. Although their flat, straplike leaves, which can grow up to 3 ft (1 m) long, appear to be very simple in form, closer inspection reveals that these plants are far more complex and highly evolved than seaweeds. The fact that they have branching roots and underground stems is a sign that eelgrasses are not algae at all, but flowering plants that have evolved to cope with underwater life.

Their land-living ancestors probably grew on mud flats and first adapted to occasional or daily inundation by the sea.

reefs and on sheltered coasts. Most common are the turtle grass (*Thalassia testudinum*), which has flat ribbon blades, and manatee grass (*Syringodium filiforme*), which has cylindrical cordlike leaves. Either together or separately, these plants colonise whole sand flats with their creeping underground stems. Growth is prolific.

CHANCE ENCOUNTERS

Like the eelgrasses, these flowering plants must reproduce under water. Inconspicuous male flowers release pollen grains in strands of mucus that may be carried miles by the currents. If by chance they encounter another patch of seagrass on their journey, the pollen grains may fertilise the female flowers of another plant. The seeds that develop from this fertilisation are contained by buoyant fruits that drift away on the current and are carried for many miles, until the flesh of the fruit disintegrates, releasing the seeds to settle on the ocean bottom. If just one seed lands in a suitable shallow spot, it can generate a whole new seagrass meadow.

The succulent seagrass pastures attract numerous grazing animals, and a multitude of filter-feeders, burrowers and scavengers that feed on plant or animal debris.

SUBMERGED PASTURES
The ancestors of eelgrass
originally grew on mud
flats, eventually evolving to
live completely under water.

Each blade of grass is encumbered with a whole community of minute algae. These tiny plants, many of which are unable to colonise the soft sediments, make use of the seagrass blades as permanent resting places in the sunlit shallows.

Grazing animals keep the grass fronds cropped shorter than they might otherwise grow, helped by the action of the waves, which tear off strands of foliage. These litter the beaches or drift out to sea. Seagrass beds export energy and nutrients when they lose leaves, providing an important supply for other communities, even in the depths of the ocean. Seagrass leaves have been found down to 25 000 ft (7600 m).

SEAGRASS GRAZERS

Turtles, birds and shoals of plant-eating fish come to browse in the seagrass meadows, which may act as temporary nurseries for the fish of neighbouring coral reefs. Large conches, spiny urchins, red starfish and orange-brown sea cucumbers are scattered over the bottom. Pipefish and sea horses, slender vertical forms in green or brown, are perfectly camouflaged in the wafting fronds. Larger fishes, such as sharks and rays, pass through in search of prey.

In the seagrass pastures of Australia and the Indo-Pacific region, the sea mammals known as dugongs come to graze. These slugggish creatures measure from about 7 to 11 ft (2.1 to 3.4 m) from broad, square, bristly snout to pointed flipper tail (the animal has no hind limbs). Their relatives the manatees inhabit the warm coastal waters, rivers and estuaries of the Atlantic.

It is estimated that an adult manatee – measuring between 10 and 13 ft (3 and 4 m) long and with a maximum weight of 3550 lb (1600 kg) – needs to eat 200 lb (90 kg) of vegetation a day to maintain its body weight. Dugongs and manatees are popularly known as sea cows, but are, in fact, more closely related to the elephant, with whom they share a common ancestor. So, like the seagrasses they graze, the dugongs are

INNOCENT VANDALS
Sea urchins sometimes
chew through kelp
stems, leaving the
fronds to drift away.

WELL DISGUISED Long, slender pipefish are well camouflaged for grazing in the vast under-sea meadows of turtle grass found in many shallow tropical seas.

descended from land-dwellers that became adapted to sea life. They, too, retain a legacy of life on land: dugongs breathe air as we do, and suckle their young.

TALL TALES AND WISHFUL THINKING

Sailors' tales of mermaids are said to have originated with this gentle fish-tailed creature – although it must have required a lot of wishful thinking on the part of the sailors to interpret its facial features as those of a beautiful long-haired maiden.

The name Sirenia given to this animal group reflects the long association with marine mythology. It is derived from the sirens of ancient Greek legend – singing seducers who reputedly tempted mariners to a watery death on dangerous rocks. Dugongs and manatees are plant-eaters, unlike the seals, dolphins, whales and sea otters. They feel for the most tender grasses with sensory bristles along the upper lip, their eyesight being weak.

One problem for animals like these, which depend on plants, particularly grasses, for their food, is that the plants contain abrasive, hardening substances that wear away the surface of teeth. In the Sirenians, this problem is solved by the older front teeth repeatedly falling out and then being replaced by new teeth that develop from behind them and gradually move forwards. This regular replacement of worn teeth continues throughout the animal's life; the same system can be seen on land in the teeth of elephants.

Dugongs and manatees have gained a reputation for being solitary, retiring creatures. But scientists believe that before they became persecuted by man they were more confident, gregarious animals. Large-scale slaughter for meat, oil and leather has left populations depleted and wary, hiding silently in quiet waters.

HEARTY APPETITE A manatee has to eat huge quantities of seagrass to maintain its great bulk.

'CONVENIENCE' FOODS — WAITING FOR A MEAL

Unlike active animals that spend their day foraging for food, many invertebrates settle in one place and wait for the food to come to them. Success depends upon straining the microscopic food particles from a vast volume of water each day. To do this, the animals draw a stream of water through some kind of intricate sieve or filter. The filter may be a mucous basket, sticky tentacles, gills or even modified legs.

FAN WORM *It pushes out its tentacles to feed.*

Such animals are known as filter-feeders or suspension-feeders. They are only found under water, in seas, lakes and some rivers. Above water, there is rarely a sufficient concentration of airborne food, nor is there any supportive medium to buoy up a mesh or sieve. Submerged seaweeds are convenient settling places for colonies of the smallest sedentary animals. Similar colonies spread in multicoloured carpets on boulders and rocky overhangs to catch the currents. These encrusting organisms are hard to recognise as animals in the familiar sense; moss-like mats are, in fact, colonies of tiny tube-shaped animals, called bryozoans, that pull in water through a comb of tentacles around their body openings. Sponges and the colourful, jelly-like sea squirts are also simple filter-feeding animals – the sea squirt's filter-basket mechanism takes up nearly the whole of its bag-like body.

Suspension feeders do not always clump together in tightly packed colonies. Tube worms and fan worms live individually in protective tubes and push out a crown of feathered tentacles to feed. One of the most beautiful is the peacock worm (*Sabella pavonina*). Its delicately coloured whorls of filaments are retracted into the tube of sand and mud at the slightest vibration or shadow.

Some of the hinged-shelled molluscs, such as the clams, scallops, mussels, and oysters are suspension feeders of a most sophisticated kind. They generate a one-way current of food-rich water by beating thousands of tiny hairs called 'cilia'. Water floods over the breathing apparatus (the gills), which doubles as a food filter. The fine gills sort food particles from inedible sand and debris. Food is carried to the mouth, while waste is flushed out with the expelled water.

PEEPING OUT *With shell slightly open, a scallop reveals tentacles and eyes.*

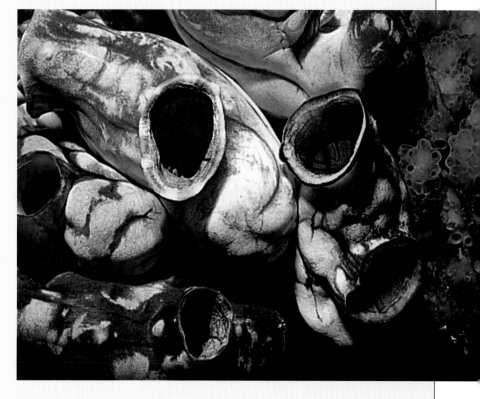

SEDENTARY DINERS *The sea squirt (top) and clam (below) are filter-feeders.*

Barnacles actually use their legs to filter-feed, as they sit between protective plates of chalky armour. Sweeping movements of their feathery branched legs draw in water, and a fine mesh of bristles catches microscopic particles that are scraped towards the mouth. Barnacles attach themselves to rocks, wooden pilings, ships and even to animals such as whales, turtles and crabs.

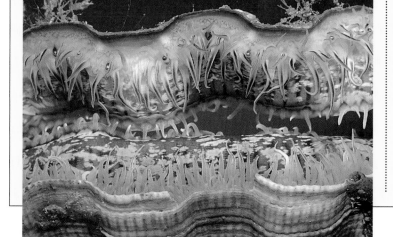

GIGANTIC 'RAFT'

A huge raft of sargassum weed in the Sargasso Sea off Bermuda is kept afloat by air-filled bladders.

In the vicinity of the island of Bermuda in the western North Atlantic is the curious Sargasso Sea. This oval water mass, almost the size of the United States, is girdled on all sides by powerful currents: to the north by the warm Gulf Stream; to the east by the Canaries' Current, and to the south by the North Equatorial Current. These swirling water masses enclose and trap a warm body of water that composes the Sargasso Sea. The sea is heavy with salt here, as there is little inflow of fresh water.

THE MYSTERIOUS FLOATING WEED OF THE SARGASSO SEA

On the surface of this vast area, float millions of tons of sargassum weed, a golden-green plant that actually belongs to the group known as brown seaweeds. Unlike the kelps and other brown seaweeds, it has no holdfast to attach it firmly to the bottom. The water of the Sargasso Sea is too deep for such a lifestyle.

Instead, great rafts of the plant hang at the surface of the sea, each of them sustaining a complete ecosystem within its branching mass. Both the sea and the plant derive their name from the bunched, air-filled bladders that keep the plant afloat. These apparently reminded homesick Portuguese sailors of bunches of grapes – *salgazos* in Portuguese – and brought back fond memories of home. Sargassum weed

COLUMBUS'S MISTAKE

On his first voyage across the Atlantic in 1492, Christopher Columbus encountered the mysteries of the Sargasso Sea. Observing the crabs and floating seaweed, he wrongly deduced that he was close to shore but in fact he was still more than 1000 miles (1600 km) away. Eventually he sailed on to reach San Salvador Island in the Bahamas, but it was not until his third voyage in 1498 that Columbus discovered the mainland. At that time America and Europe would have been 66 ft (20 m) closer together than they are today – the result of continental drift.

reproduces by breaking off tiny pieces of itself. Each fragment is capable of growing into an enormous new, self-sufficient raft.

Inhabiting this buoyant forest is a very well-camouflaged collection of professional hitchhikers that cling to the life-sustaining bundle of foliage. Below, the dark water is a 'sea desert' devoid of essential nutrients and patrolled only by transient predators waiting for a meal. In the greenish-gold branches above, the process of natural selection favours inhabitants that can cling on and look inconspicuous. The smallest organisms are able to cement themselves to the weed, with the result that it becomes encrusted with living creatures: there are single-celled plants, tiny filter-feeding tube worms and sedentary colonies of bryozoans or 'moss animals', all feeding on the plankton.

Scampering among these are tiny shrimps, crabs and other crustaceans, their camouflaged surfaces mottled and blotchy. Olive-green sea anemones, brittle stars and flatworms also find niches in the floating community. Snails rasp at algal growths with their plates of microscopic backward-pointing teeth.

Fish living in the weed may be residents or simply passing visitors. Large numbers of fish larvae shelter in the dappled refuge. More permanent residents of the sea include the elongated pipefish (*Sygnathus* species) that blends into the background of tangled stems as it hunts for small invertebrates. Best camouflaged of all, though, is the sargassum fish, *Histrio histrio*. A combination of near-perfect disguise, tempting lure and cavernous mouth make this the most cunning and fearsome of all the Sargasso's lurking predators. With jaws so large that they are capable of swallowing something very nearly its own size – about $7^{1}/_{2}$ in (19 cm) long – little is safe from the sargassum fish.

The sargassum weed is everything to these animals: a home, a hiding place and a feeding ground. Elsewhere in the open ocean, it is the phytoplankton that are the ultimate source of food, but here sargassum weed assumes equal importance in nurturing animal life, a floating pasture becalmed in the Atlantic Ocean.

CAMOUFLAGE — THE KEY TO SURVIVAL

The dappled patterns of seaweed habitats encourage some elaborate mimicry and camouflage among their inhabitants.

Kelp crabs (*Puggetia* species), though not highly camouflaged themselves, dress up in pieces of vegetation to diguise their outline. They have evolved tiny hooks on the top of their shell, to which they attach pieces of severed weed. Other decorator crabs seem almost to have made dressing up into an art form. When stationary, their extravagant costumes of fluffy sponges, wisps of algae and local debris leave them virtually indistinguishable from their surroundings.

Like the crabs, the Australian leafy sea dragon (*Phyllopteryx*) has a broken outline to camouflage it

SEA DRAGON *It floats along gently to resemble seaweed.*

among the weed. However, this animal needs no props. Its prolific leafy outgrowths are part of its body, ribbonlike projections of the living fish that perfectly resemble a torn-off piece of kelp, tattered by the waves. Also, by mimicking the colour of the weed, the sea dragon is virtually invisible to its invertebrate prey that approach so closely that the sea dragon can simply suck them into its long, waiting snout.

Sea dragons are relatives of the sea horses, an animal group (*Syngnathidae*) in which the males collect eggs from a female, fertilise them, care for them and finally 'give birth' to the young. Some sea horses have a single large pouch to contain all the eggs, but the male leafy sea dragon carries the eggs in individual capsules on his tail. When the 100 or so tiny young sea horses emerge, they are already festooned with miniature leafy

outgrowths to protect them.

Clinging to the sargassum weed of its home, the sargassum fish is another master of deception: appropriately, its Latin name *Histrio histrio* means 'actor'. Using a strategy similar to that of the sea dragon, the fish is covered by fronds of leaflike skin. However, it takes the illusions further still. The skin surface is mottled yellow-green and black, with small white patches to imitate the pattern of 'moss animal' colonies and tube worms that live on the seaweed. It dangles an enticingly wormlike lure to attract passing fish. Originally, the lure evolved from a ray of the dorsal fin, and now hangs forward so that the wormlike tip is directly in front of the gaping mouth. To capture its prey, the fish waits until the curious victim is inspecting the 'worm', then simply opens its mouth. The sudden inrush of water sweeps the helpless prey

WELL BLENDED *Sargassum anglerfish (top) and kelp crabs (above) are almost invisible – until they move.*

inside. The pectoral fins have also been modified: they form ten-fingered clasps with which the fish clutches the weed stems and laboriously pulls itself along.

SURVIVAL ON ROCKY SHORES

Where the land meets the sea, the elements are harsh and unforgiving. But the rewards are great for animals – from limpets to whelks to hermit crabs – that can withstand the conflict of rock and wave, surviving in this tumultuous zone.

Ocean breakers on the eastern edge of the Atlantic strike the sheer surface of a shoreline rock with terrifying force. Each wave pounds like a hammer onto steel, a relentless battering pulse. Any small boat, caught by a storm wave and flung onto the rocks, is smashed and splintered. A man overboard is quickly knocked unconscious, drawn down by the backwash and then thrown onto the rocks again with murderous force. It seems impossible that anything could survive, let alone thrive, in this pounding tumult.

Yet as the tide falls, and the waves withdraw to the lower shore, parts of the rock seem literally to come to life. On a greyish-white slab of weathered limestone there are bumps of identical colour and texture that look like part of the rock itself. Then, as the damp surface glistens in the sunlight, soon after high tide, one of these bumps elevates a fraction from the rock, and two tiny, mobile, pink 'feelers' start to emerge at one edge. Slowly the bump begins to glide across the rock. The bump is the worn and

WILD WAVES *The pounding Atlantic surf breaks on the shore of western Ireland.*

weatherbeaten shell of a limpet. It has long since been pounded into a gentle curve rather than the pointed, conical shape that it would develop in less violent haunts; its original ribbed surface has been smoothed out by the scouring waves, and its colour faded by the sun from a tawny yellowish hue to the same grey-white as the rock. The shell has grown thick and bone-like to withstand the force of the waves.

The limpet, carrying its shell, moves off slowly across the damp rock. As it wanders, it leaves a meandering trace of brighter rock that has been rubbed clean of the microscopic greenish-grey algae that normally cling to the surface. The limpet's sharp rasping tongue has cleared the algae away, and its stomach is now digesting these tiny one-celled plants.

GRAZING IN MINIATURE

This is the rocky shore's equivalent of a cow grazing in a field of grass, but scaled down and massively fortified for life in this punishing environment. The various algae have thick, tough outer walls and produce a sticky material that glues them to the rock. The limpet, a relative of the slugs and snails, is equipped with a large, muscular sucker (called a 'foot'), an organ of extraordinary power and tenacity, sufficient to hold its shell gripped tightly to the rock face, secure against both the storm wave and the predatory sea bird.

TONGUE TRAIL *The feeding action of the common limpet leaves a characteristic zigzagging track.*

SNUG FIT *Common limpets bed down into their scars upon a rock.*

Departing from its base, the limpet leaves behind a circular scar – or seemingly circular, for in fact there are small irregularities in the shape. The scar is formed by minute twisting movements of the shell, made when the limpet is in place. Its shell, when it is pitted against soft rocks such as limestone or sandstone, is tough enough to grind away the surface, creating a hollow that precisely fits the limpet's individual shape.

On harder rocks such as granite, the margins of the shell itself are worn down so that they fit exactly into the existing contours of the rock. A limpet gains extra protection from hazards such as the force of the breakers or the prising beaks of oystercatchers, by always settling in the same spot, with the edge of its shell locked precisely into place against the surface of the rock.

SAFETY IN STONE

Before high tide returns, the exposed rocks will begin to dry out and, if the sun is shining, become uncomfortably hot. Anticipating this, the limpet returns to base before the last of the moisture has evaporated, and clamps itself down into its homely scar on the rock. Here its tight fit can resist desiccation, keeping moisture inside even on the hottest summer day. The limpet's shell slots so perfectly into its scar that once again it looks almost like an extension of the limestone.

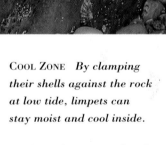

COOL ZONE *By clamping their shells against the rock at low tide, limpets can stay moist and cool inside.*

On softer types of rock, some animals find protection by actually boring into the inflexible substrate. These creatures include certain sea urchins, which grind away with teeth or spines; and segmented worms that first weaken the rock with an acid secretion, then scrape it out using their tough bristles. There is even a burrowing marine sponge (*Cliona celata*) which is able to dissolve passageways in limestone rock by the production of a mild acid. The sponge's own skeleton is made of silica and resists the action of the acid.

The truly expert borers, however, that can go deep into the rock, are found among the bivalve molluscs – shellfish from the same family as mussels and scallops, with a characteristic two-part shell that is joined by a hinge. In temperate waters, several different species of piddock mechanically drill themselves into rock. Piddock shells are something like those of cockles, but they are much stronger, elongated and asymmetrical to give a hard, angular, penetrative 'leading edge'.

This grinds into the rock first, but the rest of the shell also has abrasive powers owing to rows of tiny, hard spikes that run across the outer surface. The two parts of the shell are joined together by a ball-and-socket joint rather than the more usual hinge, making the piddock's shell a highly efficient drill: repeated rotation of the shells about the joint grinds out a circular shaft. Once lodged in the rock, the piddock sends up siphons from the safety of its chamber to sieve microscopic food particles from the water at high tide.

In warm seas, the date mussel burrows into limestone by dissolving away the rock with an acid secretion, much like that produced by the rock-boring sponge. But its own shell, which is made of the same chalky material as the limestone, must be protected from self-destruction. Such protection is given by a thick, shiny, brown coating – the colour and texture of which

EXPERT BORER *An efficient biological drill, the piddock grinds itself securely into a place in the rock.*

gives the creature its curiously date-like appearance.

Paradoxically, by tunnelling into the rocks for refuge, creatures such as piddocks, date mussels and their kind eventually undermine those rocks and bring about their collapse. The rock-borers' way of life is, in the end, self-defeating because it destroys the strength of the boulders or cliffs that protect them. Yet there is sufficient time for them to reproduce themselves before the self-inflicted disaster strikes, and the young tend to go out and colonise new areas of rock, so that the species survives.

ONLY THE TOUGH SURVIVE

Limpets and rock-boring animals illustrate the challenge of life on a rocky shore, that perilous knife-edge between land and sea. Creatures here must survive the extremes

that both environments are capable of, from the pummelling waves and harsh salt-laden spray, to searing heat at low tide in summer, or freezing temperatures in winter. Somehow they must fashion a form of protection against an unyielding backdrop of solid rock, turning its concrete hardness to their advantage.

Few creatures are as hardy as the limpet or the barnacles, which can grip the exposed, near-vertical surfaces of the rock. Most seek out the natural shelter provided by crevices and cracks, where they are shielded from the worst extremes of this habitat. Others shun the steep-sided and most wave-battered rocks, clinging instead to flatter or more sheltered surfaces.

Many seaweeds can anchor themselves here using their grasping holdfasts (the part of a plant that fastens to something else), which stick to rock surfaces by producing a strong, mucilaginous 'glue'. The rocks provide sturdy attachment sites, in contrast to the shifting uncertainties of sandy or muddy shores.

COLOUR CODING

A close look at a rocky shore reveals a surprising range of different seaweeds. There are tufts, fans, forked threads, ribbons, sheets, matted ropes and cushions. To the touch, some feel slippery, others jelly-like, tough, chalky, crisp or even velvety. And they vary in colour from yellow-green to

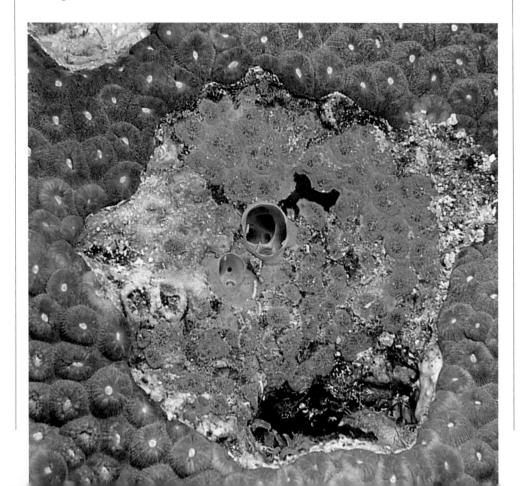

SHELTER SEEKER *A burrowing sponge eats into the hard surface of a coral with the help of acid secretions.*

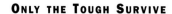

THE BIZARRE ANATOMY OF THE BARNACLE

The ubiquitous barnacle, one of the commonest animals on any rocky shore, confounded naturalists for hundreds of years. Its conical shell was reminiscent of a limpet, and the barnacle was classified alongside snails and seashells as a mollusc. In fact, the sedentary barnacle is a relative of crabs and shrimps.

The barnacle's unlikely origin was discovered in the 1920s by a British Army surgeon, John Vaughan Thompson, while he was stationed in Cork, Ireland. Thompson was a keen amateur zoologist, and dedicated much of his spare time to the study of marine animals. Familiar with the developmental stages of the common crab, from the hatching of its tiny, unrecognisable, floating larvae, to the emergence of the bottom-living adult, he turned his attention to some other crustacean larvae, similar in appearance to those of the crab. He watched them attaching themselves to stones and, after careful observation, discovered that they developed into barnacles.

When a floating larva is ready to settle, it crawls over the rock in search of a suitable site, and eventually cements itself upside-down with its antennae. The barnacle must be in suitable currents, on a firm substrate, and within mating distance of other barnacles. The choice is an irrevocable one, for once cemented in position, the little animal is there for life.

Once settled, a young barnacle secretes chalky plates of armour for protection against predators, desiccation and beating waves, and proceeds to grow and feed. It extends bristly legs through trap-door plates at the top of its volcano-shaped home. The modified legs are used to filter food particles out of passing water currents. In effect, the barnacle stands on its head and kicks food into its mouth with its feet.

LOW TIDE *The barnacles withdraw into their shells.*

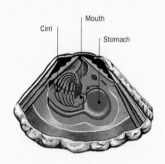

Cirri · Mouth · Stomach

BARNACLE FEEDING *Its legs filter food out of the currents.*

---

olive-brown, from dull red, pink and violet to almost black. Some have a subtle iridescence. It is by their colour that biologists classify seaweeds into basic groups: green, brown or red.

The green algae contain the same pigments as land plants, including the grass-green compound called chlorophyll. This vital pigment traps the sun's rays so that plants can make their own food. Despite the range of colours, all other seaweeds contain chlorophyll too, but they have additional pigments – red, purplish or brown – that mask the green of the chlorophyll.

Strikingly distinct bands of colour can sometimes be seen cloaking a rocky shore at low tide. The reason for this effect, called 'zonation' by scientists, is that some seaweeds can tolerate harsher living conditions than others can, and they are able to outcompete their neighbours in the daily struggle for space, nutrients and light. Zonation involves animals as well as seaweeds but the bands of green and brown created by the weeds are often the most noticeable feature.

Life is toughest for those seaweeds that are farthest up the shore and spend most time out of water between high tides. The resilient brown seaweeds survive best in this exposed zone: between wetting, some of them become crisp and dry, withstanding a loss of nearly two-thirds of their water content.

Lower down on the shore, other brown seaweeds grow in dense layers, and inadvertently they act as shock absorbers for some of the waves' energy. To equip themselves for life in this hazardous zone, the slippery fronds of the brown weeds are coated in a gelatinous slime that

SAFETY IN NUMBERS *Common mussels cling to a rock face, clustering together for protection against the waves.*

reduces damage by abrasion and stops them from drying out at low tide.

Red seaweeds mingle with the others at all levels, but are mostly scattered below the low-tide mark. Some of the very small ones coat their delicate fronds in a hard, whitish casing for protection. This is made from calcium carbonate, the same raw material

as in limestone and seashell, a product of chemicals that occur naturally in the sea water. With shell-like cylinders around each

CRAMPED CONDITIONS *Goose barnacles, sea anemones and starfish (sea stars) fight for space on a rocky shore.*

frond, the red seaweeds are actually pink in colour, and look like tiny chalk-encrusted trees, or hard cushions on the rocks.

The flimsy green seaweeds, such as the sea lettuce, thrive in places that are constantly damp. Generally, they are found on the sheltered surfaces of rocks positioned near to the sea, in rock pools or in gulleys

where fresh water runs down the rocks, since they have little to protect their fragile fronds from drying out.

In ensuring their own survival, the seaweeds – mainly the various brown seaweeds, such as the bladderwrack and serrated wrack – unwittingly modify the harsh environment of the bare rock and make the shore

a more hospitable place for animals to live in, allowing those of them that are less hardy than the limpets and rock-borers to survive. A multitude of tiny creatures take shelter beneath the piles of damp wrack as the tide goes out.

Anemones retract their tentacles; worms writhe into burrows; snails slide into their

IN WAITING Chitons, or coat-of-mail shells, sit out low tide in a rock pool.

shells; crabs scuttle beneath the moist seaweed blanket. The seaweed fronds are speckled with yellow and brown winkles and coated by gelatinous sea squirts, which benefit from the moisture held by the flaccid fronds.

Like the seaweeds, different types of animal predominate in different zones of the shore, according to their ability to withstand the hazards of exposure. Few marine animals are able to tolerate the upper shore, a zone that receives moisture only from rainfall and the hurled spray of the strongest breaking waves. Sooty black lichens coat the rocks in this region, which is beyond the range of most seaweeds. The only marine animals to thrive here are small periwinkles, residing in the cracks. Slightly lower down, the rocks are covered by thousands of acorn barnacles, which have tightly fitting chalky plates to retain moisture. At the level of the shore touched by high tides, other creatures fight for a small space among the mass of barnacles: mussels attached by sticky threads, keel worms living inside protective chalky tubes and armoured chitons.

Any movement here is limited but the chiton, or coat-of-mail shell, finds its way to and from its own particular spot in a most curious manner. It is guided by the Earth's geomagnetic field which it detects with tiny magnets on its tongue. The tongue is rasplike, the roughness provided by rows of minute teeth. Each tooth is capped by magnetite, a magnetic ore of iron. At night, the chiton moves around using its tongue to scrape algae from the rocks. But the tongue is also a remarkable navigational aid, allowing it to find its way 'home'.

EAT OR BE EATEN

In the damp zones nearer the low-tide mark, the physical environment becomes less demanding, and there is a greater variety of animal life, much of which is rarely exposed to the air. Hiding beneath rocks are sea squirts, encrusting moss animals (bryozoans), sponges, segmented worms, crabs, shellfish and sea urchins. Inevitably, this abundance of life brings many pressures of a different kind – intense competition over food and space, and an increased threat of predation.

Few creatures are safe from predators in the bustling intertidal zone. Starfish grasp prey with their suckered legs and protrude a bag-like stomach through their mouth with which to digest the helpless animal. Crabs crush shells with their pincers and pick out the tender flesh within. Clumsy,

CLOSE-KNIT COMMUNITY Dogwhelks, mussels, limpets and sea anemones crowd together on a limestone shore.

OCEAN LIFE IN MINIATURE: THE ROCK POOL

Many shores are either exclusively sandy or made up entirely of rock, but some coasts share features of both, with rocky outcrops protruding through sand, or sandy bays forming among rocks and cliffs. Often, as here, wind-blown sand dunes form the backdrop to sandy beaches, their loose sand consolidated into sturdy hillocks by the roots of hardy marram grass.

Rock pools (tide pools) are often found on rocky shores, although it takes special types of rock and particular tidal conditions to produce large pools that are vibrant with life. Such pools provide attachment sites for seaweeds and retain water at low tide, creating miniature reservoirs for anemones, shrimps, starfish and small fish. Sandy shores, in contrast, provide few attachment sites for seaweeds or for clinging animals such as barnacles and limpets. Much of the life of a sandy beach goes on beneath the surface in a maze of damp burrows and chambers.

EXPOSED ZONE *Beyond the reach of all but the highest tides, living conditions are harsh. For animals of sandy shores, some food and shelter may be found in the 'strand line' – a collection of flotsam and jetsam deposited at the highest point of the turning tide. On rocky shores, waves splash above the high-tide mark, and damp crevices may support life on otherwise barren rock.*

INTERTIDAL ZONE *This zone is exposed to the air for varying periods of time between high tides. Creatures of sandy shores can burrow deeper, or move towards the sea, to minimise their exposure. But many of those on a rocky shore, such as mussels and barnacles, are rooted to the spot. Their tough armour protects them from the drying air, the changing temperatures and the pounding waves.*

LOWER SHORE *Animals living in this zone are only exposed for a brief period at low tide. For most of the time, they are covered by water, which brings with it nutrients and oxygen, and protects them from the drying air. On rocky shores, this zone is covered with seaweeds, and when the water retreats animals take shelter in their damp tresses.*

GREAT PRETENDER: THE OCTOPUS

The fluid, flexible body of an octopus is versatile in times of need. It glides through astonishingly tight crevices to hide, or to reach crabs, worms and shellfish. What is more, it can change colour at will. Like its relatives, the squid and cuttlefish, the octopus has extremely sophisticated eyesight. All three groups have a correspondingly complex visual language based upon startling changes of colour and pattern, which indicate fright, anger, submission or sexual interest. An instant costume-change allows the octopus to advertise or camouflage its presence, depending on the circumstances.

In a rock pool, an octopus is hard to spot, as it lurks in a narrow crevice, its mottled colouring blending with the surrounding shadows. Bands, blotches, stripes, and borders of light and dark, all break up the outline so effectively that the creature can seem to vanish, even under a direct and watchful gaze.

When an octopus is provoked, successive pulses of colour and hue suddenly flood the skin. In the presence of a female, a male octopus will flush red. If threatened by a predator such as a moray eel, a normally grey-brown octopus will become red or dark brown. Octopuses, like squid, can squirt a 'smoke' screen of black ink if alarmed. Combined with a colour change, this display confuses a predator, and gives the octopus time to make its escape.

The brilliant waves of colour washing across the skin are generated by little bags of pigment that the octopus can expand or contract at will. At rest, these are spherical and almost closed, but when stimulated by nerves, their openings can be stretched by the tug of delicate radiating muscle fibres, to reveal the colour within. The result is an almost infinite variety of pattern and hue. In an even more bizarre addition to its colour changes, the octopus can make curious alterations to its texture, suddenly raising a mass of tiny lumps and projections across the surface of its smooth, rubbery skin.

CHAMELEON OF THE SEA *The octopus disguises itself well.*

NASTY NIPPERS *The bite of a moray eel is vicious enough to kill octopus and squid.*

Scattered across the rocks, and superimposed upon the pattern of zonation, are the many tide pools. These range from shallow cavities to large, deep chasms strewn with boulders, all retaining a parcel of sea water as the tide retreats. Within each is a microcosm of life, a community of plants and animals that would normally be restricted to much lower levels by their requirement for a constant covering of sea water.

NATURE'S AQUARIA

Generations of children have stalked the edges of such pools to watch their curious inhabitants. Tiny, mottled fish, transparent prawns, and the extended arms of colourful sea anemones can be glimpsed among the diffuse green seaweed. Silvery-pink topshells and beautiful cowries sometimes graze at algal growth on the rocks. Hermit crabs scuttle across the bottom, each of

long-legged sea spiders cling to their soft-bodied victims and suck out fluid food; the tiny body of the sea spider cannot contain its gut, which therefore extends into each of the eight spindly legs. Sea anemones fire paralysing, toxic barbs into any prey that is luckless enough to drift or swim into the grip of their waving tentacles.

COLOURED DOGWHELKS

One particularly effective predator found on rocky shores is the dogwhelk (*Nucella*), which bores through the hard shells of its molluscan prey using a mobile, drill-like tongue encrusted with sharp teeth. Once through the shell, it rasps out the soft body of its immobile victim within. It persecutes barnacles and mussels in particular, because they are cemented into position and are therefore unable to escape from this slow form of attack.

In the same way that pigments in the algae eaten by flamingoes tint the birds' feathers pink, so the food source of the dogwhelk influences its coloration. A diet of mussels

produces a brown or purple shell, whereas a diet of barnacles turns the whelk's shell white. At times when mussels are scarce, the dogwhelk simply switches its prey, and in doing so it undergoes a gradual change of colour. These flexible feeding habits make sure that neither barnacles nor mussels ever come to dominate their patch of the shoreline completely.

ROCK BOTTOM *A spiny lobster scavenges for food at the bottom of a rock pool.*

them wearing a secondhand shell, vacated by its original owner. Positioned on the top of the borrowed shell, an anemone may be hitching a ride. These anemones are actively encouraged by their hosts, since their stinging tentacles afford the hermit crab an extra degree of protection. Other crabs, coated in their own forms of armour, sidle under ledges or stones to hide.

But life in a tide pool is not as tranquil and well-cushioned as it may appear at first glance. Conditions in these tiny oases fluctuate wildly, with soaring changes in temperature and saltiness sometimes occurring in the hours between high tides. If it is hot,

the water may warm to near-lethal temperatures, and then evaporate, raising the concentration of salt in the liquid that is left behind. Conversely, if it rains, there is an influx of fresh water into the pool that dramatically dilutes the salt.

A LIFE FULL OF CONTRASTS

A tide pool rich in seaweeds may switch from being alkaline during the day to being acidic at night, because of changes in the amount of dissolved carbon dioxide contained in it. Carbon dioxide is released all the time by animals and plants as a waste product of breathing. In the daytime, it is used up by plants in the process of making food by photosynthesis, but at night, when there is no sunlight to fuel the process, carbon dioxide accumulates, making the water acidic.

When the tide restores conditions to normal, it does so abruptly, flooding the pool and giving the inhabitants little time to adjust. Rock-pool life is therefore closed to creatures that cannot survive changes in temperature, acidity and saltiness. These changes are particularly exaggerated in the upper-shore pools, which always suffer the longest periods of exposure.

Most marine animals would have difficulty withstanding the harsh conditions of the upper pools, but in the pools close to the low-tide mark there are many unexpected guests: starfish, for instance, are sometimes stranded by the force of a wave on the turning tide, strangers

MAKESHIFT ARMOUR
A hermit crab borrows a discarded mollusc shell as protection for its soft hindquarters.

from another world dropped into the self-contained community. They stay there until the sea returns to liberate them.

One fish that is not restrained by the steep walls of a rock pool is the frill-finned goby (*Bathygobius soporator*) of the Bahamas, measuring 4 in (10 cm) or less, which has evolved an amazingly accurate escape procedure. It is able to leap clear of any rock pool that has become too hot, salty or dangerous, and to land squarely in an adjacent pool without floundering on the dry rock in between.

The fish may jump along a series of steep-sided pools until it reaches the ocean itself – without any previous view of its goal. Experiments have shown that the fish are able to do this because they have learnt the layout of their local pools by swimming over them at high tide; they retain an exact mental map of the pools for as long as 40 days.

OFFSHORE INHABITANTS

The food-rich waters close to rocky shores are alive with predatory animals. Lobsters live in holes on rocky bottoms, where they scavenge for morsels of meat. Octopuses wait for a live meal in sheltered undersea caverns, extending their suckered arms to trap crabs, lobsters or fish in a muscular grip, and chewing their prey with a sharp, horny beak. In warmer waters, octopuses may

TINY SURVIVORS *Small prawns and shrimps are among the animals that can withstand the huge changes in temperature, acidity and saltiness that occur in rock pools.*

themselves fall prey to ferocious but beautifully patterned moray eels, that lurk in rocky crevices throughout the tropical and warm-temperate seas. Moray eels measure up to 5 ft (1.5 m), and one Pacific species, *Thyrsoidea macrura*, is known to grow to 11 ft (3.5 m). Their powerful bite and sharp teeth can trap fish, squid and cuttlefish.

Shoals of fish congregate in the shallow waters beyond the rocks. Nearby, on the narrow, rocky ledges of tall cliffs, kittiwakes, guillemots and razorbills nest in their thousands. On remote rocky islands there may be colonies of nesting gannets, and everywhere there are gulls. Each sea bird pair must catch a constant supply of food for its chicks from the stocks below the water.

Death for the fish comes swiftly and unexpectedly with the explosive arrival of a bird from the unseen world above. This bird is no more than a momentary visitor to the underwater world. Even so, its brief foray serves as a vivid reminder that the communities of land and sea are ultimately linked and interdependent.

HOME IN THE SAND

Sandy shores are a secretive environment where, with rising and falling tides, burrowing creatures emerge to feed, or retreat into dark, damp hiding places beneath the sand. Many fall prey to animals such as fish and wading birds.

From early childhood, sand has a special fascination for us. This is, perhaps, because of its unique consistency and texture: sparkling like stardust and flowing when dry; consolidated but malleable when wet. Humans are unusual, however, in their love of sandy beaches: to other life forms, these barren slopes offer an austere prospect. The characteristics that account for our enjoyment help to make the open, sandy beach inhospitable to wildlife. And a quick glance around reveals a distinct lack of animal life on the surface of the sand.

There are no crevices, boulders or overhangs for animals to use as refuges; no rock pools to retain water at the turn of the tide.

Waves dig into the shoreline and lift away layers of suspended sand grains, so that the face of the beach may be radically re-sculpted overnight. The pure, clean look of wave-scrubbed sand is testimony in itself to the absence of life on the surface.

DAILY RENEWAL *A sandy beach is re-sculpted and washed clean by each high tide.*

SHY SHELL *A razor shell uses its muscular foot to burrow rapidly into the sand for safety.*

No seaweeds stand a chance of establishing themselves on this ever-moving substrate, which runs through the fingers of a seaweed's grasping holdfast. Surface-living animals are similarly at risk of being washed out to sea. The solution, for the animals at least, is to burrow, which not only reduces the risk of being washed away by the tide, but also solves the problems of exposure, drying out and overheating: unlike us, most animals on a sandy beach try to avoid the Sun's rays.

There is little visible sign of animal presence, apart from some holes or discarded casts. But in the hidden, labyrinthine kingdom beneath the sand, there are simple animals, cloistered from each other in their burrows, silent and still, awaiting the return of the tide.

EXCAVATIONS IN THE SAND

Many different animals have evolved burrowing behaviour, quite independently of each other. Segmented worms, sand hoppers, shrimps, crabs, sea cucumbers and shellfish can all be found tunnelling into sand, as can certain heart urchins and starfishes. Bleached white discs sometimes wash up in huge numbers on tropical beaches: they are the hard outer 'shells' of sand dollars, flattened relatives of the sea urchins. Each disc is patterned with a star-shaped series of tiny holes and slits. Living sand dollars congregate in their hundreds on sandy bottoms, burrowing edgewise into the sand. Once lodged in the sand, they catch particles of food from the water currents in a sticky mucous trap.

Some animals delve far deeper than the sand dollars – they dig rapidly to escape predators or to avoid being caught up in the turbulence of an approaching wave. The razor shell (*Ensis* species), named after its resemblance to an old-fashioned cut-throat razor and measuring anything up to 8 in (20 cm) long, usually defeats the efforts of humans to capture it because it burrows faster than anyone can dig with a spade. It pushes its muscular foot into the sand, pumps the tip up with blood, and then uses this as a swollen anchor against which to pull down its smooth, elongated shell. A rapid series of such movements buries the shellfish deep below the surface in a matter of seconds.

To burrowers, the attractiveness of a sandy beach depends on the size of the constituent particles. Coarse gravel beaches are the least inviting, since burrowing is difficult and the spaces between large grains do not hold the water well, unlike the narrow spaces between small sand grains. This lack of water means that gravel beaches support only microscopic creatures, which keep a foothold by clinging to the surface of a gravel grain.

Fine sand, by contrast, does not dry out at low tide – or dries out only at the surface. Its consistent dampness offers protection from changes in the temperature, and the saltiness of the surroundings varies very little – an important advantage for marine animals. Damp sand also provides a firm medium for walking or tunnelling. As a result, hundreds of species of burrowing

INTO THE LIGHT *An Australian giant beach worm emerging from its hiding place in the sand.*

worms and shellfish prefer fine, wet sand to any other kind.

The churning of the waves introduces a steady supply of oxygen from the air. However, when the sand on a beach is not disturbed by the waves, the reserve of oxygen in the water between the grains of sand

QUICK GETAWAY *The Atlantic rock crab is an expert at rapid burrowing into sand.*

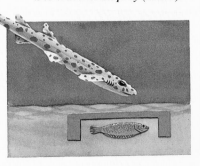

SAND SNORKELLER
*When buried in the
sand, the masked crab
breathes through a tube
that it creates by
holding its long
antennae together.*

called siphons, from the soft body within their shell. A twin set of these tubes extends up into the water at high tide, one to suck water into the burrow and one to expel it. To prevent sand from blocking the system, the siphons are equipped with special sieve-like screens.

Other animals have developed ingenious variations on the same theme, adapting whichever body parts are available. One of the most remarkable is the masked crab (*Corystes cassivelaunus*), which digs itself backwards into the sand with its hind limbs until only the tips of the antennae protrude above the surface. The antennae are held close together, and two rows of dense bristles, running the length of each antenna, interlock to make a single, clear breathing tube. This allows the crab to breathe while remaining well hidden from predators.

Food is less abundant on sandy shores than on rocky ones. Because there are no seaweeds, plant-eaters are rare, having to

begins to decline, as it is used up by the living inhabitants, and is replaced only very slowly, diffusing in from the water above. The finest sand – despite all its other attractions for burrowing creatures – suffers from

particularly slow replenishment of oxygen.

Many animals overcome the problem by making direct contact with the water above the sand. Shellfish are the real specialists, sending out long chimney-like extensions,

ELECTRIC PREY: BODY CURRENTS THAT TELL TALES

For some animals of sandy seabeds there is literally 'no hiding place'. The predators that hunt them have evolved detection skills of such extraordinary sophistication that the prey can never fully conceal themselves.

Animal movement is controlled by electrical messages, which streak along nerve fibres and stimulate muscles into activity. It is not surprising, therefore, that living bodies give out minute pulses of electric current. This happens even when animals are motionless, because of the involuntary contractions of the heart and the gentle rhythmic motions of the gills needed for breathing.

Water, unlike air, is a good conductor of electricity. To those predators that can detect it, this

faint electric hum of the heart and gills is a giveaway clue to the position of invisible prey.

Certain fish have extraordinarily sensitive organs that are capable of detecting these tiny currents at close range. They can do so in murky, silt-laden water, or even through a layer of sand. Sharks and rays are among the most skilled

ELECTRIC PROBES *Sensors on a shark's snout (right) enable it to track down prey (below).*

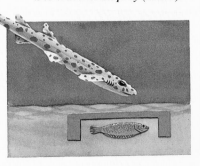

detectors of electricity, their heads pitted with special sensors called ampullae of Lorenzini.

Experiments have demonstrated how important a part electricity plays in prey location for this group of fish. A dogfish (a member of the shark group) was released in a tank where a live plaice was buried beneath sand. It quickly found the

plaice in normal circumstances. But if the plaice was covered by an insulating plastic cover (see diagram below left), the dogfish was unable to locate it. When tiny electrodes were buried in the sand, and a very weak current pulsed through them to mimic the electrical signature of the plaice, the dogfish attacked the electrodes in confusion.

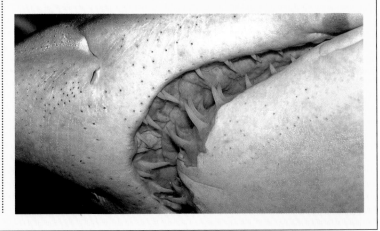

make do with a sparse supply of microscopic algae on the surface of the sand. All other food is brought in by the sea. Animals living on the shore must either scavenge food scraps stranded by the waves, or filter plankton and food particles from sea water during high tide.

SIFTERS, SCRAPERS AND MUD-SWALLOWERS

Feeding is a methodical but monotonous business for animals that live on tiny floating particles of food. To obtain enough to eat, these animals draw water through sieve-like body parts, or across feathery fans or mucous nets which retain the particles on their sticky threads. In some animals the filter system has two tasks: breathing and feeding. Hinged shellfish, such as cockles and razor shells, use their gills to extract both oxygen and food par-

CAST ASIDE *A lugworm leaves a cast of undigested sand at the top of its burrow, having first extracted all the goodness.*

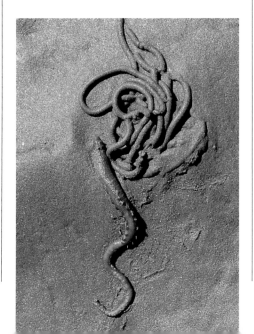

ticles from the stream of sea water passing through their siphons.

Another group, known as deposit feeders, patiently wait for food to settle on the surface of the sand. Crabs scrape up this fine detritus; worms extend groping tentacles from tubes in the sand to search for similar food particles; and certain shellfish use their suction tubes to 'vacuum clean' the sediment surface.

A third group, the sediment-swallowers, consume vast quantities of sand as they burrow, in the same way that terrestrial earthworms 'eat' through soil. One example is the lugworm (*Arenicola marina*). Living permanently in an L-shaped tube, it swallows the muddy sand above its head for five to eight hours a day. The animal digests the small quantity of nutritious material in its largely worthless meal, then backs up its burrow to squirt out the remainder in a squiggly cast. This is the cast sought out by fishermen, who dig down into the mud to harvest the lugworm for use as bait.

THE SCAVENGERS AND CARNIVORES

Farther up the shore, above the high-water level, scavengers have an erratic supply of food brought in with the tide. Dead fish, jellyfish and crabs may be cast ashore, along with the black, leathery 'mermaids' purses', which are the egg cases of dogfish, trailing from their corners the curled tendrils that originally attached them to a piece of seaweed. Torn fragments of weed are also dumped at the strandline, mixed in with all manner of inedible debris: shells, driftwood and, increasingly, plastic refuse tipped overboard from ships. Millions of shrimp-like sand hoppers (*Talitrus* and *Orchestoidea* species) hide under the flotsam and jetsam,

TERROR TACTICS *A cancer crab stirs up sand with its pincers in a desperate attempt to deter a predator.*

DISAPPEARING ACT *If a predator approaches, these garden eels will vanish faster than the eye can see.*

emerging only at night to scavenge. If their cover is disturbed, clouds of hoppers leap several feet into the air.

Coming and going with the tides is an army of visiting predators searching for the animals buried beneath the sand. Wading birds probe for worms and shellfish at low tide with sensitive, elongated bills. The exact length of the beak varies from species to species, and determines at which level in the sediment each bird feeds. Curlews have some of the longest bills, up to 8 in (20 cm) in length, with a curved tip, long enough to reach the long-siphoned furrow-shells well below the surface. Oystercatchers have stout orange-red bills of medium length, which

IN-BUILT ASSET *Curlews use their long bills to probe deep into the sand after shellfish, worms and other food.*

can reach cockles, while the short-billed plovers tend to take spire-shells from just below the surface.

The birds learn to locate good hunting areas, where their chosen prey is likely to be found: oystercatchers even seem to be able to recognise the small holes left at the surface by cockles. By exploiting a particular depth within the sand, and specialising in certain types of prey found there, each species of wader suffers relatively little competition from other predatory birds on the shore. In this way, many bird species come to coexist in the same habitat, each exploiting a slightly different source of food.

At high tide, the threat to the burrowers comes from the other direction. Fish swim over the surface of the sand at high tide and pounce on any feeding or breathing tubes extended through the sand. In the warmer oceans, rays pose a special threat to buried animals. They skim over the surface with undulations of their wing-like fins. A squirt of water from the mouth blasts away the sand particles and reveals any hiding shellfish, which are then crushed between the ray's teeth.

The arrival of a ray among a colony of garden eels projecting from their burrows resembles a

hover-mower cutting a lawn, as a swathe of eels swiftly vanishes, although it all happens too fast to tell whether the eels are devoured or escape unharmed into the seabed.

LIFESAVING MANOEUVRES

Any means of escaping predators is an asset. When threatened from above, most sand-dwellers rely on fast burrowing. If this fails and the predator catches hold, some resort to more drastic measures. For example, if grasped by a probing beak, the lugworm can shed its tail end and later regrow the abandoned segments. Similarly, the razor shell is able to cast off its protruding siphons and generate a replacement set. Starfish sometimes throw off an arm if

DESPERATE MEASURES *When faced with a predator, a sea cucumber can eject its gut and internal organs to repel, or satisfy, its attacker.*

attacked, and a predator may be content with consuming the self-amputated limb.

Sausage-shaped sea cucumbers have even more expendable body parts. For them, the first line of defence is the release of a toxin to deter predators. If this is unsuccessful, a sea cucumber can discharge a mass of sticky threads through its anus, which may confuse the predator. As a last resort, it can suddenly rupture the links with its gut and internal organs, and then expel them. Assuming that this trick succeeds in distracting, satisfying or repelling the aggressor, a sea cucumber can, amazingly, survive this violent evisceration and regenerate all the missing parts. Yet even this ability is exploited by others: a parasitic fish, which lives inside sea cucumbers, eats away at the internal organs, relying on their ability to regrow for a constant supply of food.

TIMING THE TIDES

An inherent sense of time is essential for animals everywhere. It enables them to be active when food is most easily obtained or predators most readily avoided, to keep in step with changes in their environment, to pace themselves and to stay 'ahead of the game'.

The eternal cycle of light and dark sets a daily rhythm for most animals, but on a shoreline the tides superimpose another rhythm onto that of day and night, creating a complex syncopation that is echoed by the instinctive ebb and flow of the shore-dwellers' behaviour.

Tidal rhythm is evident in the smallest of animals on a sandy shore, and even in some of the microscopic plant-like cells living between the sand grains. Each day, hordes of golden-brown algae known as diatoms (*Hantzschia virgata*) migrate upwards to reach daylight at times of low tide. Then they migrate down again to avoid the

---

FLATFISH IN CLEVER DISGUISE

Flatfish such as the sole, plaice and flounder are so familiar to us as food that we tend to forget how truly extraordinary they are, with their twisted mouths and both eyes clumped together on one side of the head. This bizarre arrangement, and their flattened shape, are signs of good adaptation to life in the sand. The flatfish buries itself in sand or gravel so that only its eyes protrude. It can then grab unsuspecting fish or other prey as they approach, as well as being protected from its own predators.

The evolutionary saga of the flatfish is revealed by the developing young. It is an ordinary-looking fry, much like that of any other fish, but undergoes a radical transformation before settling on the bottom. The body slowly becomes distorted and flattened in order that the fish may go about life lying on its side. One eye gradually migrates over the head to join the other, until both

project from the uppermost side of the head.

Flatfish are the 'chameleons of the seabed', able to adjust the pigmentation of their skin to match the colour and texture of the sand or gravel on which they lie. The colour changes of the flatfish are quite slow, however, since they are

controlled by the hormones, which cannot produce the instantaneous changes brought about by nerves and muscles in an animal like the octopus.

PERFECT MATCH *A flounder is able to change its skin colour to that of the seabed.*

---

hazards of high tide. They move through the spaces between the sand particles with a gentle gliding motion that was a mystery to biologists for many years.

Eventually it was discovered that these diatoms use a leisurely form of jet propulsion, each one of them pushing itself along by slowly expelling mucus from a pore in its hard, glassy coat. Remarkably, the diatoms maintain their rhythm of activity even if they are kept in a constantly lit laboratory, away from the influence of day and night,

waves and tides. This finding suggests that these tiny plants possess some kind of highly complex yet accurate internal clock, the nature of which is still not understood by scientists.

Green flatworms (*Convoluta roscoffensis*) living in wet sand on the coast of Brittany act in a very similar way. Their bodies contain colonies of microscopic algae, which make their own food from sunlight, as do other plants, thus providing the flatworms with a supply of food in exchange for a safe home. In order to enable their resident algae to manufacture food, the flatworms must travel to the surface in sunlit hours. A while before the incoming tide reaches them, the worms can detect the vibration caused by

COLOURFUL VISITORS *Flatworms get their green colour from colonies of algae that live in their bodies.*

the approaching waves, and wriggle back into the sand. Vibrations from approaching human feet cause whole patches of green flatworms to glide into the sand and vanish.

REPRODUCTIVE RHYTHMS

Shore animals need to coordinate their sexual activities with the tides, thereby ensuring that their eggs, sperm or young are not stranded by the waves, nor obliterated by predators. More than 2300 years ago, the ancient Greek philosopher and naturalist, Aristotle, observed that sea urchins' ovaries became enlarged at the full moon. It is now known that lunar rhythms, which control the tides, control the reproduction of many other creatures in this habitat, too.

On one particular night, during the last quarter of the moon in either October or November, a peculiar phenomenon sweeps parts of the shallow Pacific. The surface of the water comes alive with millions of green palolo worms. Events begin secretly, on the seabed, where the worms live in their burrows. Hidden from view, and coordinated by their own inherent sense of time, or by an unknown signal, the thousands of worms in their burrows simultaneously divide in two. Their tail ends then wriggle to the surface and swim about, each tail shedding either eggs or sperm.

These mingle and fertilise in the open water, generating vast numbers of fertilised eggs, which can then develop into larvae. By virtue of the sheer numbers involved,

SAFE HIDING PLACE *By synchronising their spawning with the highest tides, grunions can bury their eggs out of reach of predators.*

THE STARGAZER'S STUN GUN

In shallow water, just beneath the surface of a warm, sandy beach, the toad-like stargazer fish, measuring some 8 in (20 cm) from head to tail, lies hidden. It remains motionless below the sand with only its bulbous eyes and large mouth protruding. Anything approaching it is in for a shock, for the stargazer uses electricity to strike out at prey. A worm-like filament that is located in the creature's open mouth entices small fish towards the head end, where they are stunned by a 50-volt discharge from electrical organs behind the eye.

some of these larvae are in their turn guaranteed survival to adulthood.

Meanwhile, the hordes of spent worm-tails provide a feast for fish, sharks and local people, who consider the worms a great delicacy. The head ends withdraw into their burrows and set about regenerating new tails for another outburst of reproductive energy the following year.

One of the most curious of such synchronised mating rituals is performed by the

little silvery fish called grunions (*Leuresthes tenuis*) and takes place on the beaches of California. The ritual is triggered by the 15-day rhythm of the highest tides, or 'spring tides', and is carried out between March and September.

On a night following the new or full moon, thousands of fish ride the waves that lick the uppermost limits of their range, then hurl themselves out onto the sand, close to the high-tide mark, to spawn. The beach writhes with fish. Females bury their tails in the wet sand and lay their eggs 3 in (7.5 cm) beneath the surface, while excited males wind around them, fertilising the clutches. The fish return to the sea on another wave, before the tide falls, and the eggs develop in the sand, safe from marine predators. Fifteen days later they hatch, just in time for the young to swim out to sea on the next spring tide.

Many animals rely on these sudden abundances of food for their survival. In late spring, when the horseshoe crabs of the western Atlantic emerge from the sea to spawn on the sandy beaches of Delaware Bay in the United States, the predators are waiting for them. Millions of waders, migrating from South America to the Arctic to breed, stop off to feed on tasty horseshoe crab eggs during their long journey north. Delaware Bay has become a refuelling site for bird migrants and the horseshoe crabs (not real crabs at all, in fact, but relatives of spiders) provide the fuel.

The male crabs emerge from the sea on the high spring tides. They are packed so tightly that tens of thousands may be found on a short stretch of the beach. When the females arrive, the long, black line of males breaks up and each egg-laying female is the focus of attention for a group of males

BORN ON THE BEACH *An olive ridley turtle emerges onto a traditional breeding beach to lay her eggs in the sand. Once hatched, the young turtles return to the sea.*

jostling for the right to fertilise her eggs. She deposits 80 000 eggs below the sand and returns to the sea. Then the birds take over. In just two weeks, 50 000 sanderlings alone consume 6 billion eggs, each bird doubling its weight before resuming the flight north.

REPTILIAN RITUAL

They emerge at night, the moonlight glinting on their wet shells, and haul themselves laboriously up the sand with their flippers, sighing and grunting with effort. At a point well above the lap of the waves, each female slowly digs a flask-shaped egg chamber and lays her eggs.

These lumbering amphibious creatures are sea turtles, whose ancestry can be traced back to land-living tortoises, and whose eggs still need to develop and hatch on land. Sections of the Costa Rican Pacific coast are breeding grounds for vast numbers of olive ridley turtles (*Lepidochelys olivacea*). Females arrive in their thousands on certain nights between July and December. Allegedly, their arrival coincides with the last quarter of the moon, with a rising tide and offshore wind.

Each female turtle lays about 100 eggs, before she carefully fills in the cavity and then conceals it with scattered sand. (Fertilisation of the eggs has already taken place at sea.) The single-minded female is by no means perturbed by lights or obstacles on the beach, nor even by interference from predators. Turtles may scrabble over one another, and even inadvertently damage other deposits of eggs, in the struggle to lay their own.

After that scramble has taken place, the eggs are still not entirely safe, despite their sandy hiding places. Many are devoured by coyotes, opossums and raccoons, or collected by humans, who traditionally believe them to have aphrodisiac qualities. For those young turtles that survive the 50-day incubation period and hatch successfully, more hazards await. They must endure a terrifying journey down the sandy beach to the sea. On their way they face hungry vultures and buzzards, swooping frigate birds and the snatching pincers of crabs. Offshore, sharks lurk in the surf. Most of the turtle hatchlings make their evacuation en masse and in darkness to minimise their chances of being singled out by a sharp-eyed predator. Their instincts guide them automatically out to sea.

A number of other beach animals take advantage of the dark. For surface scavengers, night is really the only safe time for them to emerge from their hide-outs and move about. The night-time stillness of a tropical beach is broken, for example, by tiny clicks, taps and scrapes: the sounds of land hermit crabs shuffling along, dragging their shells, and of other opportunists rummaging through stranded debris.

White ghost crabs gleam eerily in the darkness with a secondhand glow that they acquire from their diet of tiny, luminescent sea creatures. The night offers all these animals a protective blanket of cool darkness, a much-needed refuge from the Sun's burning rays and from predation.

DANGERS IN THE SAND

A swimmer, wading into the sea and unaware of any danger, can suddenly receive an agonising puncture wound from one of several predatory creatures that lurk in the surface layers of offshore sand. In European waters, there are no more than a few of these hazardous fish, but the lesser weever can still inflict a painful sting should an

GIANT ROBBER CRABS

The coconut crab (*Birgus latro*) is the largest of the land-living arthropods, the multifarious group of animals that includes all the insects, crabs, scorpions, spiders and centipedes. With a leg span of up to 3 ft (1 m), this giant is actually a type of hermit crab – a name that more usually conjures up a small, scurrying creature sporting a snail shell. The coconut crab's enormous size means that it has abandoned the policy of borrowing shells, except during a short, immature period. With its thick armour and its ability to breathe air and drink fresh water, the coconut crab is able to roam quite a distance from the sea, returning only to lay its eggs. It is so well adapted to life on land that it would drown within a matter of hours if submerged.

The crab uses its strong legs and pincers to scale the trunks of coconut palms, and even to cut down the young coconuts on which it feeds – an activity which may have given rise to its alternative name – 'robber crab'. Carrion, fruit and vegetation are also part of its varied diet. Coconut crabs rest in holes in trees, or in burrows, and become nocturnal if there are people in the vicinity, since they are hunted for their delicious meat.

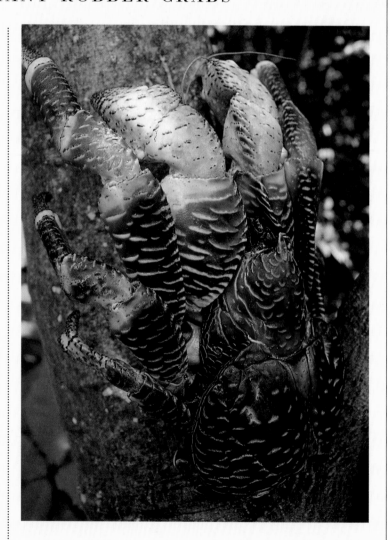

SNEAK THIEF *The coconut crab, or robber crab, can cut down young coconuts.*

unsuspecting bather step on the toxic spines protruding from its back.

The sands of the tropics are a good deal more perilous to swimmers. The apparently innocuous beauty of tropical cone shells, for example, disguises their menace. There are 400-500 species of carnivorous cone shell. Each has an extending proboscis, with which it can impale its prey and inject a paralysing nerve poison. While all cause a

DANGER LURKS *The spines on a stringray's tail are venomous and some species can kill unwary swimmers.*

painful sting, some can actually be lethal to human beings.

Some of the largest and most threatening hidden animals are the stingrays, which spend their time part-buried in the sand of shallow waters. They normally eat shellfish, crustaceans and fish. Unlike the cone shells, their poisonous barbs are not used to attack prey, only to defend themselves. However, an unwary swimmer or fisherman may accidentally provoke a resting stingray by treading on it, triggering a reaction of the whip-like tail. Its angled spines penetrate flesh and are difficult to remove. The spine of the

DEADLY APPARITION
A hatchling ridley turtle is caught by a ghost crab on its journey down the beach to the sea.

largest species of stingray may reach 12 in (30 cm) in length and has been responsible for many human deaths.

The shore, like the sea, has its well-kept secrets, and the deceptively sterile sand of a beach is no exception to that rule. There is unquestionably more life on a sandy shore than at first meets the eye. Beneath the surface, a world of concealed animals waits for the cover of high tide or of darkness. Then the barren sands are transformed into a busy stage for all kinds of breathing, feeding and reproducing actors, each of which takes its cues from the rising and falling of the tides and fulfils its own special role in the coastal ecosystem.

MANGROVE BOUNTY

Black, pungent mud and tangled, arching roots make a mangrove swamp one of the least welcoming habitats on Earth – at least for human explorers. To many animals, however, it is a place of bountiful food where life flourishes.

In 1292, after 17 years of service, Marco Polo, the Venetian traveller, finally took his leave of the great emperor Kublai Khan of China. The boat journey back to Europe took three years, by way of Indonesia, southern India and Persia. From his records, we know that Marco Polo stopped at Palembang, then a busy port on the Sumatran coast. Today, Palembang still thrives as the capital of South Sumatra province – but it now lies more than 31 miles (50 km) inland. Its change of position is due, at least in part, to natural land-building by coastal forests of mangrove trees.

THE MARCH OF THE MANGROVES

In temperate climates, sandy estuaries or gently sloping shingle shorelines are often fringed by salt marshes. The salt-marsh vegetation consists for the most part of small, hardy land-plants moving seaward that have evolved the ability to tolerate the brackish water and tough conditions of the coastal environment. In the tropics, similar types of coastline have mangrove swamps instead of salt marshes – a far richer and more complex habitat, with dense thickets of mangrove trees straddling the gap between sea and land.

Both salt-marsh plants and mangroves slow down the passing water currents, causing them to drop their load of sediment, which then becomes trapped between the mesh of plant roots. Mangroves, being larger, have a more powerful impact, accruing sediment at a remarkable speed. As the layers accumulate, so new land emerges above sea level, which in turn is slowly colonised by other plants staking out a tenuous claim on the new ground. Their presence ousts the mangroves that progress farther seaward, claiming land from the sea at a rate that can exceed some 330 ft (100 m) per year.

The term 'mangrove' embraces an unrelated mixture of species, ranging from sparse bushes to dense trees that grow up to 100 ft (30 m) tall. They are drawn together under the same label only by their shared ability to meet the challenge of life in the muddy brine, where oxygen is in short supply. Most plants cannot withstand the salty tides, lapping waves and shifting substrate. The mangroves, however, have evolved in such a way as to give them a competitive edge in this exacting environment.

SUFFOCATING MUD

The silty mud that is deposited among the mangrove roots is fine, oozing and noxious. It originates in the rivers that discharge their load into the sea, where it is carried back and forth until it settles at the slack of the tide. Below the surface layer, bacteria use up all the available oxygen as they decompose loose plant material. The mud is made acidic by

ADAPT AND SURVIVE
Mangroves survive in salty water, helped by breathing roots that are able to take oxygen from the air.

YOUNG MANGROVE *A young tree attempts to establish itself.*

porous patches are situated on elbow-like protuberances from the horizontal roots, which jut through the surface of the mud. Ventilating those roots that are deeper down, and permanently immersed in the stifling mud, is more difficult.

Some mangroves send up vertical, finger-like' extensions from the roots called pneumatophores or 'breathing roots'. These project up to 6 in (15 cm) through the surface, as a carpet of spikes. Each has a porous tip to take in air and acts as a tiny snorkel, providing the root below with a means to breathe freely.

Besides a shortage of oxygen, the mangroves must contend with an excess of salt. Land plants, like people, need a little salt, but too much salt disrupts the vital reactions of their internal chemistry. Most

GETTING A GRIP *Mangroves are stabilised by arching prop roots, like the buttresses of medieval cathedrals.*

bacterial action, and contains poisonous sulphur compounds. Such conditions would challenge any plant root that attempted to establish itself here, but for a tree, which requires especially stable anchorage, it presents particular difficulties.

Mangroves have adapted in a number of ways. Above ground, many species have arching prop roots, which emanate from the trunk and boughs to balance and support the tree. Some are branched hoops, others flange-like blades. Underground, the roots are very shallow, and spread horizontally rather than downwards. Thus they form a broad base, which rests in the upper layers of the mud, rather than threading through it at depth. Fine feeding-roots sap nutrients from the uppermost layers of silt, supplies of which are replenished with each incoming tide.

This layer is relatively innocuous, but a little deeper down the mangroves face the problem of sustaining their living roots in a medium that is almost devoid of oxygen. The problem is solved in a variety of ways. In some mangroves, the upper sections of the prop roots are above ground, and are punctured by tiny spongy patches in the bark, which allow air to pass into the root. For those mangroves without prop roots, the

THE TENACIOUS MANGROVE SEEDLING

Mangrove flowers, if fertilised, each produce a pod that contains a single seed. But the seed never escapes from the pod, as it does with most flowering plants. Instead, the seed germinates and the seedling grows directly from the pod while it is still attached to the parent tree.

These mangroves, then, are viviparous plants, a term derived from the Latin word meaning 'to bear alive'. In the red mangrove (*Rhizophora mangle*), for example, a green, spear-shaped seedling emerges directly from each pod and sprouts to a length of 6-12 in (15-30 cm). The sight of the pendulous seedlings hanging from mangrove branches has prompted the common name 'candle tree' in

some parts of the world. When the spear-like seedlings fall from the tree, they plunge downwards to a fate determined by the tide. If the mud is exposed, the seedlings become embedded in its oozing surface and begin to root immediately. Within hours, lateral roots have grown outwards and anchored the young plants against the tug of the next tide.

If, however, the tide is in when the seedlings fall, they float horizontally on the water, drifting for weeks or even months. But all is not lost. As the root end of the seedling begins to absorb water,

RED MANGROVE *The seeds germinate while the pod is still on the tree.*

it becomes heavier and the seedling tips upright, bobbing like a float in the currents until it enters shallow water, where it takes root as soon

as it runs aground. By these diverse stratagems, mangroves have colonised calm tropical shores and estuaries all around the world.

---

mangroves have more than one strategy to combat the salt. Some have a filter system in the roots to keep as much out as possible. Others let salt enter, but sequester it away safely in special stores until it can be shed in old leaves as they fall. Some species have glands to secrete salt onto the surface of living leaves, where it is washed away by rain.

Around the roots, salt tends to draw the essential life-sustaining water out of the plant. The result is a tug of war over every

molecule of water, with the root cells pulling it inwards and the salty mud pulling it outwards. The result is a paradox in which the mangroves, while growing in a swamp, are constantly thirsty for fresh, revitalising

water. Consequently, they have various water-conserving mechanisms similar to those found in desert plants, including thick, succulent leaves covered by a waxy cuticle to reduce evaporation in the hot sun.

LIFE IN THE SWAMP

It is their ability to thrive in such salty conditions that really sets mangroves apart from other plants. Mangroves do not need salt to survive – indeed, they grow better without it. But they have evolved so that they can tolerate the salt, and live on the fringes of the shore, where the briny conditions keep out less specialised plants. Farther inland, where the soil is sweeter, the mangroves lose ground to other species: their extreme specialisation to brackish mud has left them less competitive on ordinary terrain, where they

BIRDS IN ABUNDANCE *Mangrove swamps are havens for many kinds of bird life. A frigate bird (far left) displays its plumage, and a snowy egret (left) scans the water for fish.*

must battle with other plants for nutrients, space and light.

To the human visitor, a mangrove swamp offers a fearsome tangle of snare-like stems, curving stilt roots and fetid, glutinous mud. By night, it may be eerily lit with the synchronous flashing lights of fireflies. By day, biting insects whine persistently in the malodorous air, which is heavy with water vapour, sulphurous fumes and the smell of decomposition. Yet this inhospitable swamp is home to countless small creatures, which move between the knobbly roots, over the mud and up the slippery stems with ease and agility.

In this uncertain zone that is neither land nor sea, a unique combination of terrestrial and marine creatures exist side by side. Most are adapted to a lifestyle that swings with the tides – the rise and fall of the sea shaping life among the mangroves.

When the tide is in, the distinction between marine and terrestrial life seems relatively well defined. Above the water level, mangrove trees hold their own communities of animals, many of which have no

SWAMPLANDS MONKEY
A proboscis monkey feeds
on mangrove leaves.

immediate contact with the sea beneath, and show no special adaptations to this particular environment. Crickets, ants, beetles, thrips, caterpillars, centipedes and spiders all crawl across the leaves. Lizards, snakes, bats and monkeys shelter in the mangrove branches. Meanwhile, the rare proboscis monkey, native to Borneo, feeds on the tender, young leaves. Large numbers of

WARNING STANCE *An Asian mangrove snake adopts a threatening posture to deter a predator.*

noisy sea birds, such as pelicans, frigate birds, egrets, herons, cormorants and kingfishers arrive to roost and nest in the trees. Unlike some of the other tree inhabitants, these birds are directly dependent on the sea for food.

Out of sight, below water level, encrusting marine organisms coat the submerged prop roots. Oysters, sponges, barnacles and sea squirts jostle for space on the crowded woody pillars, while small colonies of coral might be found attached to underwater mangrove stilts. Five-armed brittle stars clamber over the sedentary animals. Translucent shrimps dart between the tangled roots, where there may also be a hidden octopus, a watersnake, or a jellyfish brought in with the tide. Weaving through the maze are crowds of immature fish, such as mangrove snappers, which use the mangroves as nursery grounds. Other valuable visitors include young bass, grouper, mullet, milkfish, spiny lobster, blue crab and prawns.

With the turn of each tide, the departing sea deposits sediment and carries away seeds and leaf litter. Meanwhile, the distinction between marine and terrestrial life becomes more blurred. As the waters subside,

the mud is alive with an army of scurrying creatures picking over the newly revealed morsels: crabs and snails leave the sea to scour the sediment, while birds, monkeys and snakes descend from the trees to forage. Birds probe for worms and shellfish. Snakes take crabs, fish, small birds and rodents. There is even a crab-eating monkey, the long-tailed macaque, that seizes crabs as they emerge from their holes, supplementing its diet of fruit, insects and leaves.

THE BURROWING HORDES

The bare mud is peppered with the openings to small burrows. These damp labyrinths are home to a variety of creatures that use them for refuge, for feeding and

HOLDING FIRM *The mangrove's underwater root system traps sediment and stabilises the coastline.*

THE NOT-SO-SUBTLE ART OF FLIRTATION

Male fiddler crabs (*Uca* species) each boast a large, brightly coloured claw that may equal the rest of their body in weight. It is too cumbersome to use in feeding or effective combat, but is flaunted in courtship and ritual defence, as a symbol of the owner's sex and status. Courtship among fiddler crabs is a matter of complicated sign language, in which the male communicates his interest to females by gesticulating with his enlarged pincer. As he beckons, females of his species are attracted, until one follows him down into his burrow to mate. The gestures made by the male are not random. Each species of fiddler crab has a unique set of movements which all males of that species follow. This is a type of code or password, to ensure that animals only pair up with a mate of the same species.

WARNING OFF OTHER MALES

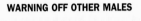

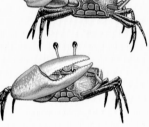

SEMAPHORE OF LOVE *The male fiddler crab courts females by flaunting a brightly coloured claw.*

COURTING THE FEMALE

for breeding. The burrowers unintentionally provide an important service for the mangroves by mixing the surface layers and allowing a little oxygen to penetrate the mud. Some of the excavators are burrowing shrimps (*Upogebia* and *Thalassina* species), that feed on worms and other tiny animals found in the mud. But it is the crabs that produce most of the tiny tunnels.

Crabs abound in the mangrove mud at low tide. They include fiddler crabs (*Uca* species), ghost crabs (*Ocypode* species), tropical land crabs (*Cardisoma* species) and mud crabs (*Sesarma* species). They are always alert to danger and will scamper into their bolt holes at the slightest hint of a predator, emerging cautiously once the threat has passed.

Ghost crabs have unusual eyes set around long, vertical stalks that project from the top of the head; these give constant panoramic vision, even when the rest of the crab's body is hidden beneath the muddy sand. Others rely more on vibrations than eyesight. Some crabs are so sensitive to ground tremors that they can detect – from deep inside a burrow – the impact of a leaf landing on the mud surface.

Mangrove-swamp crabs feed mostly on leaf litter and other detritus. Some scrape algae from the protruding pneumatophores, the 'breathing-roots' of the mangroves, using their pincers. Many roll balls of mud around in their mouths, 'licking' away the edible particles using fine, spoon-shaped hairs. The mineral grains are rejected and spat out as little spherical pellets, which litter the mud around the crabs' burrows.

FISH THAT CLIMB TREES

Certain fish in the mangrove swamp defy all conventional ideas about fish habitat and behaviour. Not only can they survive happily out of water for hours at a time, but they can also 'walk' across the mud at low tide and are even able to climb trees. These intriguing creatures are mudskippers (*Periophthalmus*, *Boleophthalmus* and *Periophthalmodon* species), lively fish about 4-8 in (10-20 cm) long, that come out of the sea to forage and to breed. Some species eat only plant material, while others are predatory, taking insects, shellfish, worms and small crabs.

Mudskippers use their sturdy forefins to haul themselves over the slippery surface of

TWO HOMES *Crabs such as the fiddler (above) and gem (right) are equally at home on land and in the sea.*

ATHLETIC PROWESS *Using their forefins for leverage, mudskippers can cross mud and even climb tree roots.*

the mud as if on a pair of crutches. Yet they are also capable of skipping and bounding, by contorting their bodies and flipping upwards with a vigorous push from the fins located on their bellies. Leaping into the air can be an escape tactic, but it is also employed by male mudskippers when they want to impress potential mates. At the height of his gymnastic leap, the male spreads two bright fins on his back, each daubed with orange and black, as an advertisement to nearby females.

Like the crabs, male mudskippers make burrows, excavating tirelessly and methodically, a mouthful at a time. Some species also scoop out saucer-shaped ponds at the tops of their burrows, surrounded by a rim of mud. The males are fiercely territorial about their dens, which they defend from other males and from intruding crabs of twice their size. It is to the burrow that a female is lured to spawn. Later, tiny larvae hatch from the eggs that she deposits on the walls of the lair.

During their hours out of water, mudskippers face the problem of how they are to breathe in air. Under water, they breathe like any other fish, passing water over their gill filaments and extracting the oxygen from it. When they are out of the water, mudskippers periodically take quick gulps of water at the sea's edge. But biologists now think that mudskippers are also able to breathe air into their open mouths, where they absorb oxygen through the damp membranes inside them.

For panoramic vision out of water, the mudskipper has bulbous, protruding eyes, placed on the top of the head – which give the fish an oddly frog-like appearance. Its delicate eyeballs are covered by a layer of thick but transparent skin to protect them from drying out. In addition, as the fish has no tear ducts, it occasionally spins the eyes downwards into their wet sockets to keep them moist. At high water, some of the mudskippers resume an aquatic existence, while others climb tree roots in advance of the rising water. They cling on with a suction pad formed from the fins on the belly, and sit out the deluge.

FLEEING THE FLOOD

Similarly, terrestrial animals also retreat to safety as the sea water seeps back over the mud. Many of the slower-moving creatures benefit from an innate behavioural rhythm, an internal clock that offers them advance

spout. As the gill covers slam shut, the tip of the tongue flicks forward to release the water, and a fast powerful jet shoots from the fish's mouth towards its target.

THE IMPORTANCE OF MANGROVES

In recent decades the acreage of mangrove swamps worldwide has been much reduced: yet the mangrove forests are of enormous ecological importance. They act as nursery grounds for edible fish and shellfish, a haven for these vulnerable larvae, without which there would be no future generations of adults. The mangroves are also home to endangered species such as the Atlantic ridley sea turtle and the brown pelican.

They stabilise coasts, protect against storm and hurricane damage, support a large marine food web, and act as a giant filter system. In trapping muddy riverine sediments, they may aid the establishment of corals in the clearer silt-free waters offshore. And in recent geological history, mangroves have played a crucial land-building role. As a bridging point between land and sea, mangroves may also have special evolutionary significance. It is easy to envisage how life forms moved from sea to land and back again in the mangrove swamps of times gone by. Those life forms may have included air-breathing fish that we count among our own ancestors. The true historical importance of the mangrove communities, which date back at least 60 million years, can still only be guessed at.

warning of the tide's return. A few land arthropods escape drowning by sealing themselves into air-filled burrows. Others take to the trees as the land disappears below water again.

In the trees, animals are safe from the danger of drowning, but not from the threat of predators. Some sea-dwelling predators can find ways to plunder the terrestrial world for food, and the archerfish (*Toxotes*) does so without even leaving the water. Lurking close to the surface, it fires a jet of high-velocity liquid at insects, as they rest unawares on a leaf or a root. The fish achieves this feat of marksmanship by pressing its tongue against a furrow in the roof of its mouth to form a narrow

ON TARGET *An archerfish dislodges an insect with a powerful jet of water from its mouth.*

COASTS OF ICE

Despite their cold, harsh climate, the ice-clad regions of the Arctic and Antarctic support a rich array of marine life. Penguins, seals, sea lions and gigantic whales are among the creatures that throng their glacial waters and thrive.

In the regions at the top and the bottom of the world where freezing wastes meet the sea, the coast is in constant flux. It is a moving, creaking, breaking zone of transition, awesome in its stark white savagery. The edges of the land are carved not from rock, but from solid ice. Far exceeding the imperceptible creep of other shores, their crystalline frontiers retreat or advance hundreds of miles

ANTARCTICA *The midnight Sun hangs low over the horizon.*

within a single season, for these are floating coasts, utterly at the mercy of the weather, expanding and contracting with each freeze and thaw.

Against all odds, life has somehow established itself in the subzero temperatures of both polar regions. Marine animals are among those that take advantage of this frozen extension to their kingdom. Some emerge onto the surface of the ice to breed, while others inhabit the calm, chill water beneath, an enclosed realm of dim, greenish, ice-filtered light by day, and utter darkness during the long winter night.

THE ENDS OF THE EARTH

Intense cold unites both the Arctic and Antarctic regions. Here, the sun remains low in the sky, so that its rays fall more obliquely and are therefore weaker than

anywhere else on the planet. Much of the feeble warmth from this sunlight goes to waste, reflected back into space by the crystalline whiteness of the ice. Because of the slant of the Earth, the sun shines for 24 hours a day during midsummer, when the polar regions experience a few brief weeks of relative warmth. But in winter the land is plunged into darkness and there is no respite from the bitter cold.

Despite the similarities in climate, there are more differences between the Arctic and Antarctic than might at first be expected. The major contrast between them lies beneath the ice. Whereas the North Pole is situated on a plate of ice capping a freezing sea, the South Pole is located on a vast rocky continent, twice the size of Australia, its jagged slopes cloaked in compacted snow and ice.

THE ICEBOUND CONTINENT

The Antarctic holds no less than 90 per cent of the world's ice, the accumulation of a good 100 000 years of snowfall – if all this ice were to melt, the global sea level would rise by about 200 ft (60 m). It is hard to believe that this land of raw winds, fog and icy blizzards once enjoyed a warm, even subtropical climate. Yet indisputable fossil evidence shows that this was the case. The rocks of Antarctica hold the fossils of birds, crocodiles, turtles, ferns and pine trees.

These fossils date from a time, millions of years ago, when Antarctica lay farther north as part of the ancient southern landmass known as Gondwanaland. About 150 million years ago, this 'supercontinent' began to break up into smaller pieces through the process of continental drift. The part of Gondwanaland that was to become South America slid westwards away from Africa. Australia and Antarctica jointly moved south, and eventually separated from each

BENEATH THE ICE *The ice cap around the North Pole overlies the Arctic Ocean, while there is a huge rocky continent beneath the ice cap of Antarctica.*

other about 65 million years ago. By 25 million years ago, Antarctica had crept even farther southwards to occupy a position over the South Pole, and in time it became covered in ice as it is now.

Today, the climate of Antarctica could not be more different from that of the other descendants of Gondwanaland. It is the coldest and windiest of all the continents, majestic in appearance, yet ruthlessly inimical to life. Ice covers 95 per cent of its

RARE SIGHT *Lichens growing on rocks along one of the few ice-free coasts of Antarctica.*

craggy coastline, but where the rock is exposed, a few lichens and grasses struggle to survive, along with some tiny insects and mites. These meagre life forms are the only ones in Antarctica that are wholly terrestrial. Much of the coastline consists of spectacularly beautiful ice cliffs, which bob with

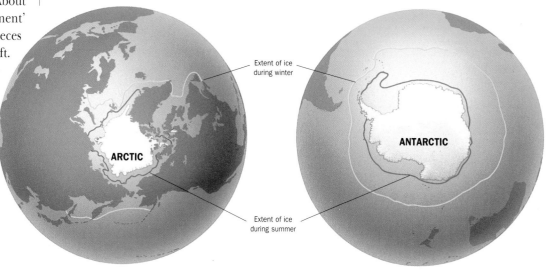

Extent of ice during winter

ARCTIC

ANTARCTIC

Extent of ice during summer

the tides. Their sheer faces 'calve' vast icebergs which periodically fall with thunderous crashes into the water below.

As summer ends, the surface of the sea begins to freeze, giving birth to new pack ice, which begins as a thin, slushy film (known as 'grease ice') before thickening and hardening into polygonal slabs. Each winter the glaze of ice spreads up to 40 000 sq miles (100 000 km²) a day, until it doubles the effective size of the continent. Ice generally protects the seabed from wave action, but in the winter months the sea ice may solidify to such a depth that it grinds against the shallow bottom.

Beyond the ice, the waters of the Southern Ocean are among the most dangerous known to man, bedevilled by storms and currents. Paradoxically, these same waters harbour the richest community of marine life in the world.

CONVERGING CURRENTS

The Southern Ocean is bounded naturally by the Antarctic Convergence, a belt of water 25 miles (40 km) wide, about 1200 miles (1900 km) offshore from Antarctica, in a zone of persistent westerly winds. Here, the cold, northward-flowing Antarctic water comes up against the warmer, circulating waters of the South Atlantic, South Pacific and Indian Oceans.

The Antarctic Convergence is a dividing line, separating water masses that are of very different temperature, chemistry and

wildlife. North of this boundary, the warm waters are comparatively barren. To the south, the colder waters teem with all kinds of life and activity.

Although temperatures in the ocean around Antarctica are close to freezing point, this has some benefits. Cold water contains more oxygen than warm water, and this extra supply helps animals such as fish and crustaceans, which 'breathe' by extracting oxygen from water. Since these animals are the mainstay of the Antarctic food web, air-breathing predators such as whales, seals and penguins also benefit, indirectly, from the oxygenated water.

THE FOOD OF OCEAN LIFE

There is also a plentiful supply of nutrients in these icy seas. The complex interplay of winds and temperature gradients in the Southern Ocean produces the phenomenon known as upwelling, whereby water from the deep ocean is drawn up to the surface in a steady flow, bringing with it a cargo of mineral nutrients that fertilise the sunlit upper waters. Microscopic plants (phytoplankton) flourish in conditions like these, especially during the summer months when there is almost uninterrupted daylight to fuel the food-making process of photosynthesis.

The phytoplankton are in turn devoured by hordes of Antarctic krill (*Euphausia superba*), pinkish-red, shrimp-like creatures just 2 in (5 cm) in length, which gather up

DAINTY MORSELS *Antarctic krill, in their million-strong swarms, are the mainstay of life in the Southern Ocean.*

armfuls of the one-celled plants in their feathery limbs. Krill congregate in millions. Vast, dense swarms of their bodies tint the ocean red, sometimes over hundreds of square miles. Each shrimp has a set of luminous organs along the body, and by night these thronging, miniature lanterns glint beneath the surface.

Krill are the crucial component of the main Antarctic food chain. They are eaten by animals of all sizes, ranging from small carnivorous squid, to penguins, fish, seals and even the enormous baleen whales. Despite their misleading name, crabeater seals (*Lobodon carcinophagus*) feed almost exclusively on krill. They take gulps of water, and strain out the tiny crustaceans using special interlocking five-pointed teeth. Crabeater seals are the commonest of all the seals, and between them they are thought to consume more krill each year than the baleen whales.

Baleen whales also employ a

WHERE OCEANS MEET *The cold waters of the Southern Ocean meet the warmer waters of the oceans to the north at the Antarctic Convergence. Waters upwelling from the depths of the ocean bring rich supplies of mineral nutrients to fertilise the surface waters.*

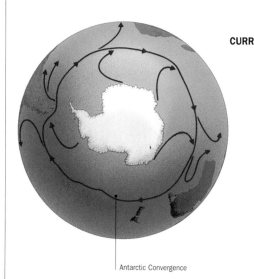

Antarctic Convergence

CURRENTS IN THE ANTARCTIC

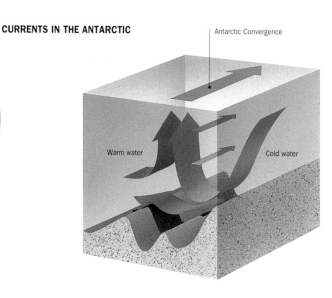

Antarctic Convergence

Warm water

Cold water

HUMPBACK WHALE *It feeds cooperatively with others of its kind to catch huge quantities of krill.*

sieving technique. Among them, humpback whales (*Megaptera novaeangliae*) have a particularly effective way of catching krill. They spiral around the targeted shoal, blowing out streams of air that bubble upwards. Because the whales are spiralling inwards, the bubbles serve as an ever-tightening 'net' that also pushes the prey inwards, thereby concentrating them into a dense mass. Suddenly, the whales burst upwards through the trapped swarm of krill, their mouths agape. As the massive jaws of a humpback close, the tongue is pressed against the roof of the mouth, and sea water is squeezed out through the surrounding fringe of bristles, thus leaving only the krill behind.

It is very unusual for a single species such as krill to sustain so many other animals; which is why each type of predator has evolved its own specialist kind of behaviour, feeding at particular times and depths, in different areas, and on krill of different ages. This reduces the amount of direct competition, with the result that there is ample to go around. However, the ecosystem is delicately balanced. Biologists are particularly concerned that the proposed exploitation of krill as a human food source might threaten disaster for the entire ecosystem of the seas around Antarctica – unless there is some control on the size of the annual catch.

CHEMICALS AGAINST THE COLD

Only about 120 species of fish are found south of the Antarctic Convergence. The numbing cold of the polar waters presents particular problems for fish, most of which, unlike the seals and whales, are unable to raise their body temperature above that of the surrounding water. Below freezing point, the liquid within their bodies is at risk of solidifying into needle-sharp crystals that are capable of piercing their skin and gills. Yet the Antarctic fish have evolved defences against this intense cold, and are able to survive at temperatures well below freezing point.

Their main defence is a chemical one. Just as we use antifreeze chemicals to prevent the water in car radiators from solidifying in winter, so these fish have a special biological version of antifreeze to stop ice crystals forming in their blood and body cells. Other survival strategies are concerned with saving energy. Many of these fish have low metabolic rates and remain relatively inactive, near to the bottom. Some have managed to achieve weightlessness in water, by having a light skeleton and storing buoyant fat deposits, thereby avoiding the use of vital energy simply to stay afloat.

BETWEEN WATER AND ICE

Sharing the underwater realm with the fish are animals whose ancestors returned to the sea from a life on land or in the air: the seals and penguins. Both

LIFE AT THE POLES *Fish living in the polar waters of both the Arctic and Antarctic have developed special protein compounds that prevent their blood from freezing.*

are streamlined and beautifully adapted for swimming but, as a legacy of their distant land-living past, each is obliged to produce its young out of water. On land or ice their aquatic grace is exchanged for an inelegant gait, the penguins shuffling and waddling, while the seals hump their blubbery bodies forward with obvious effort.

Dense seal blubber is an equally good insulator above water or beneath the surface, so seals are able to haul themselves out onto the ice without suffering from the intense cold. They use the ice floes to rest from swimming and to escape predators, or, among some species, as a place to breed.

However, certain species of seal, such as the southern elephant seal (*Mirounga leonina*) and Antarctic fur seal (*Arctocephalus gazella*), prefer to breed on sand or shingle beaches on sub-Antarctic islands. Weddell seals (*Leptonychotes weddelli*) are among the

WHALING: TIPPING THE BALANCE OF POLAR SEAS

Humans have hunted whales for centuries, attracted by the natural bounty of meat, oil and flexible whalebone (the 'baleen' from a baleen whale's mouth). For those who hunted sperm whales, there was also ambergris, a mysterious waxy substance from the intestines of sperm whales, which for a long time was used in the manufacture of perfumes to 'fix' the scent of the other ingredients.

For centuries, hunters pursued their quarry in small boats using hand-held harpoons – a dangerous business. But in 1868, an explosive harpoon gun was invented, and in time steam power allowed boats to chase even the fastest-moving whales. Before long, whale stocks in the Arctic were all but exhausted.

After 1900, the whalers' attentions switched to the newly discovered stocks of blue, fin and sei whales in the Antarctic. As the 20th century progressed, there was a boom in whaling, facilitated first by enormous factory ships, and later by the use of aeroplanes and helicopters to spot the animals. Again and again, target species were exploited almost to extinction. As one became so scarce that it was uneconomic to pursue, the next largest species was taken. The gigantic blue whales were prime targets in the 1920s and 1930s. When their numbers fell, whalers switched to fin whales, then to sei whales, and finally to minkes. By the 1960s, the number of blue whales had fallen to less than one-thirtieth of their original population, and they were eventually protected by law.

Antarctic whales have been so drastically reduced in number that the population is now estimated to be 10 per cent of its original level. As whales have a long life span and a slow reproductive rate, stocks are unlikely to recover completely, even if there were to be a complete

cessation of whaling. Nevertheless, scientific evidence shows that female whales have been reaching maturity sooner and calving more frequently since populations fell, giving greater hope of recovery. Meanwhile, the millions of tons of krill once consumed by the whales is now available to other species. The crabeater seal, Antarctic fur

DEVASTATION OF WHALES
A fairly small baleen whale being butchered on board a whaling ship.

seal, penguins and sea birds have all benefited from the additional food, and have increased to as much as three times their original numbers since the destruction of the whales.

hardiest and they stay near to the permanent ice. They spend much of the summer either sunning themselves or sleeping on the ice, but pass the winter beneath it, in the dark, chill waters.

Because they are air-breathers, the Weddell seals chisel away at the pack ice to keep air holes open in the thick layer above their heads. To compensate for the resulting wear and damage, their teeth grow – a characteristic more commonly found in herbivores such as elephants and dugongs, whose teeth are worn down by a tough vegetarian diet.

To locate both their air holes and their prey of fish, squid and krill, the seals possess a combination of strong eyesight that is able to pierce the subglacial twilight, and sonar, which guides them through the utter blackness of midwinter.

BREATH OF FRESH AIR
A Weddell seal comes to an ice hole for air. Like all sea mammals, it has to surface in order to breathe.

UNSEEN PREDATOR *A leopard seal lurks in the water, waiting for Adélie penguins to dive from the ice shelf.*

The leopard seal (*Hydrurga leptonyx*) is a fearsome predator, with a sinuous body and a head that is almost reptilian in shape. It frequents the edge of the pack ice, feeding on squid, penguins and the young pups of other seal species. With cunning and patience, the lithe seal waits by penguin rookeries, catching the luckless birds as they emerge from the water, or as they dive in off the ice. With a whipping action of the head, the seal beats the penguin against the water's surface, and violently flicks the body out of its skin before eating it.

Despite preying on these much larger animals, the leopard seal is still not above eating krill, the tiny crustaceans that are the bread and butter of all of Antarctica's wildlife. Indeed, biologists have found that krill constitute over a third of the diet of leopard seals.

EMPERORS OF THE ANTARCTIC

Penguins are highly adapted to life in icy waters and flourish in the Southern Ocean. There are seven types of penguin living in the Antarctic. Of these, the hardiest and most extraordinary is the emperor penguin (*Aptenodytes forsteri*), the only wild animal that is capable of sitting out the desolate conditions of winter on the ice, deep in the Antarctic interior.

Unlike any other birds, emperor penguins begin their breeding cycle at the start of winter. In April the adults emerge onto the expanding pack ice and walk for many miles to their breeding grounds, where they court and mate in the gathering darkness. The female lays a single egg, which is instantly scooped off the ice to stop it freezing, and passed to the male. He balances it on top of his feet and covers it in a warm fold of loose, thickly feathered skin located just above the feet. This luxuriant, downy 'hood' has evolved for exactly this purpose. Her egg laid, the female begins a long trek back across the ever-widening sea ice to feed in the sea: by this stage of winter, the open sea might be 100 miles (160 km) away from the breeding ground.

Meanwhile, the male is left to a 60-day ordeal, passively enduring the savagery of the elements while incubating the precious egg. Temperatures are known to plummet as low as –40°C (–40°F), while winds scream at up to 125 mph (200 km/h). The male penguins huddle together in their hundreds, forming a huge circle. The outermost birds stand with their backs to the gales and blizzards, changing places with other penguins from farther inside the circle at intervals. By these tactics, the emperor penguins conserve as much warmth and

THE GREAT MARCH *After an arduous winter at their breeding ground, emperor penguins have a long migration back to the sea.*

energy as possible. Over the two months of deprivation, the males lose more than one-third of their body weight, burning up fat in order to generate the heat that is needed both to warm the egg and to keep their own internal fires aglow in this bleak and hostile icescape.

When in due course the chick hatches, the male penguin feeds it on a thick, oily, nutritious liquid produced by the wall of his gullet. This 'milk' is not needed for long because the mother penguin soon returns,

ALL ALONE *As emperor penguin chicks mature, they are often left alone while both parents return to the sea for food.*

FATHER LOVE *Young emperor penguin chicks huddle together for warmth, guarded by protective males.*

with remarkably accurate timing, sleek and fat from feeding at sea.

She locates her mate, picking him out from all the others by his call. He likewise recognises her and after greeting each other, the female regurgitates fish for the hatchling. The male then sets off for the sea to feed, returning in three to five weeks' time, his own fat stores replenished, and bringing a cache of fish for the chick. Many more journeys are made by both parents

before the young are large and strong enough to leave the breeding ground.

It is a highly risky breeding strategy. If the female is late, or has fallen prey to a killer whale or leopard seal, the chick will starve. If the sea ice is slow to break up in the spring, the parents struggle to fulfil the chick's demand for food, journeying back and forth across the pack ice to the sea.

GIANT KILLER *A polar bear, foremost land predator of the Arctic, shakes the snow from its fur after a storm.*

Nevertheless, the gruelling reproductive cycle is a successful one. The chicks that survive are born into the bountiful Antarctic spring and summer, with plenty of time to develop the necessary food reserves that will see them through the devastating winter months. The emperor penguin, more than any other animal, has evolved to survive the inhospitable wilderness that is Antarctica.

In purely physical terms, the Arctic region is the antithesis of the Antarctic. Rather than a frosted continent surrounded by sea, it is an icy ocean partially ringed by land. The Arctic ice cap formed following the movements of the northern continents, which were also in transition while the southern continents were gliding into their present positions. The landmasses of North America, Eurasia and Greenland closed in around the Arctic Ocean, effectively isolating it from the warm circulating currents farther south. Under the influence of the ice ages, the waters froze. Even during the warm interglacials (of which this present time is one) the Arctic ice sheet has remained. It expands and contracts, but it never melts completely.

The northern ice sheet floats on the ocean in much the same way that a true continent drifts on a sea of magma beneath the Earth's crust: the former a thin layer of ice adrift on water, the latter a slab of land overlying semimolten rock. Each is an extension of the material underneath, yet separated, solid from fluid, through the effect of temperature.

ARCTIC ANIMALS

Whereas the Antarctic is famed for its penguins, the Arctic is perhaps best known for its walruses and polar bears. The nomadic polar bear, enormous in its white grandeur, is a powerful and patient hunter. Males may weigh up to 1600 lb (725 kg), and consume as much as 88 lb (40 kg) of flesh in one meal. A polar bear often maintains watch for hours at an air hole in the ice. Just one

swipe of its heavy paw is sufficient to kill an unwary seal as it surfaces through the hole for breath after a dive.

Ringed seals (*Pusa hispida*) are the favourite prey of polar bears, which also take Arctic foxes, birds, fish and any available carrion to sustain their enormous bulk. Female ringed seals excavate small, protective snow caves in which to give birth, but the bears' sense of smell is so acute that they can track down the concealed breeding caverns. Because the mother constructs her den close to a crack in the ice, she has an escape route to the water beneath. But the young pups, who are unable to swim until they are about a month old, may have no means of escape.

In the water, seals can outwit polar bears, which are strong swimmers but far less swift and agile than their prey. Although polar bears are land animals, they spend almost all their time at sea, either swimming or drifting on ice floes. As an aid to swimming under water, they are able to close their nostrils and open their eyes. A dense coat of fur and a layer of blubber beneath the skin give double protection from the cold. Their feet have furry soles to protect them on the ice; fearsome, curved claws help them to grip the ice.

The main hazard for seals while in the water is the killer whale (*Orcinus orca*), a predator found from the Arctic to the Antarctic. Its Latin name *orca*, which means 'sea devil', reflects ancient beliefs about this sleek, sharp-finned killer. There is no

doubt that the whales are voracious hunters, taking fish, squid and penguins, or working in packs to pursue seals and other whale species.

Killer whales are highly intelligent, communicative creatures. It is not unusual to see a pair of them collaborating to tip a seal off floating drift ice, one nudging the ice upwards with its head and the other catching the seal as it loses its balance. But it is pure myth that they slash at prey with their long dorsal fins, or that they attack human beings.

FORMIDABLE FOE *Killer whales, or orcas, are found in all the world's oceans, where they prey on seals and small whales.*

THE ELEPHANT OF THE ARCTIC

Like the elephant, the walrus (*Odobenus rosmarus*) has great white tusks of ivory, for which it has been severely persecuted by man. It is also long lived, slow to mature and very protective of its young.

Walruses are sturdy creatures, related to the sea lions, sparsely haired and square-headed. Males can reach more than 10 ft (3 m) in length. Despite their bulk and threatening appearance, they are extremely social animals, seeking close contact with others by hauling themselves out onto the ice and huddling in enormous groups. Most walruses are cinnamon brown in colour, but old bulls lose their pigmentation, and appear oddly bleached on emerging from cold water. Basking in the sun causes the walruses' skin to engorge with blood, until they blush red all over.

The diet of these sea mammals includes clams, cockles and mussels, which they find by rooting about, pig-fashion, with their snouts, or by squirting jets of water from their mouths to disturb the sediment and expose their prey. Their moustache of coarse whiskers is highly sensitive to touch, and is used to locate food in murky water. Contrary to widespread belief, the tusks (which are really elongated teeth) are not used to dig for food on the bottom. Instead, they have a social function, signifying dominance and status within the group. They may also be used as ice picks, either to hook onto the edge of an ice floe, or to break breathing holes in the ice. And they can be used as weapons in defence.

SUN SEEKER *A bull walrus hauls itself out onto the shore to bask in the sun.*

IN THE OPEN SEA

3

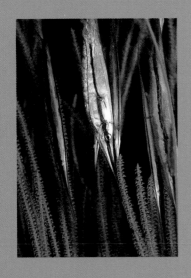

SWIMMING UPRIGHT
*A transparent shrimpfish in
night-time waters off Indonesia.*

GANNETS, CORMORANTS, SHEARWATERS AND OTHER DIVING SEA BIRDS INVADE THE SEA FROM THE AIR IN THEIR SEARCH FOR FOOD — FLYING FISH LEAP FROM THE WAVES AND SKIM ACROSS THEM TO ESCAPE PREDATORS. BOUNDARIES ARE INEVITABLY FLUID IN THE MULTISTOREY HABITAT OF THE OPEN SEAS. FLOATING CREATURES SUCH AS PORTUGUESE MEN-OF-WAR MAKE THEIR LIVING ON THE SURFACE; THE ABYSSAL DEPTHS ARE POPULATED WITH STRANGE PLANTS AND ANIMALS, FROM CUP-SHAPED SPONGES TO TRIPODFISH THAT PROP THEMSELVES ON THE OCEAN FLOOR ON STILTS. BETWEEN THE TWO EXTREMES ARE ALL THE OCEANS' VARIETY OF FISH AND SEA-GOING MAMMALS, FROM SHARKS TO DOLPHINS, SEALS AND SEA LIONS TO ELONGATED NEEDLEFISH.

BREACHING *A humpback
whale takes a breather.*

THE LAYERED OCEAN

The apparently boundless space of the ocean is, in fact, divided into layers, created by differences in temperature, light and pressure. Some animals move between layers with ease, while others are prisoners of a particular stratum.

It is mid-afternoon on a quiet Pacific lagoon. The still waters are broken only by the gentle lap of the wash from a boat. There seems to be little other activity until, in the distance, a small fast-moving bird appears, skimming the water. The bird dives beneath the surface and disappears from view. Almost immediately, another bursts from the water nearby and glides for several seconds.

There is something slightly unusual about them – can these really be birds diving for fish? Another appears and dives again, then two more emerge from the water and glide along, just above the surface. The sunlight suddenly catches their bodies, and the reflection – flashes of pure gleaming silver – reveals their true identity. These deceptive creatures are not birds, but 'flying fish'.

Their extraordinary behaviour is an attempt to outwit a persistent predator from below. By leaving the top layer of the ocean, the flying fish disappear from the view of their pursuer. With luck, the predator will become confused and abandon the chase, opting for some less tricky prey.

The outstretched 'wings' of a flying fish

SPIKY SUPPORT *Pointed outgrowths help to keep this microscopic creature afloat.*

HUNGER STRIKES *Blue-footed boobies, relatives of the gannets, dive for fish near the Galápagos Islands.*

are really taut, membranous fins, far larger than those of other fish. They can be folded flat like fans and held tightly against the body during ordinary swimming. By first building up speed under water, they are able to break the surface at an impressive 35 mph (56 km/h). In flight, the fins extend sideways, angled to catch the wind for uplift. The elongated tail is sometimes used to beat the water for extra propulsion in mid-flight.

A human, diving below water, is only

PORTUGUESE MAN-OF-WAR *Polyps on the tentacles can deliver a powerful sting.*

able to swim for a few minutes before surfacing to breathe. For a similar reason, a flying fish can tolerate only a short spell – up to ten seconds – in the air before being obliged to plunge back under water for oxygen. Its gills begin to dry out in the air and are then rendered ineffective.

Small surface-living squid, under threat from a predator, are also able to burst through the water surface into the air. Unlike the flying fish, they have no outstretched 'wings' on which to glide, but rely solely on the power of jet propulsion. They shoot from the water at speeds of over 30 mph (48 km/h), sometimes on a trajectory so steep that they land aboard ships, more than 20 ft (6 m) above sea level.

THE CEILING OF THE SEA

The surface of the water seems like a natural boundary to the marine world. But just as fish and squid escape their watery shackles to make fleeting journeys through the air, so sea birds descend into the ocean, to take advantage of the bountiful supply of marine food. Some, such as the gannets and boobies, scan the sea from a great height. On sighting a suitable meal, they draw in their wings, tip forward and drop vertically, plummeting beneath the waves like targeted missiles. The appropriately named shearwaters and cormorants bob gently on the surface, then make lengthy dives into the world below in search of fish that they actively chase through the water.

While flying fish and diving sea birds breach the frontier between air and water, there are

FAST MOVERS *Squid swim by jet propulsion. Some can even launch themselves into the air.*

a few marine creatures that make the boundary layer their permanent home, living half-above and half-below the surface. Little muscular effort is required to maintain their existence, as they have evolved floats to buoy them up and 'sails' to catch the passing wind.

These indolent creatures include the Portuguese man-of-war (*Physalia physalis*) and the by-the-wind-sailor (*Velella*). They do not even need to hunt their prey: as they are carried forward by the wind, long sting-laden tentacles trail behind them in the sea below, and small fish and other animals become trapped in these deadly tresses.

FLOATING PREDATORS

The Portuguese men-of-war and the by-the-wind-sailors are not exempt from being eaten themselves. They are at risk from smaller predators which share their home on the roof of the sea, such as the little floating sea slug (*Glaucus*), and the violet sea snail (*Janthina*), which hangs upside down on a raft of air bubbles.

Both are able to nibble at the gelatinous bodies of their floating neighbours, despite the stinging cells on their tentacles. The sea slug actually turns the stinging cells of its prey to its own advantage, swallowing them without injury to itself and storing them intact for self-defence. The

THE LAYERS OF OCEAN

330 ft (100 m)

3300 ft (1000 m)

6600 ft (2000 m)

LIVING IN HARMONY
*The plant and animal life of
the oceans is divided into many
layers: these overlap and merge
with no sharp boundaries.*

stinging cells are transported to the finger-like projections splayed on each side of the sea slug's body, where they successfully deter predators.

All these beautiful, delicate, meandering creatures are at the mercy of the wind above, and the currents tugging at them from below. In strong storms they may be blown inshore and stranded on beaches. Fragile violet sea snails are often cast up, broken and dying. Heaps of lifeless by-the-wind-sailors may be found on Pacific and Mediterranean shores, sometimes stranded by the million. Because of their inability to swim against the currents, or control their destiny, these creatures are properly included with the microscopic plants and animals as members of the plankton: the passive 'drifters' of the ocean surface.

LIFE IN LAYERS

Life in the ocean operates in layers. The flying fish arcing up into the sunshine; gannets plunging into the waves and returning with food; the by-the-wind-sailors fixed forever at the interface: all the contrasts that are immediately obvious to us at

STAY-AT-HOME *Sea pens
are among the animals
that live rooted to one
place on the seabed.*

the surface are reproduced over and again, down through a succession of ocean layers that we cannot perceive to the dark and distant seabed.

The different ocean layers are dictated by factors such as changes in light, temperature, pressure, saltiness and the availability of oxygen. The boundaries are never as sharp as those between air and water, nor are they clearly discernible, but for the creatures of the ocean they demarcate zones where life is possible from zones that are (to a number of particular species) hostile and uninhabitable.

They are boundaries that some creatures can cross while others cannot. Just as the by-the-wind-sailor is confined to floating at the surface, bottom-dwelling animals burrow in sediment and cannot survive elsewhere, and sedentary creatures such as sea pens and tube worms spend their lives attached to one spot. Such animals often compensate by living as free-floating plankton when young, in the sunlit waters far above their adult resting places. This allows them to disperse and possibly to colonise new areas of the ocean.

A FLOATING NURSERY

Among those that use the surface waters as a transient floating nursery are the tiny larvae of sponges, sea cucumbers and shellfish. Other more mobile bottom-dwelling

ATTENTION-SEEKERS *Some species of hatchet fish have luminous lures located inside their mouths.*

MICROSCOPIC VIEW *The plankton of the surface layer includes many different creatures.*

animals also spend their early lives here, including lobsters, crabs and starfish. But the larvae bear little resemblance to their adult forms. There are, for example, sausage-shaped tubes, glistening with beating bristles; spheres of jelly, girdled with gleaming hairs; and cellophane-like bells trailing wispy tentacles.

Among them paddle microscopic monsters: tiny featureless tadpole-shaped swimmers; clawed 'scorpions' with bulging eyes; and tufted flea-like creatures waving limbs shaped like rakes or combs with which they gather food. Only by studying these minute life forms extremely carefully, and by watching them mature, have biologists discovered what type of animal they eventually become.

By living at the surface, in a completely different way from that of the adults, the larvae do not have to compete with the parental generation for food and living space. At the same time, they are carried far from their birthplace by the currents and breezes of the ocean surface. Once they approach maturity and are ready to 'settle down', the larvae descend gradually through the ocean layers. This brings them to a new area of seabed, distant from that of their parents, which may offer a permanent and prosperous resting place.

However, it may equally well be a dead end, where they cannot compete with animals already established, where the conditions are not right, or where food is scarce. In either case, their travelling days are over and the future, if indeed there is one, is immobile.

PRISONERS OF THE MID-OCEAN LAYERS

Whereas the 'sessile', or immobile, creatures of the seabed are locked to one spot for the rest of their lives, some swimming animals – which are apparently free to

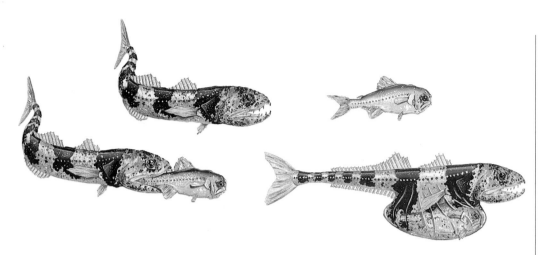

HUGE APPETITE *Loosely hinged jaws and an expanding stomach allow some fish to take prey as large as themselves.*

move about at will – are actually restricted in their vertical movements. They cannot rise above or sink below a certain level because they have become adapted to the particular temperature, pressure and food supply to be found only in that relatively narrow band of the ocean.

The tiny fish known as bristle mouths (*Cyclothone*) are extremely common in the oceans throughout the world, and they are often hauled up, thousands at a time, by deep-sea trawlers. The bristles that give them their name are actually long, fine, sharp teeth that they use to trap shrimps. The many different species of bristle mouth remain largely separated from one another by living at differing depths. In general, the species of bristle mouth that inhabit the middle layers are transparent or silvery in colour, while their counterparts in the deepest layers of the ocean are dark-coloured.

Many other animals are confined to the twilight zone: those cold, dimly lit waters between depths of 650 ft (200 m) below the surface and the farthest limit of light penetration at about 3300 ft (1000 m). These include the beautiful metallic hatchet fishes (Sternoptyx), each of which has a glowing light patch located on the roof of its mouth, so that by holding its jaws open it can lure small prey to certain death. The hatchet fish merely has to close its mouth and swallow its meal. In the same zone are slender predators known as lancet fish (*Alepisaurus* species) which, reaching lengths of 6 ft (1.8 m), are among the largest of all fish confined to these depths.

TWILIGHT OPPORTUNISTS

These permanent inhabitants of the twilight zone must be opportunistic in their feeding habits, either catching what little live prey is available, or depending upon the 'rain' of non-living food pouring down from above: corpses, food scraps, decaying plankton and the droppings of other animals that drift down slowly, drawn by gravity towards a final resting place on the ocean floor.

Many of the fish that are restricted to the middle ranges have adapted specially to take advantage of whatever food comes their way. They have highly sensitive eyes that allow them to detect prey in the faint light; stabbing teeth to maintain a firm grip; wide gapes and distensible stomachs that enable them to engulf large items, such as squid and other fish, without wastage.

Some of the twilight zone

SWIM BLADDER *Gas pressure in a swim bladder changes with depth, but the swim bladder itself stays the same size. Other fish maintain their buoyancy with special oil reserves, while cuttlefish (a kind of mollusc) have air-filled cuttlebones.*

predators are able to swallow an intact creature measuring half their own length. Barracudinas are slender fish, superficially similar to the barracudas of surface waters, but actually unrelated. They have vastly expandable stomachs, elongated jaws and a covering of delicate scales that are easily shed. Expendable scales may help them to accommodate increased girth after swallowing an occasional gargantuan meal. Indeed, some of the non-migratory fishes of the twilight zone lack scales altogether.

VERTICAL COMMUTERS

For those animals that can traverse several layers, there is always the option of seeking food elsewhere. They may move between higher and lower zones, dining in one layer and resting in another, as do the fish, squid and shrimps which make massive migrations every 24 hours, rising to the surface by night to feed, and sinking slowly to the safer waters below by day.

Most of the fish that make these daily migrations are equipped with some sort of swim bladder, the organ that enables bony

SWIM BLADDER

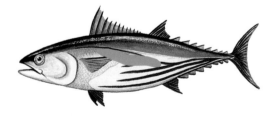

OIL RESERVE

AIR-FILLED CUTTLEBONE

OIL FLOATS *Mackerel have*
lost their swim bladders and
rely on oil for buoyancy.

fish to alter their density and therefore their buoyancy. The swim bladder occupies about 5 per cent of a fish's body, and its lightness – compared to water – balances the weight of the bones and muscles, which are slightly heavier than water. The desired effect, overall, is for the fish to have exactly the same density as the water. When it achieves this, it can float without muscular effort – a phenomenon that is known as 'neutral buoyancy'.

If the fish then swims up or down, however, everything changes. As the fish descends into deeper water, there is far more pressure on its swim bladder, which would contract substantially if the gas content were not suitably adjusted. This contraction would make the fish heavier than the water. In order to maintain its neutral buoyancy, the fish therefore needs to keep the swim bladder at the same size, so it pumps in more gas to offset the greater external pressure.

When ascending, the lessening of external pressure should make the swim bladder expand rapidly, but this effect, too, is carefully controlled, by removing gas from the swim bladder. If fish like these are brought up from the depths by fishermen, the sudden and unnatural ascent makes the swim bladder expand rapidly which can rupture the fish's internal organs or force its stomach out of its mouth. Because of these dangers of rapid expansion, the swim bladder restricts a fish's speed most strongly when swimming upwards.

Swim bladders are not ideal for fast-moving vertical commuters, because of the need to adjust the gas content. Gas is removed from the swim bladder by being absorbed into the bloodstream – a gradual process. For fish that make swift changes in level, these processes could never be speedy enough to compensate for alterations in depth and pressure. Such fish use other methods to provide buoyancy.

OIL AND GAS

Fish such as the mackerel and bonito have lost their swim bladder in the course of evolution, but instead have deposits of fat or oil in their bodies. A similar strategy is used by the sharks, which have never evolved swim bladders at all. Sharks store fat in the form of an oil-rich liver, but other fish accumulate reserves in their muscles or around their internal organs. Oil is 10 per cent less dense than sea water, and if there is enough oil in a fish's body, it can contribute substantially to achieving neutral buoyancy.

Some fish use a combination of a swim bladder and oil to maintain lift. The herring, for example, is able to rise from any depth to the surface without hesitation, and can ascend more rapidly than some of its predators, such as the cod, which depends upon the slowly adjusting swim-bladder system alone. Rather like the flying fish, leaping from the surface, the

GIANT CUTTLEFISH *It can*
adjust to different depths
using the gas in its 'cuttlebone'.

PUTTING ON THE CLOAK OF CONCEALMENT

More than nine out of ten of all mobile creatures in the ocean eventually become the prey of others. In the exposed, sunlit zone there are no hiding places, and animals are particularly vulnerable. This is the haunt of some of the fastest marine predators: sharks, tuna, marlin and swordfish. Animals are susceptible to attack from all sides, from below, and from the air. As a result, they have evolved strategies to make their bodies as inconspicuous as possible – often by exploiting the very transparency and reflective properties of the water itself.

HATCHET FISH *These fish from 1300 ft (400 m) depend on their light organs for camouflage.*

Jellyfish and the Portuguese man-of-war combine translucency with a rich iridescent blue sheen – a reflective, watery camouflage common to many drifting creatures of the surface layer. Similarly, the tiniest animals of the plankton have evolved completely transparent glass-like bodies to render themselves virtually invisible against the clear water.

The muscular, swimming animals of the surface layers can never be transparent. Many of these fish have silvery mirror-like scales, which scatter sunlight and minimise the formation of giveaway shadows. Others depend on the use of colour and shading to protect them from both above and below. Due to the filtering effect of the water, a predator looking down from the upper layer would see dark green or blue in the depths. But a predator looking up from below would see, during the daytime, the pale expanse of distant sky above the surface. For this reason, many swimming animals have a dual colour scheme: a dark

upper surface to blend with the depths, and a light underside to merge with the well-lit surface.

Animals of the twilight zone take this countershading even further. The hatchet fish (*Argyropelecus* species) and lantern fish (*Myctophum* species) have a battery of lights beneath the body to disguise the conspicuous silhouette which would betray their presence when viewed from below. The light emitted is altered to match exactly the dim light filtering down from above.

SEEN FROM BELOW *The silvery scales of surface-swimming fish help to conceal them.*

Little or no light penetrates beyond about 3300 ft (1000 m). In the black abyssal depths, deep-water fish tend to be heavily pigmented with brown or black, while crustaceans are vivid red. Both are effectively invisible in a zone where any glimmer of ambient light will be in the blue part of the spectrum.

---

herring can leave its predators behind by rising into a different layer.

Swim bladders and oil deposits are not the only means of making a marine animal less dense. Cuttlefish, for example, have a spongy air-filled cuttlebone (often fed to parrots and other cagebirds) which might be described as a 'bony balloon'. Internally, the cuttlebone is divided into as many as 100 thin layered compartments.

Unlike a swim bladder, the cuttlebone has a fixed size, and does not expand or contract with changes in depth. Instead, the cuttlebone operates rather like a ballast tank on a submarine. By exchanging the gas in some of the compartments of the bone with water, it can increase the overall fluid content of its body, thereby

making it heavier and capable of descending lower in the water. By reversing the operation, the cuttlefish can ascend nearer the surface.

This process is simple enough in the surface waters, but becomes far more difficult in the depths below, where the high external pressure tends to force liquid into the spaces within the bone. In order to maintain the correct amount of water in the bone at this depth, the cuttlefish has to resist this pressure by relying on the power of salts to control the flow of water.

Using a special network of blood vessels, the cuttlefish extracts salts from fluid in the bone with the result that the bone fluid itself becomes less salty than the blood. It is one of the simple laws of nature

that water tends to flow from a less salty solution into a more salty solution, in an attempt to equalise the two – a phenomenon known as 'osmotic gradient'. By lowering the salt content in the bone fluid, the cuttlefish sets up an osmotic gradient that draws water out of the bone and prevents the cuttlebone from being flooded with fluid from the blood. The system works extremely well as far as depths of around 790 ft (240 m). Beyond this point, the osmotic gradient can no longer balance the increasing external pressure, with the result that the cuttlefish is excluded from most of the twilight zone.

When animals enter the sea from the world above, air can get trapped in their outer covering of fur or feathers. This is what gives most diving sea birds their buoyancy and helps sea otters and fur seals to return to the surface. Some sea birds, however, have 'leaky' plumage that becomes sodden with water as they dive. This enables them to descend more rapidly in pursuit of fish, although the birds will have to work harder to regain the surface afterwards. Cormorants are the most notable practitioners of this diving technique – but they need to dry their plumage once they have finished diving for food. They can frequently be seen, perching on rocks, with their black wings held out, angel-fashion, to catch the sun.

With their sophisticated mechanisms for controlling bodily processes, mammals

BORN TO DIVE *Air-breathing animals, such as these sea lions, have to surface regularly.*

have evolved into supreme diving machines. The seals, whales and porpoises all have their expert divers, but without doubt the ultimate example is the sperm whale (*Physeter macrocephalus*), the deepest-diving sea mammal.

Despite being an air-breathing mammal, the sperm whale is able to stay submerged for between 50 and 80 minutes, reaching astounding depths. Sonar has confirmed dives of up to 7380 ft (2250 m), although it is believed that the farthest dives reach considerably deeper still. The extent of these marathon descents can only be inferred from the stomach contents of the whales, which include bottom-dwelling animals in areas where the seabed is at a depth of nearly 10 000 ft (3050 m).

To achieve dives of this kind of depth and duration, the sperm whale is armed with some remarkable adaptations. First,

DRYING OFF *A cormorant stretches out its wings to dry after a prolonged dive.*

the whale must be able to control its depth. Although it has a powerful tail for downwards and upwards propulsion, scientists believe that there is another mechanism involving far less effort. In its vastly enlarged, bulbous head is a large reservoir of a special waxy substance, called spermaceti, which melts to an oil when warmed to a slightly higher temperature. It is thought that this wax solidifies or melts under the

LOCOMOTION IN THE OPEN OCEAN

So many types of animal swim, and with such apparent ease, that we could easily be deceived into thinking of swimming as relatively effortless. Yet movement through water – even for animals whose bodies have been sculpted by natural selection to its demands – poses more problems than might be assumed.

To begin with, water is 60 times more viscous (that is, stickier) than air, which means that it is more difficult to force the particles apart and to allow an object to pass through. Water particles have a tendency to stick to one another and to other substances (which is why things 'get wet'). For microscopic animals, viscosity is an overwhelming problem. Water clings to their surfaces with syrupy adhesion. Swimming for them might be compared to human beings trying to flounder through treacle. Many of these creatures are unable to propel themselves through water, and instead, drift with the currents.

SIDE TO SIDE *Fish such as sharks (below left) and barracuda (below right) swim with side-to-side undulations of tail and body.*

Larger animals suffer less from the effects of viscosity, but to move forward, they still have to summon up the energy to push aside the weight of water in front of them. Since the ocean is some 830 times denser than the atmosphere, powering a body through it requires much more effort than propelling one through air. For a large animal, the most effort-saving shape for forging a path through the water is that of a teardrop or torpedo. The evolutionary paths of creatures from fish and whales to seals have all converged upon this body form.

As for the swimming itself, animals use a variety of movements, but the majority of them can be reduced to a few

WING-LIKE FINS *Rays propel themselves through the water by flapping their large triangular fins like wings.*

basic 'strokes'. The most widespread is undulatory movement, which throws the body, or part of the body, into a series of rippling waves. Variations on this theme are employed by animals over an enormous range of body sizes throughout the ocean layers. Many of the smallest planktonic animals propel themselves with wriggling undulations of tiny hair-like appendages called flagella.

Some larger animals involve their whole bodies in smooth, serpentine movement. They do this by flexing and relaxing the muscles on alternating flanks. As the muscular waves move backwards along the animal, they propel the body forward, creating a sinuous glide through the water that is much like the movement of a crawling snake over sand. The eels and water snakes all swim in this fashion, as do many of the different kinds of marine worm.

Most fish also swim by undulating the tail fin from side

EEL-LIKE MOVEMENTS *The sea snake, like the eel, undulates through the water.*

FLOWING MOTION *Sea creatures' swimming techniques range from the graceful undulations of most fish to the paddling of turtles and jet propulsion of squids.*

principles as any human oarsman – the only difference being that the oars cannot be lifted from the water on the recovery stroke. Instead, animals twist their 'oars' on the return, so that the narrow edge is leading, and presents minimal resistance to the water. Underwater rowers range from the tiny 'oar-footed' copepods of the animal plankton, to the paddling crabs, marine turtles and penguins. Sea lions pull themselves through the water using their paddle-like front flippers, whereas seals use pulses of pressure from their webbed hind feet. Some animals are able to row extremely fast: penguins perform as many as 200 strokes per minute with their paddle-shaped wings. Jet propulsion is the major alternative to undulation or rowing, and is a popular method of transport among the invertebrate animals – those that have no backbone. By squirting water from their bodies in one direction, animals are able to produce thrust in the opposite direction. Jellyfish weakly pulsate their gelatinous bell-shaped bodies to produce a gentle backwards and downwards thrust.

Octopus, squid and cuttlefish, with more muscular, streamlined forms, use jet propulsion to greater effect. They draw water in through a wide frontal slit and then expel it through a much narrower funnel. The funnel is at the head end, sticking out from beneath the head, with the result that the animals normally move 'backwards' through the water.

However, the funnel is adjustable and can be curved to point in any direction, as necessary. Squid are the fastest of the jet-propelled animals. Large oceanic squid are able to sustain cruising speeds of 20 mph (32 km/h) – a fine achievement for a relative of the slugs and snails.

to side, sweeping its flattened blade hard against the water to push them forward. Whales swim in a similar way, except that the tail swings up and down. When carrying out tricky manoeuvres, fish may use just their side fins to move along. Some oddly shaped fish, such as the rigid bracket-like sea horses, the flattened manta rays and the massive discoid ocean sunfish, depend upon their side fins all the time.

An alternative to the propulsive tail is the use of 'oars' or 'paddles'. Some animals row through the water, pushing against it with broad strokes. They use the same

FLIPPER-PADDLE *Turtles, such as this green turtle, row themselves along.*

DIVING CHAMP *The sperm whale can descend to phenomenal depths.*

influence of temperature changes that are controlled by the whale's nervous system, to alter the density of the animal and act as a buoyancy control.

PROBLEMS OF PRESSURE

Human divers who surface too quickly, without proper decompression procedures, may be paralysed or even killed by a phenomenon called 'the bends'.

This is caused by nitrogen, the major ingredient not only of the air we breathe but also of the compressed air inhaled by divers from underwater cylinders. Nitrogen dissolves more readily in blood at depth, with the result that the blood acquires an additional load of dissolved nitrogen during the dive. As the diver rises to the surface, however, and the pressure is lowered, the extra nitrogen comes out of the blood, escaping gradually through the lungs with each exhaled breath during a slow ascent. If the diver comes up too fast and the pressure declines quickly, then the nitrogen is released suddenly, forming tiny bubbles in the bloodstream. These are potentially damaging and dangerous.

Something similar happens when the top is opened on a fizzy drink – the same trigger, a rapid release of pressure, causes a surge of bubbles throughout the liquid in the bottle.

To avoid this problem, sperm whales have collapsible lungs that fold harmlessly inwards under increased pressure. As they collapse, gas from the lungs is forced up into the windpipe and then along the nasal passageways. These have thickened linings that prevent extra nitrogen from entering the bloodstream.

To survive under water, an air-breathing mammal has to carry a portable supply of oxygen. Although diving whales do not have particularly large lungs for their size, they have more blood in relation to their body size than other mammals – and this blood is particularly rich in the red pigment haemoglobin that holds oxygen and transports it about the body.

Sperm whales also have an abundant supply of a similar pigment called myoglobin which stores oxygen in the muscles. Altogether, sperm whales are able to store and use 90 per cent of the oxygen from a breath, whereas humans utilise no more than 20 per cent.

A sperm whale's internal chemistry is well adapted to tolerate low oxgen levels, and much of its body can function even when the blood supply is cut off. As a whale dives, it lowers its heart rate by half to conserve oxygen, and reduces the blood supply to all but its most vital organs (the brain, nervous system and heart) in order to stretch the limited supply even farther. On returning to the surface, its airways and lungs are cleared of spent air in an enormous exhalation through the blowhole, before the lungs and blood are recharged with fresh oxygen.

With so many adaptations for hunting at depth, the sperm whales are able to exploit food sources beyond the reach of the other toothed whales, seals or sea lions.

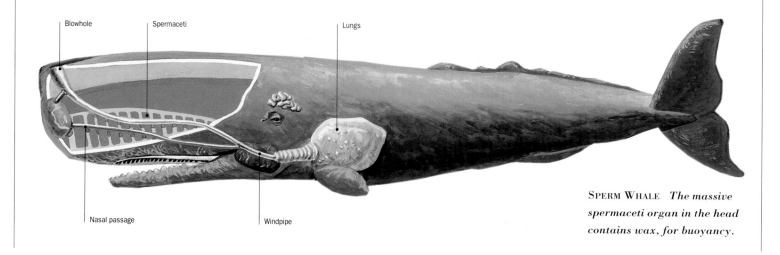

Blowhole   Spermaceti   Lungs

Nasal passage   Windpipe

SPERM WHALE *The massive spermaceti organ in the head contains wax, for buoyancy.*

The staple diet of sperm whales is squid, but the stomachs of captured specimens have been found to contain small sharks and even tin cans, as well. The stomachs' contents have also confirmed evidence of giant animals in the depths, once known only from rumour and legend: giant squid.

HUNTING FOR SQUID

Their immense size implies that sperm whales tap into a rich food source during their deep dives. Indeed, it seems that they do not even chase their quarry, but stay in the same spot (once they are at the right depth) and simply wait for the squid to swim within reach. Sperm whales usually surface within a few hundred yards of the point where they embarked on their dive, having spent just over half an hour in much the same spot (descent and ascent take about 15 minutes in total).

Those spots are usually to be found on deepwater slopes at the edges of the continental shelves, where the seabed falls steeply away towards the abyss. It is here, on this precipitous cliff-like seabed in the mid-ocean layers, that many species of squid lay their eggs. There are dense shoals of them in such areas, many with luminescent organs making them visible in the murky twilight or perpetual darkness. The sperm whale rests motionless at this level, waiting for a shoal of squid to approach, whereupon it snaps its 6 ft (1.8 m) long lower jaw to capture as many of the squid as possible.

The superabundance of these squid remains a mystery. Why are they not more heavily exploited by resident predators? There are some medium-sized sharks at this level, but these seem to be rather sluggish animals and they would probably not be able to capture

LIFE ON THE OCEAN FLOOR
A sea cucumber caught in the lights of an unmanned submersible.

DEMONS OF THE DEEP

The existence of monstrous giant squid (*Architeuthis*) used to be dismissed as maritime myth, until several bodies were washed ashore in Newfoundland during the late 1800s. Since that time, evidence has been found suggesting that some giant squid weigh more than 550 lb (250 kg) and measure 70 ft (21 m) from tentacle tip to the end of the body.

The sperm whale is thought to be the only animal to prey upon the giant squid (evidently, giant squid do not give up without a fight, for many sperm whales bear battle scars from their clawed suckers). Sperm whales have regurgitated suckered tentacles as thick as a man's arm. The horny beak-like jaws of the squid remain inside a whale long after the rest of the meal has been digested, and from the size of some massive beaks retrieved so far, it is believed that there must be squid in the depths far larger than any yet washed up on land.

the fast-moving jet-propelled squid. Smaller and faster sharks, only about 12 in (30 cm) long, hunt in schools, and appear to prey on individual squid that are roughly twice their size, surrounding them and attacking in unison. In general, however, these resident predators seem to have little impact on the massive schools of squid, leaving rich pickings for visiting sperm whale.

Perhaps the high pressure and the low temperature in these deeper waters impose such powerful constraints on the biological functions of fish that few really successful resident predators have evolved: neither medium-sized, fast-moving fish that could chase the squid, nor large powerful fish that could lie in wait and ambush them as the sperm whale probably does. The sperm whale can overcome the problems created by the cold because, being a mammal, it has its own internal heating system.

We may never know the answer to this puzzle, however. The deeper layers of the ocean, from the twilight zone down to the abyssal depths, are territory that humankind can only investigate with difficulty, let alone conquer. Our knowledge of these enigmatic zones is based upon echo-sounding, on the scant observations made by deep-water submersibles or underwater cameras, and on the creatures brought up by trawl nets. The fact that these nets regularly yield entirely novel species reveals how little we know. In time, we may discover new species and find out new facts, but much about these levels of the ocean – from which man is excluded by the invincible, crushing pressure of the water above – will remain forever mysterious.

FISH OF THE OPEN SEA

A pancake-flat, flapping manta ray is a fish, but so is a sinuous eel, a globular pufferfish or a stolid ocean sunfish. A dazzling and bewildering array of shapes and forms reflects a diversity of lifestyles among the different fish species.

They call the creature the devilfish. It flaps slowly past on vast, taut wings, a sinister, black, diamond-shaped shadow that glides in eerie silence through the ocean. At the front of its head, two strange appendages project forwards like fleshy, devilish horns. On either side of them, dark eyes stare out into the emptiness of the sea. A mouth gapes between the horns, constantly open. For a while, the spectre disappears into the inky blue, then materialises again from the void, an awesome presence that dwarfs any human diver.

On occasions, these colossal fish gather in groups of three or four, circling, swooping and gliding like huge underwater kites, each of which trails a straight, cord-like tail. As they loop and somersault, the creatures expose the flashes of white that cover their undersides.

These enormous fish – some of them have been known to measure 23 ft (7 m) across – are Pacific manta rays (*Manta hamiltoni*), whose Latin name derives from *mantus*, meaning 'cloak' or 'mantle'. This refers to their vast, wing-like fins lying outstretched in the current like a black cloak in the wind. At the base of these immense triangular fins, a ray's body is slashed by five pairs of symmetrical, parallel gill slits.

Water floods into the mouth as the animal cruises along, and flows through the gill arches – where small food items are

SINISTER PRESENCE *The manta ray's mouth, seen at the bottom of this picture, is flanked by two fleshy horns.*

POLKA-DOT PARTY *A group of spotted eagle rays feeding together.*

sieved – then out through the gill slits. The process is so efficient that the huge bulk of the manta ray is sustained solely on a diet of tiny fish and other animals that live suspended in the open waters.

For all its seeming menace, the devilfish is no danger to human swimmers.

THE SIGNIFICANCE OF SHAPE

Measuring, on average, 20 ft (6 m) across and weighing a good 2 tons, the black kite-shaped manta ray challenges most people's idea of what a fish should look like – that is, torpedo-shaped, silvery and no more than a few feet long.

Through millions of years of trial and error, natural selection has produced torpedo-like body forms in many kinds of fish, as well as in other underwater animals such as the dolphins, the seals and the extinct reptiles known as ichthyosaurs. The predatory tuna, marlin, swordfish, mackerel and billfish have all evolved this sleek body form, enabling them to cut cleanly through the water in pursuit of shoals of plankton-feeders such as anchovies and herrings, which, in their turn, are streamlined for a rapid escape.

Fastest of all is the tropical sailfish

(*Istiophorus platyperus*), a powerful racer that can reach top speeds of more than 60 mph (96 km/h). Various computer-simulated designs for machines have converged on a similar solution for fast aquatic travel: the same streamlined form is used in the design of modern ship and submarine hulls.

So why is it that some fish, such as the manta ray, do not conform? Basically, it is because speed is not necessarily the top priority for every species. This is particularly true of those species living in sheltered coastal habitats or lurking on the seabed. Over the eons, natural selection has favoured other shapes in response to the demands of different habitats or lifestyles: bodies have become flattened into discs, moulded into globular forms, or stretched into ribbons, cords and cylinders.

Flat bodies, similar to that of the manta ray, are mostly found in bottom-dwelling species. This allows them to lie concealed on the seabed, half buried in the sediment. When they need to swim, an undulatory action of the body and fins produces movement, and the fish travel through the water like the flying carpets of Oriental fairy tales: reasonably effective, but not speedy. The manta ray is unusual in having abandoned the bottom-dwelling habits of its ancestors; instead, it spends most of its time swimming freely or floating at the surface. Its huge size protects the manta ray from predators, so concealment and speed are no longer necessary. And its food source

WALKING ON FINS *A red-bellied batfish crawls across the ocean floor.*

requires it to operate in open water. The sideways extension of its fins into triangular 'wings' has improved on the swimming performance of the flattened body shape.

THEMES AND VARIATIONS

In producing a flattened body from a conventional fishy form, there are two evolutionary options: top-to-bottom flattening or side-to-side flattening. Manta rays, stingrays, eagle rays and skates are all flattened from top to bottom, as are the strange triangular or circular deep-water batfish (family Ogcocephalidae) that crawl over the sea floor on stumpy leg-like fins. The flatfish that are familiar to us as food, such as plaice, sole and flounder, are flattened in the opposite way, their bodies being compressed from side to side. Their evolutionary journey is retraced by the young ones, which begin as ordinary fish with a torpedo-like form. By a peculiar series of developmental migrations and contortions, both the eyes of these young flatfish come to be on the same side of the flattened head, rather like a Picasso portrait. The adult spends its life lying on its opposite side, eyes uppermost.

Not all fish that are flattened from side to side are as bizarre as the plaice and flounder: many have their eyes in the normal position and go about their lives in an upright posture. The beautiful angelfish and butterfly fish of coral reefs are typical examples: their bodies broad and colourful when glimpsed from the side, yet pencil-thin when seen from the front. Compressed body

narrow triangular fins one of which projects straight up from its back, the other pointing down from its belly. Both fins are positioned just ahead of the tail-end, giving the sunfish a curiously unbalanced look, yet the fins seem to work well enough, propelling the strange creature slowly through the water. The reason for the sunfish's peculiar body form is something of a mystery. No other fish looks quite like it.

LOOKS CAN BE DECEPTIVE

Pufferfish and porcupine fish are fundamentally torpedo-shaped, but plump. These slow, apparently vulnerable creatures have a surprise in store for any attacker. If provoked, they can dramatically change shape, swelling their bodies with water so that they become balloon-like objects that are virtually impossible for a predator to bite into or swallow.

In addition, the porcupine fish is armed with an impressive array of prickly spines. These normally lie flat against the body,

PROBLEMS WITH SWIMMING
Batfishes are poor swimmers who often have to bury themselves – rather than swimming away – when disturbed.

shapes are common on the coral reef, and in habitats thick with weed cover. Their slender shapes are useful for making fast, sharp turns, and for slipping quickly into narrow hiding places, or between strands of foliage.

Despite its similarly flattened body, hiding is not really an option for the enormous ocean sunfish (*Mola mola*). Nor are quick, sharp manoeuvres. Fortunately, a fish that weighs up to 2200 lb (1000 kg) has few predators to evade. What is more, it

feeds on slow-moving jellyfish or other drifting plankton that it can grasp unhurriedly with beak-like jaws. Its huge body is flattened from side to side and looks, in profile, like the head of a giant fish with the body removed, as if by a fishmonger, for it ends sharply, just behind the fins, in a vertical edge that has a narrow fringe of fin running down it. This does little to move the fish forward, the real work is done by the long,

SPHERES AND BULLETS *By blowing itself up into a ball the pufferfish (top) can escape its enemies. The odd shape of the sunfish (below) is unique in the marine world.*

SHARP NOSES *Razorfish, like needlefish, have pointed, rapier-sharp jaws.*

but on inflation they bristle outwards, creating a fearsome deterrent. Many pufferfish, the death puffer (*Arothron hispidus*) included, have another line of weaponry, for a virulent poison is contained within their blood and organs. Since they have so many forms of defence, these fish can well afford a rotund body and the loss of streamlining and speed that this inevitably entails.

STRAIGHT AND NARROW

Stories of giant sea serpents have been told for centuries and continue to this day, perpetuated by alleged sightings of long, serpentine creatures offshore. The origin of the serpent legends may well lie with certain large, elongated fish: the beautiful ribbon-like oarfish (*Regalecus glesne*). Its sleek, silvery body is more than 20 ft (6 m) long, and is adorned with a feathery red crest running the length of the spine. Sightings of this exotic snake-like creature are not very common because it normally remains in deep water, where it feeds on shrimp-like crustaceans. No purpose behind its extraordinary size and shape has yet been identified.

Elongated fish are a varied collection, ranging from the eels to the spear-like needlefish. Needlefish, found in tropical waters, are slender, hyperstreamlined relatives of the flying fish. They have a narrow pair of jaws, tapering to a sharp point, with which they grasp fast-moving fish prey. In frenzied pursuit of smaller fish in the upper layers of the ocean, needlefish occasionally fling themselves clean out of the water. They fly like a missile and have been known to lance fishermen inadvertently through the legs, chest or abdomen. This happens more often at night, when the fish are presumably attracted by the artificial lights of fishing

boats. The largest species of needlefish is the houndfish (*Tylosaurus crocodilus*). It reaches up to 5 ft (1.5 m) in length, and could cause considerable injury to any person unlucky enough to be caught in its flight path.

Closer to the shore, hidden among weed or in coral reefs, lives another group of long-snouted, elongated fish. These, however, are very slow swimmers, because their bodies are held almost rigid by a covering of armour plates. They include the tube-like pipefish and the sea horses, both of which lurk in seaweeds, sucking into their long snouts any plankton that passes by. They are reliant on their slender

body forms for camouflage among the strands of vegetation.

Sea horses are among the most oddly made of all fish, their bodies permanently upright and their heads bent at a sharp angle to the body Their tails are curled in a spiral, specially adapted for grasping underwater perches. Their relatives, the

OCEAN HITCHHIKERS
A Queensland grouper carries remoras (left) which attach themselves by suckers (below).

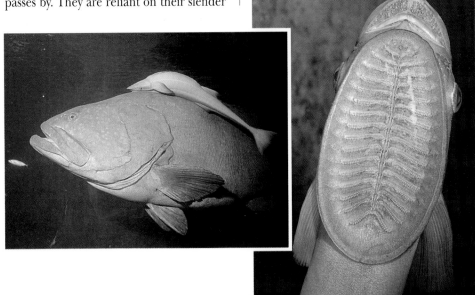

A HARMLESS GIANT: THE WHALE SHARK

From the dim blue of the distant water, a colossal shape looms ominously into view. A rectangular mouth, 6 ft (1.8 m) across, cuts across the front of a broad, flat head. The brown-grey flanks are patterned with white polka dots the size of tennis balls. Not only is the beast more than 30 ft (9 m) in length, it is also a shark – a combination sufficient to inspire paralysing terror in those who encounter it for the first time.

Yet this, the largest type of fish in the world, poses absolutely no threat to humans. It is a whale shark (*Rhincodon typus*), a tropical species first described in 1828, but probably observed several times previously as an unknown 'sea monster'. So far, the longest reliable measurement of a whale shark is 39 ft (12 m), but they are rumoured to reach at least 60 ft (18 m) in length. Despite their size, whale sharks feed only on shrimps and

JONAH BEWARE *A diver is dwarfed by the monstrous open mouth (left) of a whale shark, the world's largest fish.*

small fish. Divers can safely hitch a ride with one of these enormous fish, clinging precariously to the fin on its back, or holding onto the tail as it lashes from side to side.

Second only to the whale shark is the basking shark (*Cetorhinus maximus*), which reaches lengths of up to 33 ft (10 m), and also has a bulk measured in tons. This languid giant cruises gently at a top speed of about 3 mph (5 km/h) near the surface of the cooler seas, feeding entirely on plankton. Behind the head on either flank are five long gill slits, giving the strange impression that the head is partly severed from the body. Food-laden water passes over the gill filaments, where plankton is trapped and oxygen is extracted. A basking

BASKING GIANT *The massive gape of a shark as it feeds.*

shark can process 1000 tons of water in an hour.

Basking sharks are probably responsible for many stories about sea monsters. Sometimes they swim in lines, nose to tail, giving the illusion of a single, enormous serpent looping through the water. Mysterious carcasses washed up on beaches have sometimes been identified as the remains of basking sharks. In an advanced state of decomposition, the gill arches are absent, leaving a tiny skull on the end of a long 'neck': the overall appearance resembles a massive prehistoric monster with paddle-like limbs.

shrimpfish, have straight, flat bodies, streaked with black markings along each side. They often hang motionless among the dark spines of sea urchins, head downwards, camouflaged by their stripes.

The remoras, another elongated group – measuring 1-3 ft (30-91 cm) – have a very different lifestyle. They hitch a ride with larger fish, attaching themselves by means of a modified fin on their back, which acts as a vacuum-type sucker. Remoras are not parasites, but simply save energy that might be spent swimming, and gain scraps of food from the meals of larger fish.

Lampreys, on the other hand, are parasitic. There are about 36 species of these slender, worm-like fish, some living in fresh water, others in the sea. Marine lampreys leave the sea to spawn in rivers – a migration similar to that of salmon – after which the adults die. Filter-feeding larvae called ammocoetes hatch from the eggs, and then live inside

BLOODSUCKER *The rasping disc-like mouth of a lamprey, among the most primitive of all fish.*

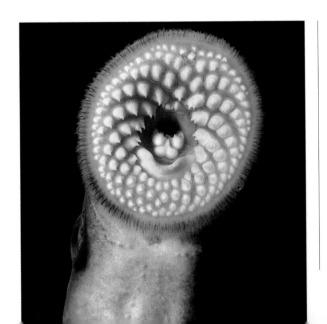

burrows on the bed of the river. Sea lampreys (*Petromyzon marinus*) remain in the larval stage for up to seven years, before undergoing a complicated metamorphosis to adulthood, and a long journey back to the sea. Adult sea lampreys have a disc-like mouth, lined with concentric circles of rasping teeth. The mouth acts as a sucker, enabling the lamprey to lock onto the body of a larger fish, puncturing the victim's flesh and feeding on its blood.

WORM-SHAPED HAGFISH

Although they are not closely related, hagfish share many superficial similarities with lampreys: both are worm-shaped, and have a simple suction disc, rather than hinged jaws, for a mouth. However, unlike lampreys, hagfish are almost blind and have to seek out their food on the seabed using sensory tentacles around the mouth. They eat marine worms and crustaceans, but also consume dead and dying fish, boring through the skin of their prey, and then devouring it from within, leaving only skin and bone.

To gain additional leverage on its prey, a hagfish is able to tie its pink, rubbery body into a knot as it feeds, lubricated by an unpleasant slime that deters other animals from joining the feast or eating the hagfish itself.

Even from this great variety of shape and form, it would be hard to guess that

FINS WITH SPOKES *This striped goby belongs to the largest group of living fish, the ray-finned bony fish.*

fish species outnumber all the species of birds, mammals and reptiles put together. In total, there are many more than 21 000 known species of fish, of which 58 per cent live in the sea. They range in size from the most colossal 8 ton whale sharks to the smallest of marine fish (*Eviota zonura*), tiny gobies that mature at just 0.6 in (15 mm) – scarcely longer than a fingernail. At the same time, new species are still being discovered and described – at a rate of more than 100 each year.

This enormous collection of animals, herded together under the heading of 'fish', is not even one group, but is made up of several very different ancestral lines. These ancestral lines probably do have a common origin, if one goes back far enough in the distant evolutionary past, but by Silurian times (438-408 million years ago), there were already at least two separate, well-established major groups. The first of these lines gave rise to the lampreys and hagfish, the second to all other living fish, plus the amphibians, reptiles, birds and mammals. Consequently, while an eel may look at a cursory glance much like a hagfish, it is actually more closely related to an ostrich. There is more in common between the DNA of a tuna and a tiger, than between the DNA of a tuna and a lamprey, even though both tuna and lamprey are called 'fish'.

As with all other animal groups, the path of fish evolution has been deduced, in part, from fossil evidence collected over many years and much can also be gleaned from studying modern fish. The lampreys and hagfish are particularly useful

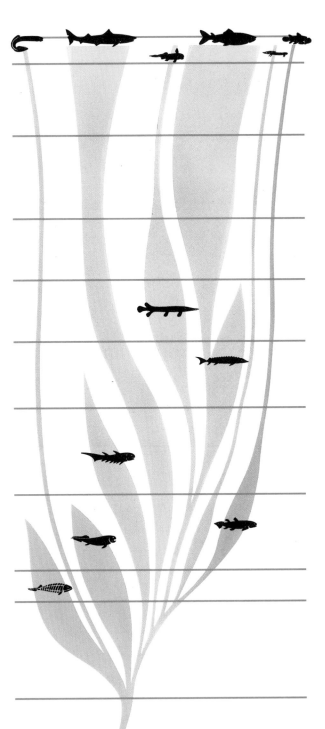

FISH EVOLUTION *The fish of today's oceans, rivers and lakes belong to many quite separate lineages that are only distantly related. From their earliest common ancestors living more than 500 million years ago in the Cambrian Age, their 'family tree' branched out into creatures such as the 'shell-skinned' fish of the Silurian Age and the lobe-finned fish of the Devonian Age. Some of today's fish have evolved greatly since then; others, such as the coelacanth, have changed remarkably little.*

PRIMITIVE SURVIVOR *A Pacific hagfish, a slimy eel-like animal with a slit-like mouth, horny teeth and no jaws.*

in this respect because they are the only modern fish which do not have jaws. From the earliest fossil fragments, dating back as far as 500 million years, we know that the jawless condition was the original one.

All the very earliest fish – armour-plated creatures called ostracoderms, meaning 'shell-skinned' – lacked jaws. Like the hagfish and lampreys of today they would have sucked at their food rather than actively chewing it. Some were mud-dwellers, with bizarre flattened, shield-shaped heads, others were more classically fish-shaped. All were encased, to some degree, in cumbersome bony plates, either shielding their head and trunk, or enclosing the entire body from the mouth to the tip of the tail.

This thick armour offered protection against the various predators, principally the sea scorpions, or eurypterids, that roamed the oceans of the time. Although these animals are often described as giant scorpions, they were in fact quite small. The largest ever recorded, however – a New York State species from the Silurian Age, measuring 10 ft (3 m) long – does indeed fit the popular description.

Lampreys and hagfish are relics of the ostracoderms, which otherwise became extinct many millions of years ago. Apart from the absence of jaws, they show little resemblance to the body form of their forebears. The bony armour has been lost, and a worm-like body has evolved in both the modern groups of jawless fish. Clearly this body form has certain advantages in the life of the ocean, which is why it has evolved repeatedly.

JAWS: AN EVOLUTIONARY BREAKTHROUGH

If fish evolution had come to a halt with the ostracoderms, cows would not chew the cud, human beings would not be able to chew their food, and there would never have been a horror movie called *Jaws*. Tens of millions of years after the evolution of the first fish, a number of groups gradually developed jaws. Fossil evidence suggests that the jawbones were derived from the hinged gill supports, but no one knows for sure whether this development occurred just once, or a number of times in different fish groups.

Jaws were an extremely significant innovation, opening up a whole range of new dietary possibilities for the early fish, which could now bite and capture other animals, crush and eat hard body parts, as well as using their jaws in self-defence. Along with jaws, these fish also developed controllable, paired fins, an asset for swimming that gave them much increased mobility and agility, both when they were chasing prey and when they were evading capture themselves.

From the earliest jawed fish, several quite separate fish groups eventually became

established. Some of these, such as the spiny-skinned sharks (Acanthodians) and the bizarre, armoured placoderms, both of which first appeared about 400 million years ago, flourished for a time and then became extinct. However, other lines, that became established at about the same time as these creatures diverged, proliferated and survived.

Two of them continue to the present day. The larger of the two is called the bony fish (Osteichthyes), characterised by a hard, calcified skeleton. This vast group encompasses almost all of the most familiar fish: goldfish and minnows, piranhas and barracudas, eels and sea horses, flounders and angelfish. The smaller group, known as the cartilaginous fish (Chondrichthyes), is easier to define because it includes only a few species: the rays, skates, dogfish, sharks and chimeras.

Cartilaginous fish do not have hard, calcified bones. Instead, as the name implies, their skeletons are formed from cartilage, a lighter, more flexible, almost rubbery material. Made from tough fibres of protein, cartilage forms the skeleton of all vertebrate embryos, but in most it gradually develops into bone as the embryo grows.

The process by which cartilage becomes bone involves many changes, one of the most important being calcification, in which hard little crystals of calcium phosphate salts develop within the network of cartilage protein. The protein fibres of the cartilage remain, but the calcium salts take away the rubbery, flexible quality and give the structure a new hardness.

These fish, such as sharks, retain a cartilaginous skeleton throughout their lives – in other words, calcification never occurs. The consensus among scientists is that the ancestors of sharks and their kin had bony skeletons, so that the cartilaginous

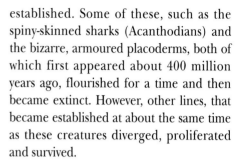

EARLY JAWS *Skins armoured with bony plates and primitive jaws were the new features of the placoderms of the Devonian Age about 400 million years ago.*

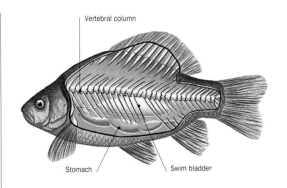

Vertebral column

Stomach   Swim bladder

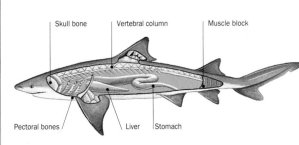

Skull bone   Vertebral column   Muscle block

Pectoral bones   Liver   Stomach

skeleton is no longer seen as a primitive condition. Rather, it is seen as something that natural selection has developed, beginning with fish whose skeletons were bony and then gradually eliminated the calcification process. Exactly why this should have occurred is not fully understood.

LOBE-FINS AND RAY-FINS

It was from a subdivision of the bony fish – called the lobe-finned fish – that amphibians, reptiles, birds and mammals eventually evolved. The collection of small chunky bones inside the stumpy lobed fins became the raw material from which natural selection modelled the various limbs of land-dwelling animals: the legs, arms, wings and flippers. Modern representatives of the lobe-finned fish are scarce, but they include the freshwater lungfish and the marine coelacanth that was rediscovered this century having been thought extinct.

The study of these extraordinary survivors can help us to understand the evolutionary process by which the ancient lobe-finned fish conquered the land.

All the other bony fish are 'ray-finned',

UNDERWATER FENCER *The swordfish uses its fearsome rapier to slash at prey.*

INTERNAL STRUCTURES *Most common fish have hard, calcified skeletons (left, above). However, some species, notably the sharks, have skeletons made of lighter, more flexible cartilage (left, below).*

meaning that their fins are strengthened by fine bony pins or 'rays'. The ray-finned fish themselves are divided into several groups, but most of these groups, which include esoteric species such as the sturgeon and bowfin, are small. The vast majority of ray-finned fish belong to the teleost group, the hugely successful and widespread scaly fish with which we are most familiar. The most notable attribute of the teleosts is a complex mouth which can be pushed forward to suck in food – a familiar feeding manoeuvre to anyone who has ever watched aquarium fish sucking food from the glass walls of their enclosure.

KEEPING AFLOAT

The material of which their skeletons are made is just one of the differences between the bony fish and the cartilaginous fish, and it provides a convenient distinction by which to name them. But there are various other differences. For example, most bony fish have an air-filled buoyancy organ called a swim bladder that is absent in cartilaginous fish.

Swim bladders probably evolved from an early type of lung, first developed by freshwater fish that inhabited shallow, stagnant pools, during a period when the Earth's climate was unusually hot and dry. In stagnant water there is relatively little oxygen. Any lung-like adaptation to secure an extra supply from the air would have been advantageous.

Later, these air-breathing bony fish returned to colonise the oxygen-rich sea. Here, lungs would have been redundant, at least in their original role. But gas-filled lungs probably had incidental advantages as 'floats'. Gradually, by the process of natural selection, it seems that lungs became modified into swim bladders, allowing bony fish to keep afloat without expending energy on swimming.

Because cartilaginous fish do not have swim bladders, sharks, whose bodies are heavier than water, must keep swimming if they are not to sink, just as humans must. Sharks propel themselves forward solely by means of a muscular, lashing tail. Upward lift, to counteract sinking, is provided by the tail's asymmetrical, upturned shape, and by the angled fins on the side of the

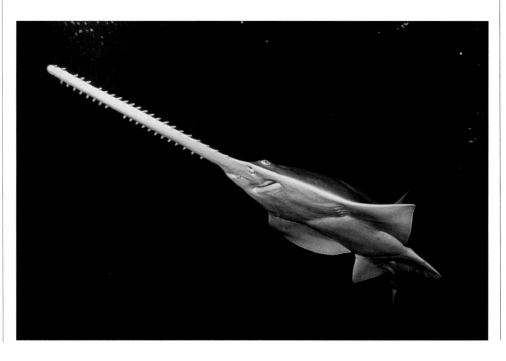

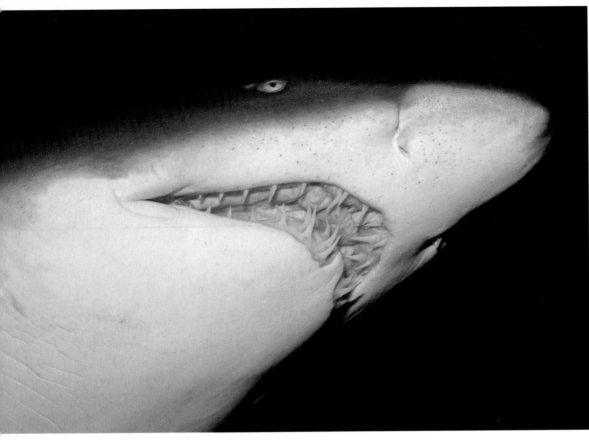

DISPOSABLE BLADES
A shark's teeth are constantly being shed and replaced.

material that forms human teeth. Modified denticles form the spines of spiny dogfish, and the 'sting' on a stingray's tail. Where denticles protrude over the edge of a shark's jaw they are enlarged to produce the rows of triangular teeth characteristic of a shark's gape. Surprisingly, these knife-sharp assets are expendable: sharks loose teeth at a rate of one every few days, and replace them by a conveyor system, which may issue thousands of replacements in a lifetime.

body – structures comparable with the tail and wings of an aeroplane.

Constant forward motion in sharks also provides a plentiful supply of oxygen, since water continually floods into the mouth and across the gills. It is said that sharks suffocate if they stop swimming, but this is not completely true. A number of species, such as the nurse sharks, carpet sharks and cat sharks, spend much of their time motionless on the seabed with no apparent ill effect. It is thought that they use muscular contractions to pulse water over their stationary gills. Bony fish similarly achieve a constant flow of water over their gills by opening and closing a bony gill cover called the operculum.

In bony fish with swim bladders, tails and fins do not need to provide lift. Freed from this function they can take on different shapes and roles. The tails of most bony fish are symmetrical and sickle-shaped to give the best forward propulsion. Their paired, manoeuvrable, rudder-like fins help in balance and steering. Unlike sharks, some bony fish can hover, and even swim backwards.

The most manoeuvrable of the bony fishes must be the sea horse. Though not a strong swimmer it undulates its tiny fins and propels its stiff body upwards or downwards among the seaweeds where it lives. Likewise, the snipefish, which swims with its body vertical and its head down, can travel forwards or backwards. And the triggerfish, which moves by flapping its fins in unison, can reverse neatly into a crevice where, each night, it jams itself in by erecting the spines of the fin on the top of its back.

FROM SCALES TO TEETH

Whereas bony fish are usually covered in smooth, petal-like or disc-shaped, overlapping scales, cartilaginous fish are covered by thousands of much smaller, sharply pointed triangular ones. The coating of some species is so rough that sandpaper has been made from it. The tiny scales are called dermal denticles, literally meaning 'skin teeth', and they are indeed made of dentine, the same

SNEAK THIEF *The cookie-cutter shark feeds by snipping chunks of flesh from unsuspecting larger fish.*

SHARK ATTACKS

From the serrated blades of the great white to the curved fangs of the mako, the teeth of sharks have done much to reinforce their reputation as grisly flesh-tearing man-eaters. In reality, of the 350 different species of shark, only 30 have ever deliberately attacked humans. Attacks are usually meant

WHY FISH SWIM IN SHOALS

More than 200 species of fish swim in shoals. Some, like the herring family, congregate in numbers approaching a million. The fish, which are all of a similar size, and all of the same species, swim parallel to one another, equally spaced and perfectly synchronised. They flit, stop and turn with such precision as a group that they appear from above like a single flowing organism, as if each fish were attached to the rest of the group by invisible strings.

If a predator approaches, the shoal splits and neatly bypasses the hunter, or appears to explode about its intruder, scattering instantaneously before melting back together. It is as if the performance is rehearsed to perfection, and it differs from one situation to another – yet biologists have concluded that the movements of the fish are instinctive.

There are several good reasons why it may benefit fish to shoal. First, a fish swimming with a mass of others is less likely to be snapped up by a predator. Secondly, there are mating advantages; the fish of a shoal simply release their sperm and eggs into the water where they are guaranteed a high chance of fertilisation. In addition, there may be hydrodynamic benefits to swimming in a shoal – each fish can swim faster and with less energetic effort than if it is alone, rather like birds flying in a V-formation.

Some predatory fish also shoal. This is thought to increase their chances of capturing prey, rather like wolves hunting in a pack. Interestingly, tiny prey fish have been seen to cluster around individual hunters such as tiger sharks, to protect themselves from patrols of hungry barracudas. The large predators, for their part, ignore such small fry.

MOVING AS ONE *The synchronised balletic movements of a shoal of fish look rehearsed but are thought to be instinctive.*

to frighten away a human intruder. When a shark strikes to kill, it probably mistakes people for seals, especially if they are paddling on surfboards. Sharks may break off an attack after discovering their mistake: a distasteful bite of a rubber wet suit or an unpleasant taste of suntan oil is often sufficiently off-putting.

The cinema perpetuates the standard image of sharks as sleek, sharp-nosed hunters. Yet the sharks, like most other groups of fish, are full of variety. Some, such as the whale shark and basking shark are huge, wholly innocuous filter-feeders. Others are tiny animals less than 1 ft (30 cm) long, the very smallest shark being the dwarf shark, *Squaliolus laticaudus*, which is fully mature at 5 in (12.5 cm).

One of the most peculiar is the little cookie-cutter shark, a weak swimmer that feeds by taking bites out of unsuspecting fish, dolphins or whales. It waits for a passing victim, and then sinks its grasping teeth into their flanks and swings around in a circular motion, neatly removing a hemispherical scoop of flesh.

DIFFERENCES AND SIMILARITIES

A mako shark and a marlin come from different evolutionary lines. One is a cartilaginous fish, the other a bony fish. Yet both are swift hunters, top predators in the ocean hierarchy. Both are sleek, streamlined, torpedo-shaped swimmers. A flatfish and a ray are equally unrelated, yet have evolved similar bottom-dwelling habits and flattened body forms. Eels and lampreys, separated by a huge chasm in relationship terms, have hit on the same snake-like body, one that can provide swimming action by a sinuous side-to-side motion.

Inevitably, by evolving to meet the challenges presented by their common watery environment, fish from completely different ancestries have sometimes arrived at comparable solutions: a process called convergent evolution. But 'fish' is just a term used by humans to refer to all those swimming vertebrates that are not mammals, birds, amphibians or reptiles. In imposing our human viewpoint on the animal kingdom we are sometimes blinded to the extraordinary richness and variety of animal life.

RETURN TO THE SEA

Over millions of years, a number of mammals and reptiles have moved from the land to the sea. None of them has become completely independent of their terrestrial roots, yet they are among the most successful of all the ocean animals.

Of all the sounds heard in the animal world, the mournful cry of a seal is one of the loneliest and most human. According to Gaelic folklore, seals are people whose form has been changed and who are trapped under a tragic spell: doomed to yearn for the shore whenever they are at sea, and to long for the sea when on land. Legend tells of seal people slipping out of their skins at night and emerging onto the beach in human form. It is said that men, enchanted by the beauty and haunting brown eyes of transformed seal women, can only lure them into marriage by locking away their cast-off skins. If such a woman ever finds her former skin, she is irresistibly drawn back to the water, abandoning her husband and children.

The seals' urge to come ashore is an integral part of their life cycle, an annual return to the habitat of their distant ancestors. It is only on land that they can give birth and suckle their young. This is a consequence of an evolutionary link so strong that 25 million years has failed to break it. The forerunners of seals were indeed land-dwelling mammals, not human in form, as myth would have it, but animals related to the present-day otters, mink and badgers (the Mustelid family). As they took to a diet of fish and acquired an increasingly marine lifestyle, natural selection moulded these ancestral mustelids to the requirements of a novel environment: their bodies gradually became more smoothly streamlined, while their limbs and tails became shorter and broader, adapted to swimming rather than walking.

However, seals have only made a partial transition to the sea, unlike whales and dolphins, an unrelated group except that they too are mammals. Whales have lost their hind limbs entirely but seals still have stubby limbs, set close to the tail, as do their close relatives, the sea lions, which share the same mustelid ancestor. Another vestige of life on land can be seen in the

LIONS OF THE SEA *Sea lions are so called for the bulls' manes and their roaring when mating.*

sea lions, which have small, scrolled external ear flaps. These ear flaps are something that the seals, on their evolutionary journey, have finally lost, although they still have functional ears.

Most significantly of all, newborn seals and sea lions are generally unable to swim, and in the few species that can swim from birth the young have insufficient blubber to keep them warm. Consequently, all seal and sea lion parents are obliged to give birth out of water. The same is true of the walrus, a third member of the seal and sea lion group.

Hauled out on ice, rocks or beaches, seals are rendered awkward and ungainly by their shape, short limbs and blubbery mass. To counteract their resulting vulnerability and to minimise danger, they breed in large colonies at secluded sites, some on rocky islets or drifting ice floes, others on mainland beaches with a steep cliff backdrop, or in remote coastal caves. What these sites have in common is an absence of natural predators large enough to attack them. Each female gives birth to a single pup, which emerges wrapped in a dense, soft coat of fur. Pups are fed on a very rich milk and become strong and independent in a remarkably short time. Some species are deserted by their mothers after a matter of weeks, by which time they have shed their juvenile coats and are ready to join the adults at sea. The young of other species

MOTHER'S MILK *A young sea lion is raised on milk in common with other mammals.*

FLIPPER FOOT *A sea lion, in grooming, displays its greatly shortened hind leg.*

remain dependent on their mother for up to six months.

Female seals mate again soon after their pup is weaned, or sometimes earlier. Their fertilised egg can remain dormant for several months in the womb, staying in 'storage' until the time is right for it to begin development. This postponement, called delayed implantation, means that birth and mating are achieved during one annual gathering on land, minimising the time seals need to spend out of water.

THE FIRST SEA MAMMALS

Seals were not the first mammals to return to the sea – that achievement belongs to the whales and dolphins. Fifty-million-year-old fossils of primitive whales, found in Pakistan, suggest that the ancestors of whales and dolphins predated the seals by about 30 million years. Fossils show that some of the earliest whales were small and porpoise-like, others were gigantic eel-like creatures reaching 50 ft (15 m) in length and probably represented an evolutionary

'dead end'. Among these early marine mammals were the ancestors of all modern whales and dolphins, although the exact steps along the path of whale evolution are still a mystery.

Fossil clues suggest that the very first whales were descended from early land-dwelling ancestors of the modern hoofed mammals (ungulates). Because there are so few fossils, we can only speculate about the evolutionary stages that linked these land-dwellers to fully aquatic whales. In the aftermath of the catastrophic extinction of the dinosaurs about 65 million years ago, a great variety of mammals spread across the land, colonising habitats from the tops of mountains down to the coasts. Huge sea-going reptiles, known as ichthyosaurs and plesiosaurs, though not part of the dinosaur tribe, had died out at about the same time, so there was probably a superabundance of fish and, therefore, rich opportunities for any large land animal that could adapt to an aquatic existence.

ADAPTING TO AQUATIC LIFE

Natural selection is the mechanism that brings about evolutionary change. It works because there is always some variation between different individuals of the same species: slight differences perhaps in the

HOSTILITIES ON THE BEACH

Two and a half tons of roaring, shuddering, brown blubber hurtles across the beach towards an equally vast, moving mountain of flesh. The two clash and spar, bellowing and snorting, butting and biting one another. These are male northern elephant seals (*Mirounga angustirostris*) in combat, and the stakes are high: the winner is set to gain access to an entire harem of fertile females. The loser will gain nothing but bloody wounds, and may not mate at all during this breeding season.

Northern elephant seals breed on islands off the Californian coast in December each year. Miraculously, the population survived near-extinction in the late 19th century, following years of ruthless hunting. At its lowest point, fewer than 100 animals remained. Somehow there was a recovery, and in recent times the population has doubled every five years. It is estimated that by the year 2000 there will be in the region of 250 000 elephant seals, quite possibly competing with people for space on mainland beaches.

Male elephant seals are at least three times larger than females, at 16 ft (5 m) in length. Each has a dangling proboscis of skin, which inflates into a grotesque balloon and resonates with his guttural war cries. The neck and chest is padded by fat and by tough, wrinkled skin, often scarred by previous fights.

Constant rounds of ferocious battle create a strict hierarchy among the males. Only one in nine becomes a successful 'harem master', and while there are occasional mating successes by daring interlopers, it is mainly the harem masters that impregnate the females. Consequently less than 10 per cent of mature males mate with 90 per cent of the females. Some unfortunate males die without ever having managed to pass on their genes.

Dominant males are relentlessly

aggressive in defending and mating with the members of their harem. As the females emerge onto the beach, heavily pregnant from the previous year's impregnation, an eager male may not wait before exercising his mating rights. He roughly mates with any available female, whether pregnant, giving birth or suckling young. Many of the new-born pups are crushed and trampled by the rampaging males in their haste to

RAGING BULLS
Surrounded by females and their pups, two male elephant seals fight.

mate or oust a threatening intruder.

So exhausting are their exertions that dominant males are able to maintain their position for no more than four years. Some die after a single season, burned out with the constant aggression and effort.

length of their limbs or the strength of their muscles, in the thickness of their fur or fat layer, the capacity of their lungs, or the sharpness of their vision. Individuals best suited to meet the challenge of life in a particular environment tend to survive longer and produce more young than others of their kind (they are the 'fittest'). Some of their offspring inherit the genes for many of the beneficial features that helped their parents to survive, and, in turn, produce more young, passing these advantages on to future generations.

Thus, under the strong influence of natural selection, the bodies of the earliest whales and dolphins gradually became more streamlined. Over many generations, the forelimbs evolved into flippers and the tail broadened to form wide flukes for propulsion. The nostrils gradually became sited higher on the muzzle, and eventually on the very top of the head, to allow a quick breath to be snatched at the surface without pushing the head clear of the water. Hind legs were unnecessary in the sea, and the insulating fur, so effective on land, was a drawback for a streamlined swimmer. Both hind legs and fur were eventually lost, although there are relics of these ancestral features even today. Whale embryos still have sparse fur, while adult whales possess a few bristles around the mouth. These, and the tiny, useless remnants of hind-leg bones that are embedded deep within the whale body, are the only reminders that whales, like us, evolved from four-legged, fur-coated land animals.

Modern whales and dolphins number more than 70 species, which fall into two distinct groups according to their feeding habits. The majority are in the group known as toothed whales: fish and squid-eaters such as dolphins, porpoises, killer and pilot whales, sperm whales, beaked whales and white whales (beluga and narwhal). The other group, baleen whales, encompasses about ten very large, plankton-feeding species, including the grey whale, rorquals (such as the blue, sei, minke and humpback whales) and right whales. These huge animals have no teeth. Instead, enormous plates of baleen (whalebone) hang vertically from the upper jaw, packed close together, so that there is a narrow space between one

FOSSILISED ICHTHYOSAUR *These marine reptiles became extinct over 65 million years ago. They were examples of creatures other than fish that adapted to life at sea.*

plate and the next, forming a grille-like barrier between the whale's mouth and the outside world. On this grille thousands of krill and other tiny prey are caught.

All modern whales are supremely adapted to life at sea. Their eyes are protected from the salt by a greasy secretion from the tear ducts, and their blowholes can be closed off by a special ring of muscle to prevent water flooding the nasal passages. Their muscular bodies are smooth and streamlined, yet insulated from the cold by a thick layer of blubber beneath the skin.

Buoyed up by the water around them, whales have reached sizes that would be unsustainable on land, where animals have to support their body weight on a set of limbs in order to move about. When a whale is stranded on the shore, it is usually unable to survive. Despite being an air-breather, a beached whale may quickly suffocate, as the force of gravity crushes the vast body under its own weight and collapses the lungs.

REPRODUCTION AT SEA

In contrast to seals and sea lions, whales mate and give birth in the water. Courtship may be a prolonged affair. Males show off their swimming skills, leaping, splashing and sometimes hitting the water surface with a flipper or tail fluke to gain a female's

FISH EATER *A pilot whale shows off its teeth, used to catch fish.*

attention. If she becomes interested, the pair caress and stroke one another before mating begins.

After a lengthy gestation of between nine and seventeen months, whales usually calve in warm seas to protect the hairless young ones from cold. As soon as the single calf is born, tail-first, it is nudged to the surface by its mother to take an initial breath, and then guided to her teats to suckle. The mother often lies on her side to feed the calf, so that it can breathe while feeding. Milk is forcibly squirted into the calf's mouth by the contractions of the mother's body muscles. Calves can swim instinctively, and cruise close to their mothers for many months.

As they gain strength and confidence, calves may periodically part from their mothers to frolic in the water. Young southern right whales roll upside-down, and perform long sequences of 'breaches' – leaping clear of the water and landing with a resounding splash on their backs. This behaviour may help to develop their muscles. Breaching is also seen among adult whales, including humpbacks, right whales, grey and sperm whales, but its

exact purpose is still a mystery. It is probably a form of courtship display, or a show of strength among males. An alternative suggestion is that the underwater reverberations of the whales crashing down onto the surface could be a form of long-distance communication.

FAMILY BONDING

Maternal devotion is particularly strong in whales and dolphins. Female belugas that lose their young sometimes adopt a piece of driftwood for a while, as a replacement. Sadly, the intense bond between mother and young has been exploited by hunters of right whales, humpbacks and belugas. Mothers of these species follow their harpooned young into close range of a whaling ship when they, too, are captured.

Caring behaviour among whales and dolphins extends beyond parental ties, however. If an adult animal is injured, others of its *(continued on page 128)*

BALEEN PLATES *The fringed baleen plates of a grey whale (below left and below) allow it to sieve food items from the sea.*

OCEAN-GOING REPTILES

Between 200 million and 65 million years ago, many types of swimming reptiles thronged the oceans, some of them reaching enormous sizes. Among the first were the turtles which, by 100 million years ago, were as big as motor cars: a fossil turtle, Archelon, measured 12 ft (3.7 m) from head to tail. The early turtles shared the fish-rich seas with large hunters such as the plesiosaurs, broad-bodied creatures with paddle-shaped limbs and sharp pointed teeth. Some plesiosaurs had extraordinarily long, snake-like necks (these were the prototype for artists' impressions of the 'Loch Ness monster'), bringing their total body length up to 40 ft (12 m). Alongside them were the most highly adapted of the marine reptiles, the dolphin-like ichthyosaurs, streamlined, long-beaked active hunters up to 30 ft (9 m) long, that preyed on squid and fish.

By colonising the sea these early reptiles were returning to the home of their distant ancestors, the lobe-finned fish that emerged from the ocean onto land about 375 million years ago. Like the whales and dolphins many eons later, the ichthyosaurs and plesiosaurs quickly became the top predators – clearly a period of evolution on land confers survival qualities that are a

major asset in the sea. However, one major obstacle hindered the reptiles from making a complete return to a marine existence. The reptilian egg, well suited to terrestrial life, did not function in the sea: its porous, leathery shell allowed water to enter, drowning the enclosed embryo. This legacy of a terrestrial life meant that plesiosaurs and turtles were bound to the shore for reproduction.

The ichthyosaurs, however, evolved an alternative solution to the problem. They retained the eggs in their bodies until the young were fully formed and could be born alive, at sea. Fossils of female ichthyosaurs, found with tiny fossilised young ones within, were the first indication that they bore live young. But there was a grimmer interpretation – that they ate smaller icthyosaurs whole, and the tiny fossils were in the stomach. It is difficult to know the location of soft organs from a fossil, so the position of the stomach could not be pinpointed. The dispute was solved when a fossil was found of a female ichthyosaur that had died while giving birth – a young ichthyosaur was half-in and half-out of her body just below the tail.

Despite their excellent adaptations to

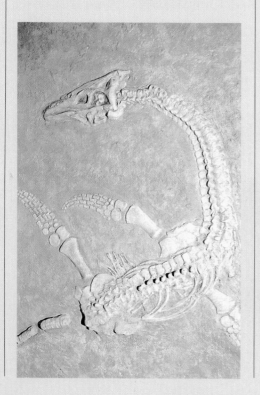

FOSSILISED GIANT *The plesiosaurs probably emerged onto land to breed, as seals still do.*

SEAGOING SNAKE *A banded sea snake lies coiled on a rock. It has to surface regularly for air.*

marine life, and for reasons not yet known, the ichthyosaurs went into decline about 100 million years ago. At about the same time, huge marine lizards called mosasaurs evolved rapidly to fill the same fish-eating niche, reaching lengths of 16 to 33 ft (5 to 10 m). But their success was short-lived on the scale of geological time: even though none of the dominant marine reptiles were members of the dinosaur tribe, they suffered the same fate. By the time of the mass dinosaur extinction, about 65 million years ago, the mosasaurs, ichthyosaurs and plesiosaurs were also extinct.

Today, marine reptiles are much scarcer and smaller, represented by a few species of turtles, the estuarine crocodiles, the sea snakes and two species of lizard, the marine skink and the marine iguana. Like their early counterparts, some are more independent of the land than others. The turtles are an ancient reptile line, and were thriving in the sea alongside the plesiosaurs and ichthyosaurs. Somehow they survived the great reptilian extinction. Other marine reptiles such as the marine iguana have probably returned to the sea more recently.

Of all the modern marine
reptiles, the lizards probably
spend the shortest periods at
sea. The marine skink dives
into the sea to escape predators or to grasp the tiny crabs
and shrimps on which it feeds.
Marine iguanas, by contrast,
are vegetarians. Along the
volcanic, rocky coast of the
Galápagos Islands hundreds of
these blackish, dragon-like
creatures bask in the sun in
order to raise their body temperature before venturing out
into the cold water to feed on
seaweeds. Once in the water,
they are powerful swimmers,
capable of diving to depths of
50 ft (15 m).

Both marine iguanas and
sea turtles bury their eggs in
sand for protection and incubation. But in contrast to the
iguanas, which remain close to
their home territory, some
turtles actually travel thousands
of miles to special egg-laying
sites. Because turtles spend the
rest of their lives at sea, their
body armour is generally lighter
than that of related land-living
tortoises for greater buoyancy
and less strenuous swimming.

It is the sea snakes that are
the most independent of land:
they can sometimes be found
hundreds of miles from the
shore, and most species give
birth to live, swimming young,
like the ichthyosaurs before
them. Sea snakes inhabit tropical waters, from the Red Sea
and the east coast of Africa to
the Indian Ocean and Pacific,
reaching as far as Japan and
northern Australia.

group will swim around their wounded colleague and attempt to push it away from the source of danger, or buoy it up at the surface for air. They may also try to bite through a harpoon line or even attempt to overturn a whaling boat.

This is just one sign of the profoundly social nature of whales and dolphins.

Some, such as killer whales, stay with the same group of individuals all their lives. Since their natural life span is estimated at 50-100 years, their society is probably more stable than that of any other social mammal, including modern man. The closely knit family groups are called pods, each containing several generations of related

whales. To stay in communication with others of their kind, particularly when hunting, killer whales use a language of whistles, clicks, groans and squeals. A collection of pods that shares the same basic language is known as a clan. However, microphone studies have shown that each pod, even within the same clan, has its own identifiable dialect. And this dialect is transmitted from parents to young.

Most whales and dolphins emit complex sounds for communication. Some, such as the dolphins, also use sound for navigation and for homing in on prey. Blue whales can produce noises louder than any other creature, the reverberations travelling over 500 miles (800 km) through the water.

Most famous of all whale vocalists is probably the male humpback, whose haunting, melodious song of repeated phrases may last all day, and can be so loud that it will resonate through the hull of a nearby ship. Like the killer whales, humpbacks have regional dialects, all those in an area singing the same basic song.

WATER SPORTS

It is all too easy to make wrong assumptions when interpreting the social behaviour of whales and dolphins, in particular to attribute human motivations or emotions to their actions: a dolphin's 'smile', captivating though it might be, is more a reflection of the animal's anatomy than of the fact that it is happy. Yet even sceptics cannot deny that, on occasion, whales and dolphins appear to have a sense of fun.

HUMPBACK EMERGING *Gulls circle a humpback whale as it breaks the surface.*

HOW DOLPHINS SEE WITH SOUND

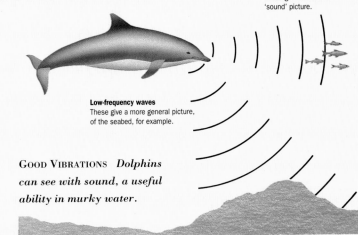

High-frequency waves
These give a detailed 'sound' picture.

Low-frequency waves
These give a more general picture, of the seabed, for example.

In murky or deep water, where little light penetrates the gloom, vision is of limited use in detecting prey and keeping watch for predators. Dolphins have evolved a different means of 'seeing' their surroundings: like bats they use echolocation, or sonar, to build up a picture entirely from sound. Sound travels five times faster through water than through air, and covers much greater distances. So it is no coincidence that ships use a sonar system based on the same principles as dolphin echolocation to survey the seabed.

Dolphins emit whistles and squeaks, many beyond the range of human hearing. These pulses of high-pitched sound are produced by squeezing trapped air through passages and valves beneath the dolphin's blowhole. The sounds are then passed through the melon – a waxy 'lens' in the forehead, which condenses and 'focuses' the sound. The concentrated stream of sound is projected outwards like a search beam. As the sound waves hit objects in their path, they are reflected, and bounce back. Dolphins do not have earflaps as we do, because these would interfere with streamlining. Instead, the returning echoes are picked up through cavities in the dolphin's lower jawbone, and travel through oil-filled channels to the inner ear.

GOOD VIBRATIONS *Dolphins can see with sound, a useful ability in murky water.*

Details of the echoes can be interpreted by a dolphin to determine the exact position and shape of a nearby object. The sound 'picture' built up by a dolphin of a fish is not quite like the visual image we would see. The sound waves pass right into the body of the fish, and bounce off the skeleton and air-filled swim bladder, returning an impression more like an X-ray than a photograph. Most detail is obtained from echoes of very high frequency sound, in the range of 270 000 cycles per second (270 kHz). Dolphins also emit frequencies as low as 0.25 kHz. These sounds have a long wavelength, and give a more general picture of the seabed, for use in navigation.

There is still much to be learned about dolphin sonar. Current evidence suggests that the beams of ultrasound may be so powerful that they can also stun prey at a distance – an echolocation device doubling as a 'ray-gun' of sound.

BUILT FOR SONAR *Trapped air is squeezed through passages and valves inside the dolphin's head, to create pulses of high-pitched sound. The bulbous 'melon' at the front of the head then focuses the sound beam.*

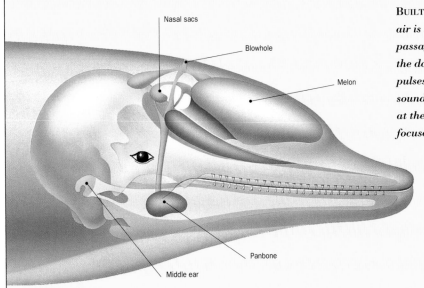

Nasal sacs

Blowhole

Melon

Panbone

Middle ear

There are accounts of southern right whales repeatedly riding storm winds, their tails held vertically out of the water as sails, and of dolphins surfing, apparently for sheer enjoyment. Young male belugas have been seen playing tag with a frond of seaweed, or trying to balance a stone on their head while others in the group do their best to nudge it away.

To some extent, however, socialising or 'play' probably has important survival functions in the wild, since it helps young animals to acquire life skills, and enables the adults of a group to know one another well enough to hunt as a team or to present a united defence against any predators.

Without the lure of food – or any reward other than companionship – solitary wild dolphins occasionally come inshore and interact with human beings. They seem curious and may, after a time, initiate play. The famous bottle-nosed dolphin of Dingle Bay on the south-west coast of Ireland has sought human company for years, arriving at the signal of a rubber flipper being splashed on the water surface, and leaping playfully around his human visitors, sometimes letting them scratch his chin.

Less frequently, groups of wild dolphins will accept a human swimmer, chattering excitedly at high volume, and peering inquisitively from all angles, before involving their strange companion in games of tag. Darting tantalisingly close, or hanging still in the water, apparently waiting for their companion to catch up, they seem to invite play. Tales are still told of dolphins rescuing drowning men, fending off sharks, and even driving fish into nets.

But why should a wild animal seek out the company of humans? Until anyone establishes a language of communication with dolphins, the real motivation behind their friendly encounters with humankind will remain a mystery.

THE OCEAN'S ABYSS

Where sunlight cannot penetrate the ocean's depths, life itself makes light. These flickering stars of the deep are generated by squid, fish and other animals, which inhabit a mysterious, slow-moving world of scavenging life forms.

Utter darkness is a concept that is hard to imagine. Absolute darkness is the sooty black that is found deep in an underground cave, far from the entrance and away from any illuminating chinks of daylight that pierce the roof. This is a smothering blackness, so oppressive and so disorientating that it feels like being physically enveloped and constrained by some intangible substance. The eyes do not even begin to adjust, and all sense of direction and scale are completely lost. For us, survival in these conditions, without the aid of light or sonar, would be virtually impossible.

Yet the largest living space on the planet – three-quarters of the ocean's immense volume – is constantly engulfed by exactly such an eerie, inky blackness. Below a depth of 3300 ft (1000 m), where the last glimmer of sunlight has faded, the water is not only shrouded in constant darkness, but is also gripped by perpetual winter temperatures: a chill 5-6°C (41-43°F). Below roughly 13 000 ft (4000 m) through to the deepest trenches, temperatures stabilise near freezing – a mere 1-2°C (34-36°F).

Until the 1870s, it seemed inconceivable that anything could live more than a few hundred feet beneath the surface of the sea. The first discoveries of life in the ocean's depths came with the expedition of HMS *Challenger*, a British ship that carried out a survey of the ocean depths in 1872-6. *Challenger*'s trawls and dredges brought up grotesque forms of life never seen before. With the benefit of modern, manned submersibles, remote-controlled vehicles and underwater photography, we now know that there is life throughout the deep, right to the bottom of the greatest trenches at depths of well over 33 000 ft (10 000 m).

FOOD FROM AFAR

For those creatures subsisting precariously in the depths, the intense cold and pressure are not the only hardships. There is also a severe shortage of food. Below about 650 ft (200 m), the glimmer of sunlight is too weak to support microscopic plant plankton or, indeed, any other plant life. Consequently there is no food supply being generated in this zone, and such

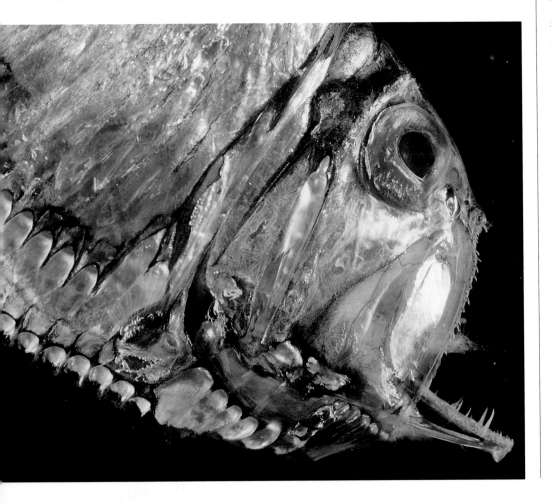

MONSTER OF THE DEEP *The head of a hatchet fish, one of the many bizarre fish of the abyss.*

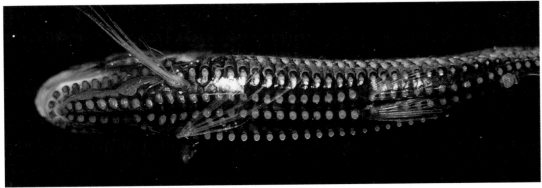

FAIRY LIGHTS *Strings of light organs decorate the body of this deep-sea fish of the* Ichthyococcus *species.*

nourishment as there is drifts slowly down from above, a thin drizzle of dead material that was originally produced in the surface layers, composed of fine detritus, dead plankton and droppings, fragments of coastal vegetation, and rubbish dumped by ships. The sinking food must be caught in passing by those that do not live on the ocean floor, a difficult task indeed. The animals that pursue this way of life are eaten, in their turn, by predators, but these too are ultimately dependent on food that is generated in the sunlit realms of the sea.

Since most food particles originate in the surface layers, they must pass through successive zones of the undersea before reaching the depths. This slow descent takes them through the bright, densely populated domain of the tuna, the sailfish and the dolphins, then on into the twilight zone, where the last remnant of sunlight is still present as a dim glimmer of indigo, but even that gradually fades with increasing depth.

For the inhabitants of the twilight zone – that uppermost part of the deep sea between 650 and 3300 ft (200-1000 m) – food-finding is profoundly influenced by the waning light. Since sunlight comes from above it is easiest to spot potential food in silhouette from below. Many fish, including the hatchet fish (*Argyropelecus*) and the argentine *Opisthoproctus soleatus* (a salmon relative), have bizarre, tubular, upward-pointing eyes, with which they scan the water above their heads.

Their own bodies are flattened from side to side, presenting a slim, discreet outline that decreases the chance of detection by potential predators still further

below. In addition, special light organs on their bellies emit a gentle glow that virtually cancels out any silhouette that might be apparent from beneath. For the camouflage to adapt to the passing of night and day, or to changes in depth, the intensity of light produced by the fish is carefully controlled so that it exactly matches light filtering down from above.

BIOLOGICAL LIGHTS

On land there are glow-worms and fire-flies, but these luminescent animals are rarities. By contrast, the sea is ablaze with the glimmer and flicker of homemade light. Shallow tropical seas sparkle with the luminescence of microscopic marine plants, and coral reefs glow with the oval lights of flashlight fish feeding at night.

But biological lights reach spectacular proportions in the barely lit waters of the twilight zone, where at least two-thirds of the fish species produce light. In addition to hatchet fish, other light-producing fish include the menacing black dragon fish (Melanostomiatidae family), the curious silver lantern fish (*Myctophum*), the fanged viper fish (*Chauliodus*) and various species of the ubiquitous bristlemouths (*Cyclothone*). Each species has a distinctive

DRAGON FISH *The gape of a black sea dragon engulfs prey that swims too close to its lure.*

pattern of tiny lights that enable it to recognise and attract a mate, or to join in schools with others of its kind in the semi-darkness. In fact, everything that is achieved by colour and pattern in the shallow waters of a coral reef can be done with lights at depth, from camouflage to warning signals, from mate recognition to territorial displays.

Fish are not the only creatures to produce their own light. Many otherwise defenceless animals of the deep use lights to frighten or confuse predators. Small animals that travel passively on the deep-sea currents, such as jellyfish, spherical comb jellies and tiny copepod crustaceans produce flashes of light on contact with other animals. The effect seems momentarily to startle and disorientate a potential predator. Others make use of a decoy. Certain scarlet shrimps and prawns can squirt a luminous cloud from their mouths, and then flip their bodies in the

opposite direction, to escape in the confusion. Similar tactics are used by some deep-water squid, which throw out a luminous cloud comparable to the black discharge of 'ink' produced by their shallow-water relatives. One family of fish, the Searsiids, is even able to squirt a blue-green 'smoke screen' of glittering, luminous particles.

While some lights in the gloom are used to deter predators, others are employed to attract food, probably mimicking the sparks of light produced by small, deep-sea animals such as comb jellies and copepods. In this way, large predators capture medium-sized predators by simulating the lights of tiny prey. Brightly lit patches embellish the inside of gaping fish mouths, while luminescent lures dangle temptingly in front of dark, hidden jaws. All are variations on the lure-and-ambush system exemplified by the grotesque deep-sea angler fish that inhabit the deeper, darker waters below the twilight zone.

Females of most deep-sea angler species dangle a glowing bulb on a 'fishing rod', made from a modified fin on their back. When an animal comes to lunge at the 'bait', the angler fish flicks back its lure and closes its cavernous jaws on the helpless prey. Male angler fish generally have no need of this complex feeding apparatus for, in many species, they are parasitic on the females.

Viper fish of the twilight zone operate a similar 'fishing' system, flexing the cord-like second ray of the fin on their back so that its luminous tip hangs just in front of the mouth. These fish possess an array of stabbing teeth and impaling fangs. When an item of prey is caught, it is transferred to the stomach by a ratchet of mobile teeth in the throat.

Luminous chin barbels are probably a variation on the same theme. Many fish of the middle depths, including the black dragon fish and the star-eaters or snaggle-tooths (Astronesthidae), are very elaborately

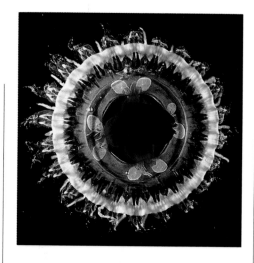

CIRCLE OF LIGHT *A luminous jellyfish pulsates in the depths to distract predators.*

equipped: some have a veritable beard of branched tassels, others possess a single whip up to six times the length of the body. The barbels not only attract prey, but also seem to sense its presence through tiny movements in the surrounding water.

In the lower twilight zone, where the barely lit water fades into blackness, some animals with powerful luminescent organs simply use them as search beams. This is a serious threat to the smaller creatures that are sought as prey, and most have non-reflective surfaces to avoid detection in the glare of predatory headlights. Fish in these depths tend to be a velvety black or deep brown colour; squid and jellyfish vary from brown to purple. Prawns, however, may be vivid red. Since biological light is normally bluish, as is the dim light of the twilight zone, red objects are invisible, absorbing blue light.

Scarlet, therefore, is a colour of camouflage in the ocean depths. But one group of predators has evolved a means of

LIVING TRAP *The open jaws of this deep-sea angler fish create a suction strong enough to vacuum in any creature investigating the lure that sticks up above its body.*

HOW ANIMALS PRODUCE LIGHT

Up to 90 per cent of the energy from a conventional lightbulb may be lost as heat. New energy-saving bulbs create less of this wasteful heat, but some animals long ago evolved a way of generating light that is even more efficient, outperforming any commercially made device. They convert chemical energy into light energy with virtually no heat loss. Biological light is produced when a special chemical called luciferin reacts with oxygen in the presence of a catalyst or enzyme. Many worms, squid and fish produce light from this process in their own cells, under the control of the nervous system. The more advanced kinds have special lenses, reflectors and colour filters to control and modify their output.

Others animals, including some of the deep-sea fish and squid, borrow the light produced by bacteria, keeping the luminescent microbes in special pockets or organs. The glowing bulb at the end of the female angler fish's lure is exactly such an organ. The arrangement is a reciprocal or 'mutualistic' one: the bacteria receive food from their host, and, in return, the larger animal obtains its light source. The drawback of this system is that luminescent bacteria produce light all the time. To 'turn them off', fish draw across eyelid-like shutters or restrict the blood supply to their bacterial compartment. Some predatory fish have inky black stomach linings so that the luminescence of swallowed prey does not shine through their body wall and give them away.

SHINING EYES *The eyes of this deep-sea squid are bioluminescent – that is, they emit light.*

penetrating this security, by producing red light. These are fish, known as rat-traps or loosejaws (*Malacosteus*), that produce a red-tinted beam from just below their eyes. Unlike most other deep-sea animals, these fish have eyes that are sensitive to red wavelengths. They can therefore illuminate and see a red prawn while the prawn remains completely oblivious (prawns having blue-sensitive eyes).

THE DARKEST DEPTHS

Beyond the dusky twilight zone, glinting with the sparks of bioluminescence, is the abyss. As one zone grades gently into the next at about 3300 ft (1000 m), the flashes of luminosity become less frequent. Living inhabitants take up less than 100 millionth of the water volume here.

With life so sparsely spread throughout this vast habitat, there are not enough food particles suspended in the water to satisfy filter feeders. Almost all animals of the open water at abyssal depths are predatory species. But encounters between animals are still rare, and predators may have to endure long periods of fasting. For this reason, saving energy between infrequent, unpredictable meals is essential. Many of the creatures in the deep have watery muscles and weak

skeletons to minimise their weight and thus approach neutral buoyancy so that they can stay suspended in the water without constant swimming action. Because of their insubstantial frame and muscles, these animals rely on stealth and ambush, rather than speed, to catch their prey. An example is the long, black gulper eel *Eupharynx pelecanoides*, which has vast pelican-like jaws, joined by a stretchy membrane: the jaws take up one-quarter of its body length. Like the deep-sea angler fish, it has become a floating trap, seemingly all mouth and teeth, with a much reduced body and tiny eyes and brain.

For the opportunistic predators of the deep, it is important to capitalise on every single encounter with potential prey. Fish have curved fangs to grip their catch, hinged jaws that open wider than their own bodies, and enormously distensible

SHELLFISH SHUFFLE   Prawns swim by using the limbs located on their abdomens.

impossibly large items. Many deep-sea fish can swallow prey as large as themselves, if not larger, dislocating the specialised hinged jaws to engulf the prey, which then stretches the elastic stomach and body in a grotesque fashion. One particularly distended specimen of the giant swallower (*Chiasmodon niger*), caught off Madeira at a depth of 5900 ft (1800 m), had swallowed an eel nearly four times its own length.

The depths reach their most thinly populated by about 8200 ft (2500 m) below the surface, where gelatinous, weak-muscled life forms are isolated from one another by vast stretches of uninhabited water. Things remain that way until immediately above the deep-sea floor, which, away from the edges of the continents, is at an average depth of 13 100 ft (4000 m). Here, the population of fish and squid suddenly increases again. Animals swimming near to the sea floor are relatively robust and large, having stronger muscles and greater power than their relatives in the open water, just a few hundred feet above. Many have swim bladders or fat deposits for buoyancy, so that they may swim easily just above the seabed.

Oxygen is not in short supply in this region, despite the fact that the air, from which the oxygen supply is replenished,

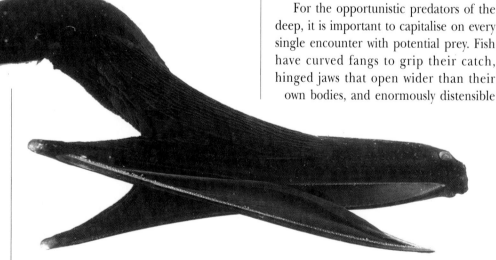

FOLDING JAWS   The jaws of gulper eels are like collapsing campstools, capable of opening out into a massive gape.

stomachs. When their prolonged famine is broken by an occasional feast, size is rarely an obstacle to consumption, and predators gorge themselves on what appear to be

RODENTS OF THE DEEP
Rat-tails or grenadiers are the most abundant fish of the deep ocean floor.

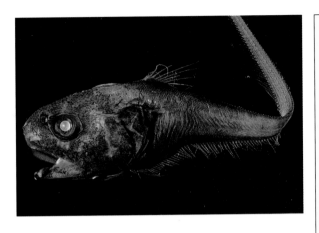

lies so far away. Cold surface water from the polar regions sinks to the deep seabed and flows in great, slow currents across it, carrying oxygen as it goes. Feeding possibilities are much greater here than in the open waters of the abyss as fish can hunt and scavenge on the sea floor.

VULTURES OF THE ABYSS

Automatic underwater cameras, baited with dead fish, have revealed that there is a population of cut-and-thrust scavengers patrolling just above the seabed. Furious gatherings of shrimp-like crustaceans, octopus and fish attack any sunken bait until only bones remain. Such abyssal opportunists probably detect food by its scent. Large scavenging sharks have been photographed down to depths of about 6500 ft (2000 m), dismembering what remains of the carcasses.

Featuring in almost all photographs and trawls taken near the ocean bed are fish of the Macrouridae family known as rat-tails or grenadiers. Typically, they have large heads, and long slender bodies tapering almost to a point, fringed by rayed fins above and below the narrow tail. They swim nose-down over the sediment, snapping up bottom-dwelling creatures or burrowing into the silty detritus to find worms. However, should a sizable meal arrive from above, rat-tails are capable of tearing out large bites alongside the other scavengers. Male rat-tails make drumming noises by flexing muscles against their swim bladder, possibly to attract mates. Sound travels well at depth, and may be an alternative to chemical or visual communication in the deep. Shy fish called brotulids, that hang back from underwater cameras and are rarely glimpsed, also communicate with drumming sounds.

Rat-tails and brotulids share their living space with other fish, such as the spiny eels (Notacanths), elongated, scaly fish with a row of spines along the back. Spiny eels bite off pieces of sea pens, sea anemones and other bottom dwellers, while their relatives, the sharp-snouted halosaurs, pick crustaceans from the sea floor.

LIFE IN THE OOZE

The abyssal sea floor is an undulating plain, occasionally rising into steep ridges and peaks, or plunging into deep trenches. This surreal landscape is blanketed in a deep ooze, a layer of soft sediment containing centuries of accumulated debris from the thousands of feet of water above. Those creatures that rest permanently on the bottom, such as sea anemones and sponges, live out their lives at an even slower pace than their relatives in coastal regions, for they are oppressed by the weight of water above and chilled into ultra-slow motion. Movement, growth and colonisation of new areas all proceed at an almost undetectable pace.

Animals on the soft bottom either have to lift themselves clear of the ooze, or abandon themselves to a life in its clutches. Those that are stationary tend to be raised on upright scaffolds and anchored in the sediment by root-like outgrowths. They include cup-shaped sponges, perched tulip-like on slender stems, and sea lilies that are relatives of the feather stars. Their undemanding lifestyle is sustained by food brought on the sluggish currents.

Strange tripodfish (*Bathypterois*) also make use of the slow, sustained water movement. Each tripodfish props its body above the bottom on a set of stilts, formed from the elongated rays belonging to fins on the

STRANGE MATING HABITS

In the blackness of the deep ocean, finding a mate is not an easy task. The deep-sea angler fish have several solutions to the problem. In most species, the female is much the larger of the sexes. She has poor vision, but attracts prey into her waiting jaws using a luminous lure. The pattern of this lure is unique to each species and may also be used by the better-sighted males to identify an appropriate mate. In addition, the females release powerful chemical substances that can be detected in minute quantities and tracked to their source by an interested male.

Deep-sea angler fish males are dwarfs in comparison with the females, but they mature precociously, and reach sexual maturity while still looking like juveniles. These small males have pincer-like jaws, with which they grasp onto a female once they have found her, to make sure that mating is guaranteed. In other species (for example, *Edriolychnus*, *Linophryne*, *Cryptopsaras* species) the males take this one stage further, and actually become parasites on the females. Burrowing his jaws into a female's skin at any point on her body, a male remains in position until his mouth fuses with her skin and their blood systems intermingle. Eventually, the tiny male body completely merges with the female, receiving all nutrients and oxygen from her, and producing sperm under the control of her hormones. The fact that the female's immune system does not reject this imposition is of interest to organ transplant research, where rejection of a 'foreign' body is a common problem.

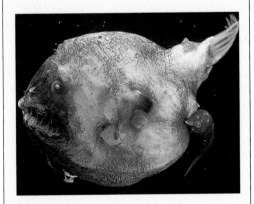

PARASITE FISH *The male angler fish fuses with the female.*

pelvis and tail. Two more fins, situated just behind the head, are spread, like the wings of a bat, across the approaching current. They are highly sensitive, and are probably used to detect the small swimming crustaceans on which the fish feed.

Other animals perambulate slowly over the ooze, or plough their way through it, sifting out nutritious morsels. Worms and sea cucumbers are particularly common, munching through the sludge, and there is even an ooze-eating fish, *Lipogenys gilli*, that vacuums up mouthfuls of the muddy deposit. Starfish, brittle stars, sea urchins and woodlouse-like crustaceans leave their tracks in the soft sediment.

Many sea-floor creatures are small and incredibly fragile. Shells are frequently thin and brittle as the strengthening material calcium carbonate has a tendency to dissolve out into the water under such intense pressures. Since they fall apart when caught in the net of a trawl, most of these frail animals have only been observed since the advent of submersible vessels and underwater cameras. Even then, some gelatinous creatures are so insubstantial that they simply disintegrate under the glare of a submersible's headlamps.

THE HADAL ZONE

Submersibles have revolutionised our ideas about the deep. Just as manned and unmanned spacecraft have allowed the exploration of space, so submersibles, carrying observers to depths where no diver could ever survive, have given insights into deep-sea life that would have been unimaginable 100 years ago. Scientists have journeyed across the plains and ridges of the sea floor, and have been able to witness living animals operating in their true environment. They have even been able to descend into the deepest trenches, previously known only from soundings.

Oceanographers imaginatively named the deep-sea trenches – reaching depths of 20 000-33 000 ft (6000-10 000 m) – 'the hadal zone', a word that is derived from the Greek Hades, the invisible, mysterious and terrifying Greek god of the nether world.

HOTSPOTS OF LIFE

In 1977 came the most exciting underwater discovery of all. The deep-sea submersible *Alvin*, later famous for its discovery of the *Titanic* in 1985, was exploring an area lying about 200 miles (320 km) north-east of the Galápagos Islands in the Pacific. Unexpectedly, at a depth of 8530 ft (2600 m), the crew of geologists stumbled across a group of hot-water geysers, properly known as hydrothermal vents, spouting from the sea

floor. Immediately around them were dozens of different species – and at densities never before thought possible in the deep sea.

Giant white clams, towering tube-worms with scarlet tips, blind crabs, yellow mussels, delicate dandelion-like animals and tangles of spaghetti worms clustered around the vents, while beyond them, in the cold, dark abyss, the region was almost barren of life. Thriving on the edges of this remarkable oasis were fish, shrimps, squat lobsters, limpets, and octopuses, all benefiting from the abundant food.

EATING MUD *Silt on the sea floor contains morsels of food on which sea cucumbers feed.*

The vents were situated on a submarine ridge, a tiny link in the vast undersea chain of spreading ridges that mark the edges of diverging crustal plates. Where these slabs of Earth's crust are moving apart, the spreading seabed is moulded by volcanic activity, its convoluted surface the product of lava welling up from below. As the plates wrench slowly apart, deep fissures are created in the crust. Sea water, seeping down into the fractures, meets the searing heat generated by the molten magma beneath.

Heated to temperatures of about 350°C (660°F), and thick with minerals that it has dissolved from the rock, the sea water duly re-emerges as a superheated jet. Billowing,

dark clouds of underwater 'smoke' are composed of tiny particles of iron, copper and zinc sulphides. As the emerging geyser meets the chill water at the bottom of the sea, it cools instantly, dropping its chemical load, which blankets the surrounding rock in colourful deposits. Some of the minerals solidify so fast that they form a solid chimney-stack around the water spout.

So why is it that animal life flourishes so

DEEP SEA *Life is generally sparse in the ocean's remotest depths. Cup sponges poke up from the seabed like surreal wine goblets; spotted rat-tails (on the right), hagworms (left) and deep-sea sharks prowl for food. Hydrothermal vents (on the right) provide the basis for unusually rich concentrations of animal life.*

abundantly around the submarine hot springs? Clearly, the warmth could be one factor – the water around the vents is in the range of 10-20°C (50-68°F), compared to the average deep-sea temperature of about 2°C (36°F). But scientists have shown that temperature is not the important consideration here. Instead, it is an unusual source of food. That food originates with a chemical known as hydrogen sulphide (smelling characteristically of rotten eggs) formed in the hot abyssal springs.

AN UNUSUAL ENERGY SOURCE

Almost everywhere on the planet, plants sustain animal life – trees and grasses, mosses and waterweed, seaweeds and the microscopic plant plankton of the ocean surface are all near the bottom of the food chain. All make their own food, using energy from sunlight, and that food is consumed by animals, or broken down after the plant's death by decomposed organisms such as bacteria and fungi.

There are a few exceptions to this rule: ancient bacteria from the dawn of life, living in unusual habitats such as deep, oxygen-deficient marshes and mangrove swamps. These bacteria can use a variety of simple chemicals and, by releasing energy from the chemical bonds, create food.

Around the hydrothermal vents there are similar bacteria that sustain the rich gathering of animal life. These bacteria 'burn' hydrogen sulphide with oxygen to produce water and energy. The energy is used to build far more complex molecules such as sugars and proteins, which the bac-

teria need in order to grow and reproduce. These bacteria, then, are the 'plants' of the deep-sea oases, and the sulphide is their equivalent of sunlight, the energy source upon which all the other animals of the oases ultimately depend.

Here at the depth of the sea there is an exceptional situation, unlike any other on our planet: life-sustaining energy is being derived, not from the Sun, but from the molten core of the Earth.

Further exploration has confirmed that the bacteria are the food source for all the other animals in vent communities. Some animals filter the bacteria from the water, or scrape them from the surface of the rocks. But others, including beard worms, mussels and the largest clams, culture bacteria inside their bodies in a mutual partnership.

Of all these species, the beard worms are perhaps the most interesting. Instead of a mouth or digestive system, these strange animals have evolved a special body compartment for their bacteria – in effect, it is a food factory. Raw

OASIS LIFE *A rich variety of animals cluster around hydrothermal vents.*

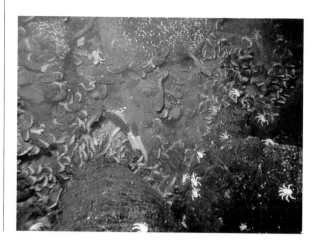

BEARD WORMS *The red tips of these beard worms contain bacteria that make their food.*

materials such as hydrogen sulphide are brought into the factory through the gills, and conveyed in the bloodstream to the bacteria. For a while, the mechanism behind this process remained a mystery: let loose in the bloodstream, sulphide, like cyanide, is highly toxic to most animals. However, biologists discovered that the tube worms have evolved a special carrier that renders the sulphide harmless while it is in transit.

Since 1977, more hydrothermal vents have been found. Most have been teeming with life, just like those first discovered on the Galápagos Rift. But others have been eerily lifeless, scattered with the remains of dead animals. Scientists believe that each vent has a lifetime of only decades. Then the gradual onward movement of the crusts bring the hot-water vents to an end, though new vents may burst through elsewhere.

Despite their transience, communities like these have existed for at least 200 million years. Somehow, before their vent is snuffed out, the animals must produce enough offspring to ensure that some will colonise a new vent, perhaps thousands of miles away. Exactly how they achieve this remarkable feat remains an enigma.

REEFS BUILT OF CORAL

4

CLOWNISH COLOURS *A clown fish nestles into sea anemones in reefs off Borneo.*

COOPERATION LIES AT THE HEART OF LIFE IN THE CORAL REEF. THE REEF ITSELF IS THE PRODUCT OF A REMARKABLE PARTNERSHIP BETWEEN THE TINY, IMMOBILE CORAL POLYP IN ITS CHALKY CASING AND A MICROSCOPIC PLANT KNOWN AS A ZOOXANTHELLA. THE POLYP PROVIDES THE PLANT WITH ESSENTIAL MATERIALS, INCLUDING MINERAL NUTRIENTS; THE PLANT KEEPS THE POLYP WELL FED. TOGETHER, POLYP AND PLANT HAVE, OVER THE LAST 170 MILLION YEARS, CREATED THE THOUSANDS OF SQUARE MILES OF CORAL REEF THAT STUD THE WORLD'S OCEANS. THESE, IN THEIR TURN, PROVIDE A

IN CORAL *A long-nosed hawk fish off Papua New Guinea.*

REFUGE FOR NUMEROUS OTHER SPECIES OF PLANTS AND ANIMALS IN ONE OF THE MOST COLOURFUL AND BEAUTIFUL CARNIVALS OF MARINE LIFE.

UNDERWATER GARDENS

No other natural spectacle can compare with the brilliant colours, constant movement and complex textures of a coral reef. This rich pageant of life has been acted out in the same shimmering sunlit waters for many millions of years.

The first astronauts who walked on the Moon looked back to Earth and saw swirling masses of cloud, the familiar shape of the continents, the vast oceans of our planet – and some tiny sea creatures no larger than a child's fingernail. These extraordinary life forms are visible from space because they have huddled closely together, generation after generation, the living congregating on the dead, so that their sheer numbers make a massive, conspicuous structure. Known as coral polyps, they are tiny animals, but animals that live an unenergetic life rooted to a single spot. Each one resembles a miniature sea anemone, although its soft body is hidden within a homemade cave of chalk, a protective retreat into which it can withdraw its delicate tentacles. After it dies, this strong chalky casing remains – a small but significant addition to one of the largest constructions ever built by animals.

Beneath those coral polyps now living are the empty homes of billions upon billions of their forerunners, long dead but providing the foundations for the latest generation. Since they first colonised Australia's northern waters as much as 18 million years ago, untold numbers of coral animals

CHANGEABLE CORALS
Gorgonian corals can grow in these whip-like forms, or as flattened fans, depending on local conditions.

have contributed their efforts to the Great Barrier Reef, the massive edifice of coral that the astronauts could see from 238 850 miles (384 400 km) away. The Great Barrier Reef – actually a string of some 2500 separate reefs – lines the north-east coast of Australia for more than 1250 miles (2010 km), towering to a height of 394 ft (120 m) from the seabed, and measuring as much as 90 miles (145 km) across in places. Other coral reefs cluster in the warm shallow waters around coasts and islands of the tropics, including the Pacific and the Indian oceans, the Red Sea and the Caribbean.

Closer to each reef, from the perspective of a diver rather than an astronaut, is a fantastic multicoloured landscape of domes and columns, pinnacles, ledges, caverns and canyons. Small, delicate coral colonies balance on sturdier ones. Pointed 'antlers' reach out above flattened plates and curved boulders, their surfaces convoluted into folds or sprouting, branched finger-like projections. Sea fans spread their intricate latticework across the current. Deeper down, bouquets of soft coral grace the walls of the reef, nestling against enormous, vivid sponges. There is a profusion of hiding places, a labyrinth of secret channels and hollows, providing innumerable secluded

LIVING COLOUR Fairy basslet fish swarm over a cluster of lettuce coral on a Malaysian reef.

GREAT BARRIER REEF The most massive coral reef in the world is visible from the Moon.

niches in which seaweeds, sea anemones, shrimps, clams, sea urchins, fish and other life forms can flourish. Coral reefs, not surprisingly, are the richest and most varied of all the oceanic habitats.

AN IMPOVERISHED PARADISE

Paradoxically, this rich celebration of life takes place in waters that, like most tropical seas, offer little in the way of food. The sparkling clarity of water that allows divers to enjoy the superb colours of the reef also indicates how sparse the available nourishment is – sea water that is full of nutrients has a more soupy, cloudy appearance. At night, the beam of a torch reveals the colourful coral polyps extending their slender, stinging tentacles to trap a few tiny animals from the drifting plankton. But this is a meagre diet, providing no more than a tenth of the polyp's daily food needs.

Reef-building corals can survive here only because there are unseen helpers within their bodies – microscopic single-celled plants known as zooxanthellae (pronounced 'zoo-oh-zanth-ell-i'). These tiny green cells

benefit from the protected environment within the coral polyp, and are the true providers, making their own food with the energy of the Sun, just as other plants do.

The coral animals reap much of this food, but the zooxanthellae benefit from a supply of essential raw materials, such as carbon dioxide and mineral nutrients, in return. Animal and plant are locked together in a mutually beneficial relationship – neither can survive for long without its partner. It is a partnership that dates back at least 170 million years. Over this time, the coral and its microscopic plants have set up an efficient system of recycling resources, a stringent economy where nothing is wasted.

With the help of its internal guests, a coral polyp has enough energy to grow in size and to extend its chalky coating regularly. The hard white construction material is calcium carbonate, the same substance that forms seashells and limestone. The coral polyp produces this by extracting naturally occurring chemicals from the sea water around it. The plants' contribution is considerable: the chalky growth of corals is up to 14 times faster in the sunlight, when the zooxanthellae produce food, than in the dark, when they provide no help.

The corals multiply as well as grow.

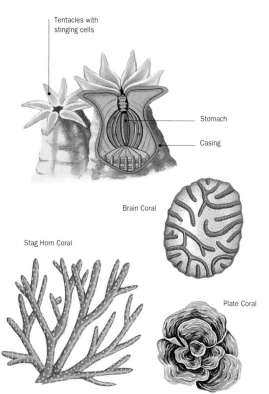

Tentacles with
stinging cells

Stomach

Casing

Brain Coral

Stag Horn Coral

Plate Coral

IMMOBILE ANIMALS *As they
multiply, coral polyps build
elaborately shaped colonies,
ranging from turrets (above)
to the distinctive 'stag horn',
'brain' and 'plate' forms.
Each polyp constructs a
hard outer casing (left,
above), expanding out of it
when feeding. It uses its
tentacles to trap food.*

Individual polyps are able to clone exact
copies of themselves by a process called
'budding', simply pinching off a small sec-
tion of an existing polyp to produce a tiny
new polyp that grows alongside. In time,
this produces a mass of genetically identical
polyps all living in one chalky mass: a coral
colony. The exact pattern in which each
polyp duplicates itself helps to determine
the ultimate shape of the colony – whether
branching or fluted, bulbous or plate-like.

The underlying pattern is characteristic
of the particular species of coral. As the
water surges through the channels of the
reef, a coral colony's ultimate form will be a
version of the species pattern modified by
the local conditions: a trade-off between
resisting the power of the currents and
gaining as much light as possible. The
former is best achieved by compact shapes,
the latter by spreading and branching
growth. Millions of coral colonies belonging
to hundreds of different coral species
combine to make the living mass of a coral

COLOURFUL PLANTATION
*A colony of tube worms
burrow in the coral.*

reef. Australia's Great Barrier Reef alone is
estimated to contain between 200 and 350
species of coral.

CONSTRUCTION, ABRASION AND EROSION

Corals are not the only creatures building
the reef. Numerous others contribute their
quota of calcium carbonate: barnacles and

clams, tube worms and moss animals (bryozoans) all huddle on the reef, while little
snails called vermetids also opt for a sedentary life, fusing their tubular shells to the
coral framework. Less obvious, yet highly
significant, is a group of plants known as
the encrusting algae. Spreading themselves
thinly across the reef under a chalky
shield, and looking more like knobbly pink
stone than vegetation, they are the cement
of the reef, welding together rubble and
sand and so reinforcing the whole reef
structure against the power of the waves.

As fast as the corals and algae add to
the hard structure of the reef, other creatures, directly or indirectly, wear it down –
a process known as bioerosion. Sponges,
fungi, burrowing sea worms and molluscs
bore holes in the coral structure for protection, mining mechanically, or dissolving
away the limestone with acid. Grazing
molluscs and sea urchins inadvertently
scrape away the surface of coral as they
browse on short tufts of seaweed.

Other reef inhabitants prey directly on
the coral itself, undeterred by the hard
chalky armour with its many razor-sharp
edges. Parrotfish (Scaridae) have exceptionally tough, horny beaks with which
they snap off pieces of coral, then crunch
through the outer casing to feed on the
soft polyps and algae (continued on page 148)

REEFS UNDER THREAT

For thousands of years, coral reefs have survived periodic destruction by natural forces: hurricanes and earthquakes frequently take their toll, shattering delicate arms of limestone or breaking off whole coral colonies, which tumble to the seabed and pile up as lifeless rubble. The destruction makes way for new growth and maintains a healthy mixture of species, ensuring that no single species comes to dominate

CORAL BLOCKS *Hard, compacted limestone from the base of coral reefs is used for building.*

the reef. Coral has a remarkable ability to self-repair, and under normal circumstances a reef will return to its former glory within a few decades.

However, in more recent times, coral reefs have been subjected to all kinds of additional damage from human activities. Mining and blast-fishing are probably the most conspicuous, although other, more subtle, causes may be equally devastating in their effects.

As a raw material, coral has many uses. It yields lime, and is valuable as a building material for the construction industry. Ironically, the

UNSEEN DAMAGE *Fishermen have unwittingly damaged this barrel sponge.*

demand for new buildings is often fuelled by a growth in tourism, as people flock to marvel at the beauty of the reef – and tourism easily damages the very reef on which a resort's popularity is founded. Careless snorkellers may stand on the frail polyps, or damage the brittle coral with the uncontrolled kick of a flipper. Even the accumulated suntan oil from hundreds of swimmers harms the normally resilient reef.

In addition, corals and decorative shells, especially those of conch, abalone, clam and cowrie, are collected in large numbers to be sold as curios. Alongside them in the souvenir shops there may be dried starfish and stuffed turtles, while 'precious' red and black corals are gathered to make pieces of jewellery.

Although traditional fishing methods cause little damage to a reef, they are inevitably being superseded by more efficient and ingenious techniques. These new methods catch more fish, and therefore supply not only the local food demand but also the expanding export markets. However, they are also more destructive.

To increase their catch, spear fishermen have taken to using bleach (an irritant) to flush reclusive

AT RISK *The animals of the coral reef include many with beautiful shells, whose survival is imperilled by souvenir hunters.*

fish from their hiding places. Commercial fishermen now frequently trawl reefs, and even use dynamite explosives to kill fish – shattering the very framework of the reef. There is also increasing demand for colourful aquarium fish. Sodium cyanide, which is toxic to coral, is used by aquarium collectors to stun fish temporarily so that they may be caught alive.

Underwater activities are not the only ones to harm coral. The development of adjacent land, for agriculture, hotels or roads, can

have devastating results. Removal of trees, particularly coastal mangroves, means that freshwater run-off bearing soil, pesticides and sewage, flows unimpeded into the sea. The silt smothers the coral, shading it from the sun and choking the tiny polyps. Their usual cleaning system – a conveyor belt of beating hairs flushing silt particles out on a film of mucus – is overwhelmed by the deluge.

Some reef death has no local cause. During the 1980s, there was a mysterious decline in the reefs of the Caribbean and Indo-Pacific region. Some of the corals ejected their zooxanthellae, the microscopic plants that turn sunlight and sea water into food, turned white and died – a phenomenon known as bleaching. There is a suggestion

DYING CORAL *This coral has become bleached on one side, a deadly blight that is spreading to reefs throughout the world.*

that the thinning ozone layer is allowing more ultraviolet light to reach the zooxanthellae and damage them.

Bleaching seems mainly to take place, however, for reasons that are not understood, where water temperatures have risen above 30°C (86°F). Its widespread occurrence may be an indicator that the seas are warming up, just one aspect of global warming caused by the build-up of 'greenhouse gases' from the burning of fossil fuels.

TEEMING WITH LIFE *Coral reefs may be home to up to a third of all known species of sea fish. With their endless nooks and crannies, they are* an ideal refuge for fish, as well as other animals and plants, from sea urchins and sponges to sea slugs and octopuses.

1. Imperial angelfish
2. Pufferfish
3. Leather jacket
4. Triggerfish
5. Parrotfish
6. Basslet
7. Damselfish
8. Butterfly fish
9. Moorish idol
10. Stonefish
11. Moray eel
12. Octopus
13. Triton snail
14. Crown of thorns
15. Clownfish
16. Sea slug
17. Grouper
18. Cleaner wrasse
19. Barracuda
20. White-tip reef shark

LIVING TOGETHER

In the overcrowded tumult of life on the coral reef, living in close proximity with others is inevitable. Some animals have taken the close association one step further, evolving relationships with members of a quite different species. Although such teamwork is usually to the mutual benefit of both parties, the participants are not actively or intentionally 'cooperating' – it is a system that runs on instinct and selective advantages, not intelligence or idealism.

In the sandy bottom adjacent to the reef, a small shrimp works furiously to excavate a burrow which, on completion, is promptly taken over by a cream-coloured goby (*Smilogobius*). The goby, reluctant to leave its new home, remains on sentry duty at the entrance, snapping up odd morsels exposed by the shrimp's efforts. Meanwhile, the shrimp continues to put in hard physical labour, diligently maintaining the shared burrow. It is clear that the goby benefits, but at first sight there seems to be no advantage to the shrimp in allowing the intruder to stay. On closer observation, however, it becomes obvious that the shrimp is virtually blind, and that the goby, with its bulbous eyes, scans the area for predators. The shrimp, which trails an antenna over the back of its bodyguard, senses danger through the movement of the fish. Faced with a threat, both disappear into their joint bolt hole in an instant.

Even less likely relationships have evolved between fish and giant stinging anemones. On the Great Barrier Reef alone, 29 species of fish convene with 13 different species of anemone. The tangled tentacles of sea anemones are endowed with sprung, poisonous barbs that fire on contact, injecting toxin into any creature unwary enough to stray into their deadly caress. Yet the little clownfish (*Amphiprion* species) and others enjoy apparent immunity, passing unharmed through the lethal thicket, and sinking deep into an anemone's tentacles if danger threatens.

The tiny clownfish, typically yellow, orange or red with white bands, have to work for their privileged position safe within the arms of the anemone. Anemones secrete a special slime for self-protection, a substance that stops the stinging cells on one tentacle from discharging when they contact other tentacles or the anemone's body. Rather than acting as a bullet-proof vest and deflecting the stings, the slimy mucus prevents them from firing at all. Dicing with death, a clownfish must endure fleeting encounters with an anemone, deftly brushing against a tentacle or two, until it

SAFE FOR SOME *The stinging tentacles of a sea anemone form a safe refuge for the clownfish.*

CLEANING SERVICE *A grouper fish is being cleaned by members of two different species: a shrimp and a wrasse.*

evolved for this purpose, they now double as an advertisement to attract customers. Cleaner fish usually establish cleaning stations at prominent coral protuberances.

The patrons do not usually need much persuasion. Large fish of all kinds – goatfish, parrotfish, groupers, moray eels and jackfish – all evidently uncomfortable with their burden of parasites, gather at the station to wait their turn. The tiny cleaners work over the body of each impassive client, picking off clinging parasites, meticulously removing pieces of damaged skin – and obtaining a meal in the process. Despite darting provocatively inside the mouth and between the sensitive gills of large predators, the cleaners are almost never eaten while undertaking their risky job.

The cleaning service is clearly an invaluable one: some large fish apparently spend as much time being cleaned as they do looking for food. In the West Indies, when the cleaner species were experimentally removed from a reef, many fish left the region. Those that remained became unhealthy with sore and tattered fins.

One animal cheats the system. The sabre-toothed blenny (*Aspidontus taeniatus*) imitates both the colour patterns of the cleaner wrasse and its characteristic jerky movements. As trusting fish allow the fraud to approach, it leaps forward, and instead of removing a parasite, takes a chunk of flesh from a fin or a gill.

has acquired enough slime to coat its surface and trick the anemone into accepting the fish as part of itself.

By sheltering amid the hundreds of tentacles, a fish is protected from predators. It is not certain what, if anything, it offers in return for its safe haven, but it may drop morsels of food that the anemone picks up, and defend its anemone territory from butterfly fish (*Chaetodon* species) which bite at the tentacles, seemingly indifferent to the stinging cells. Clownfish have even been seen apparently tempting predators with bold displays in order to lure them into the mass of stinging tentacles where they become an easy meal for the anemone. Most clownfish stay with the same anemone for their entire life, never straying more than a few feet away to feed, and laying their eggs at its base for safety.

Several species of shrimp also live in association with anemones. Many of them, such as the banded *Periclimenes* species, find morsels of food in their anemone partner, and also provide a beneficial cleaning 'service', removing, with their tweezer-like pincers, wedged particles that the anemone cannot dislodge for itself. The service is often extended to other willing recipients,

be they fish or human divers. As it clambers over a fish, the shrimp removes parasites, mucus and loose scales, and cleans wounds, sometimes actually cutting into the skin to remove infected areas. Most of the detritus can be used as food, so the shrimp's 'motives' are not altruistic ones, but it aids the larger animal, nonetheless, and the shrimp probably enjoys some protection from predators by the company it keeps.

The shrimps are among a number of animals that make their living from grooming others. Several species of fish, typically small, slender, brightly coloured animals, are also in the cleaning business. They include the cleaner wrasse (*Labroides*) of the Indian and Pacific oceans and the neon gobies (*Gobiosoma*) of the Caribbean. Like shrimps, they usually have a distinctive pattern of stripes that may well protect them from attack by their larger companions. Although the stripes no doubt

PAIRING UP *Teamwork means survival for the blind shrimp and its sighted goby companion.*

LOW TIDE *The coral polyps retreat into their hard cases when exposed by low tide, as here on the Great Barrier Reef off Australia.*

within. The ground-up casing of the coral is passed through their digestive tract and returned to the reef as a shower of fine sand.

Thus the constant building of the reef is balanced by a steady attrition, not only in the crunching, rasping and boring of the reef's inhabitants but also in the constant pounding action of the waves that crash relentlessly onto its outer ramparts.

THE ATOLL ENIGMA

Because of the light demands of their plant partners, corals are only able to grow in water less than about 165 ft (50 m) deep. Consequently, most hug the shallow margins of continents or islands – except, that is, for coral atolls, those perfect circles of coral characteristic of the Indo-Pacific region that seem to rise out of the deep ocean, miles from the nearest land. Their origin puzzled the young Charles Darwin as he sailed across the tropical seas in HMS *Beagle*. Indeed, it was Darwin who correctly guessed the answer to this mystery.

He proposed that each atoll was originally an ordinary reef, fringing a tiny circular island – an island that was the tip of a volcanic peak towering up from the seabed. Darwin suggested that over time such an island might gradually subside and sink beneath the waves. If the island sank slowly enough, its coral reef would continue to grow, and would keep pace with the surface of the sea. To begin with, the reef would become separated from the shrinking island by a widening lagoon until, in the end, the island would drop completely out of view, leaving behind the circle of coral, like a halo without its saint.

At a time when science knew nothing of plate tectonics – how powerful movements in the Earth's crust could result in the uplift or subsidence of the seabed – people were sceptical about Darwin's theory. It was not until 1953 that he was proved correct. Drilling through Eniwetok atoll in the Marshall Islands, scientists found volcanic rock beneath 4308 ft (1313 m) of coral limestone. This was just the evidence they needed to prove that the volcanic rock had once been near enough to the surface to support coral growth.

REACHING FOR THE LIGHT

Although some reefs, such as the one at Eniwetok, may be tens of millions of years old, others are geologically quite young: the southernmost portion of the Great Barrier Reef was not established until 2 million years ago, and many reefs in the Atlantic are only 10-15 000 years old. When these younger reefs first began to form in tropical seas, the northerly and southerly latitudes were a bleak, frozen landscape, devastated by the last Ice Age. At the height of the most recent glaciation 18 000 years ago, the glaciers and the polar icecaps had captured such huge amounts of the planet's water, solidified into ice, that the sea level throughout the world was about 390 ft (120 m) lower than it is today. The land extended further and the corals grew a short distance from the shore.

Gradually, as the world thawed and glaciers retreated, sea levels everywhere began to rise. For the corals this was potentially disastrous – the zooxanthellae must have sunlight to make their food. Where possible, the answer was to grow upwards, building towards the light, and thus eventually forming barrier reefs some distance from the modern shoreline.

Mostly the rise in sea level following the end of a glaciation was sufficiently gradual – a process taking thousands of years – for the reef corals to keep pace, always maintaining their upper pinnacles in the sunlit surface waters. But it was not always that way. Sea level has risen and fallen many times in history, sometimes at a much faster rate, 'drowning' reefs that could not keep up with a rapid rise, or stranding former reefs out of water as the sea level plummeted, leaving them open to erosion by wind, rain, tides and coastal river outflows. When the sea rose again, fresh corals

TUBE CORAL *Coral polyps release packets of sperm or eggs into the water.*

THE MATING GAME *Coral polyps form eggs and sperm within their bodies in huge numbers. They release them from the single body opening that serves as mouth and anus.*

grew on the sculpted foundations of formerly stranded reefs, so that the ghost of the old shaped the pattern of the new. Today, stranded reefs can still be found on many coral coasts, including Barbados, Jamaica and New Guinea.

The age-old struggle to reach the light results in a daily battle between coral colonies. As they slowly grow, coral colonies encroach on their neighbours' space, shading them from the precious sunlight streaming in from above. Different species of coral employ different strategies in the fight: some extend tall limbs up above the thicket of their competitors to obtain light and nutrients, others extend the colony sideways over the rocks at an early stage to exclude trespassers from below. Many engage in local chemical warfare – poisoning, stinging or even digesting any trespassers that try to invade their space.

After seven to ten years of growing and dividing, the coral polyps reach an age when they can reproduce sexually. Unlike budding, sexual reproduction generates swimming coral larvae that can disperse over long distances, allowing the new generation to flee the overcrowded reef and colonise new shores. For the coral this is highly advantageous: the larvae, carrying some of their parents' valuable genes, have higher survival chances if they are spread over a wide area.

Because they are unable to move about to find a suitable mate, coral polyps rely on the water to do the work for them, releasing their sperm or eggs into the currents. It is a game of chance, in which the odds of survival are increased by sheer numbers. The extravagant release of millions upon millions of eggs and sperm ensures that some will be spared from the small crabs, fish and other plankton-feeders that feast on such delicacies.

MASS REPRODUCTION

To increase their chances of successful mating – which relies on encountering sperm or eggs of the same species in the vastness of the ocean – many coral species have evolved a remarkable synchronicity in their spawning. The phenomenon is at its most dramatic on the Great Barrier Reef. Here, just once a year, on a warm, still night following the full moon in November or December, there is a flurry of silent activity among the polyps along the entire length of the reef. Prompted by some mysterious, invisible cue, the spectacle begins. Everywhere, tiny parcels of eggs and sperm are jettisoned into the currents – pink, green, red and orange. Like miniature parachutes in reverse, they sail upwards to mingle with the rest of the plankton. In this kaleidoscopic deluge, the packaging melts away, and clouds of spawn intertwine and merge.

Those eggs encountered by sperm of the same species are fertilised and develop into tiny, globular larvae, propelled by near-invisible beating hairs. After hazardous days or weeks in the open water, when most perish, a very few sense a suitable place to settle, probably guided by chemical cues. They spread the base of their flexible body into a disc, and cement it down onto a hard surface that will become their permanent resting place. In time, these young polyps begin to secrete their chalky casing and to generate copies of themselves – the start of a new colony, and, perhaps, of an entirely new reef.

LIFE ON THE REEF

Night and day, there is always some kind of activity going on among the enormous variety of creatures that make their home on a coral reef. In this labyrinth of the sea, life assumes some of its most gorgeous colours and intricate patterns.

A frilled gash of emerald and turquoise, marbled with black, pulsates gently in the shallow water. The intense blue-greens of the scalloped lips contrast strikingly with the pinks, browns and yellows of the sponges, sea squirts and delicately tinted moss animals that form a living patchwork on either side. As a shadow falls across the reef, the brilliant zigzag of flesh shudders and withdraws inward behind the ancient, fluted edges of a large double shell. Unmistakably, the ridged and encrusted shell is that of a giant clam (*Tridacna* species); its base is sunk out of view, apparently engulfed by the spreading body of the reef.

Giant clams are the very largest of the hinged-shelled molluscs, a group that includes oysters, scallops and mussels. At its most colossal, the largest species of giant clam (*T. gigas*) reaches lengths of more than 4 ft (1.2 m) and weights of over 500 lb (227 kg). However, contrary to popular legend, giant clams do not snap shut to trap the feet of incautious divers. The hauling together of their gigantic hinged valves is actually a slow, laboured reflex, which any swimmer could easily evade. Nonetheless, a person would struggle to wrestle open a large specimen once it was closed.

The muscle that clamps the shells together thus serves to protect the delicate flesh from predators and from the drying effects of low tide. Like corals, giant clams have tiny plant cells in their bodies, from which they obtain a proportion of their food. The food produced by the plant cells through photosynthesis supplements the clam's diet of plankton. This is filtered from large quantities of sea water that is drawn in through an intake tube and passes across the sieve-like gills where the food particles are trapped. The sea water is then forced out through the exit tube.

The clam's internal plants, like all others, need light. It is for this reason that the body of the clam has become contorted over evolutionary time, so that the richly coloured flesh of the mantle, which in most other clams is tucked safely away inside the base of the shell, protrudes into the sunlight. The clam's bright pigments act as a sunscreen for the vulnerable flesh, filtering out the Sun's harmful rays, but allowing enough light to enter to fuel the food-making process conducted by the internal plants.

A LIVING LANDSCAPE

Giant clams live in shallow reef flats – sand-filled lagoons on the shoreward side of fringing reefs, scattered with isolated clumps of coral, coral rubble and patches of seagrass.

Between the mosaic of coral outcrops, starfish, sea cucumbers and conch shells litter the sandy bottom. Tuskfish (*Choerodon*) dig in the sand for tiny crustaceans and worms, attracting crowds of smaller fish that swoop in to grab any leftover morsels. From time to time, an elegant angelfish

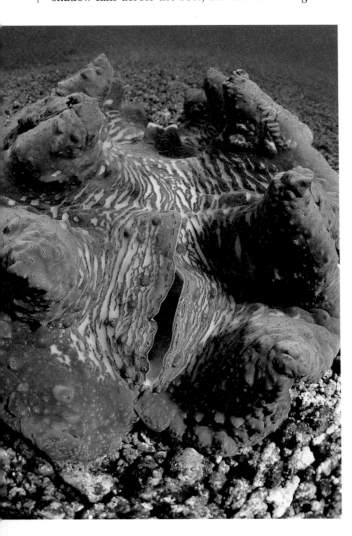

HOUSE PLANTS *A giant clam's rippling lips contain minute plants that make food.*

CORAL CRUNCHER *Parrotfish*
break off pieces of coral with their
horny beaks and eat the polyps.

(*Pomacanthus*) swims by, or a blue-hued parrotfish (*Scarus*) arrives to crunch at the coral polyps. Around an isolated coral sculpture, a cloud of small, striped damselfish (*Abudefduf saxatilis*) hangs in the clear water. Should danger threaten, they dart for cover, vanishing suddenly into hiding places in the coral.

On the coral itself, every inch of space is occupied. Gleaming cowries slide across patches of fine algal turf, anemone tentacles sway between coral fingers, and the feathered crowns of serpulid tube worms (*Spirobranchus*) spiral above their burrows like miniature Christmas trees. Pincushions of dark sea urchin spines (*Diadema*) extend menacingly from cracks.

Elsewhere, the green eyes of multicoloured mantis shrimps (*Odontodactylus scyllarus*) peer from crevices, seeking prey. These beautiful 6 in (15 cm) crustaceans are armed with a pair of bludgeon-like forelimbs that can strike so fast and powerfully that they are able to shatter the glass of an aquarium, and can easily crush the shell of a crab, snail or small clam.

The reef flat, which stretches out from the sandy shore as far as the backbone of the reef, is sheltered from the full force of the waves by the reef crest. The crest is the breakwater of the reef, where waves curl into a

BRIGHT AND BEAUTIFUL
Cowries are molluscs, and
among the most spectacular
inhabitants of the reef.

white foam over a ridge that is reinforced by layers of smooth encrusting coralline algae. On the crest itself, corals may be stunted or absent because conditions are too rough for them to survive, but away from the direct impact of the waves, they grow in profusion, benefiting from the oxygen and nutrients that are brought by the churning waves.

Lively butterfly fish, triggerfish, wrasse,

snappers and angelfish throng the reef-top passageways, flitting between the coral heads in search of food. Parrotfish, filefish and pufferfish feed on the coral polyps, while the majority of predators pick at any invertebrate that reveals itself from a crevice for a split second. Fewer than 15 per cent of the fish species are plant eaters, yet so effective is their grazing that seaweeds are kept short and hardly any greenery is evident on the reef.

Some species of the tiny damselfish (*Pomacentridae*) are meticulous grazers, pulling out any tough or unpalatable plants on their particular patch of reef and discarding them. This 'weeding' maintains a crop of young, nutritious algae. The fish defend their seaweed allotments with zeal, chasing off any intruders that might hope to steal a mouthful.

On the seaward side of the reef crest are the spurs and canyons of the reef's outer slope, broad buttresses of coral alternating with narrow, eroded gullies, that serve to diffuse the destructive energy of approaching waves. From the base of

the buttresses drops a plunging wall, wreathed in flexible soft corals, spectacular sponges, plumes of crinoid feather stars and trailing sea whips. Hundreds of colourful fish dance across the cascade of coral, and shoals of silvery anchovies hover near the top of the wall.

Lower down, caves and recesses offer hiding places for some of the larger reef fish, such as big groupers and enormous Napoleon wrasse (*Cheilinus undulatus*), which may reach lengths of 6 ft (1.8 m). Sharks, jackfish (trevally) and barracudas patrol the drop-off, alert for reef inhabitants straying from the safety of the coral. Occasionally, other open-sea visitors loom out of the void: schools of mackerel, tuna fish and even vast, flapping manta rays.

COMMUNICATING WITH COLOUR

Colour is everywhere. In the clarity of the tropical waters, reef inhabitants seem to flaunt their vivid hues, embellishing the scene with a riotous exhibition of scarlet and jade, lilac and indigo, ochre and citrus – many emblazoned with patterns in contrasting shades. Lurid sea slugs, decked out in pink, blue and orange, glide over

HOME ON THE REEF *A reef offers homes to many creatures from Napoleon wrasse (above) to feather stars (right).*

PLAID FISH *The rectangular patterns of this long-nosed hawkfish camouflage it against sea fans.*

the rocks, a sprout of feathery gills blazing on their backs. These shell-less snails feed on sea squirts, sponges and sea anemones.

Glowing colours and bold patterns serve many purposes on the reef. For some animals, like the giant clam, colours act as protection from ultraviolet light. For others, colour and pattern constitute an effective sign language, acting as advertisements for mates of the same species, as warning signs that they are not pleasant to eat, or as identity tags. Colours often become more intense at breeding time, when the need to be recognised by a potential mate across a crowded reef seems to outweigh the added risk of being spotted by a predator.

In the unusual conditions of the coral reef, bright colours and camouflage are not necessarily incompatible. Here, camouflage is not restricted to the muted shades and drab tones associated with concealment on the seabed, since the corals and sponges themselves provide a colourful backdrop against which green, blue, yellow or pink animals can blend anonymously. The tartan hawkfish (*Oxycirrhites typus*) and long-nosed hawkfish are decorated with grids of bright interlocking lines that make them virtually indistinguishable from the spread of a similarly coloured sea fan.

Seemingly bold patterns, especially strong bands of the kind worn by the Moorish idol (*Zanclus cornutus*), help to

break up the outline of an animal, and make it less obvious to predators. Butterfly fish (*Chaetodon* species) are brilliantly coloured, and often have markings that look like an eye near to their tail fin. Their real eye is camouflaged by a dark vertical band. Predators have difficulty differentiating head from tail, particularly as the butterfly fish can swim backwards. When a predator dives for the false 'eye', the fish accelerates forwards, usually escaping with its vulnerable head end intact.

SHADES OF DANGER

Brazen colours and striking motifs may, alternatively, be used as a warning of danger to others – a sign of toxic stings, unpleasant taste, irritating secretions or aggressive territorial behaviour. Most of the flagrantly exposed invertebrates on a reef have poisons or stings as predator deterrents, and they are highly coloured to advertise the fact.

FALSE EYE *The spots on butterfly fish deflect attacks to their tail end providing a chance of escape.*

There are the multicoloured stinging anemones, the aptly named fire sea urchins coloured flame-bright orange and yellow, and the particularly ostentatious sea slugs, whose stinging cells are carried in their backs, ready to discharge at any perceived threat. In addition, more than half of the various showy tropical sponges are poisonous to fish.

An attacker, suffering an unpleasant encounter with any of these creatures, usually learns its lesson and, remembering that particular combination of colour and pattern, avoids it in the future.

Despite first impressions, not all creatures on the reef are brightly coloured. Behind the flamboyant characters that catch the eye of the diver, there lurk more self-effacing forms of life in muted dress. Some creatures wear the drab tones of rock or shadow, others conceal themselves in the cloak of darkness, or lurk deep inside the coral structure for safety.

UNDERCOVER OPERATORS

Some of the reef's deadliest creatures, the scorpionfish (*Scorpaenopsis, Scorpaena*) and the stonefish (*Synanceja*), do not employ warning coloration. Although their venom is only used in defence, any attacker that

HIDDEN DANGER *The scorpion fish (left) is camouflaged to resemble a coral surface with encrustations of seaweed. When swimming, the lionfish (opposite) resembles an exotic bird.*

enough for tiny particles of food to drift in on the currents of water, and for the diminutive males of the species to pass back and forth.

CREATURES OF THE NIGHT

Among the lurkers in coral dens and lairs are many nocturnal animals, temporary residents that leave their refuge only under the cover of night. They include squirrelfish (*Holocentrus*), soldierfish (*Myripristis*), cardinals (*Apogon*), sweepers (*Pempheris*) and bigeyes (*Priacanthus*), plus a whole range of reclusive invertebrates.

Night transforms the reef. The sweep of a torch shows that most of the daytime fish are at rest, hidden away in caves and under ledges. Their places are taken by wide-eyed nocturnal fish and numerous invertebrates. Crabs, lobsters and octopuses emerge to clamber over the coral. Urchins browse at seaweed, and featherstars crawl from crevices to festoon the reef with their fern-like arms. Hunting lionfish (*Pterois*) take cover among featherstars, their plumes of spines inconspicuous in the upward-pointing thicket. And everywhere, the colourful coral polyps themselves blossom from their cups of chalk, tentacles blindly grasping for minute planktonic animals in the current.

So it is that the coral reef never really sleeps: rather the animallife works in shifts, taking turns to rest, forage, eat and reproduce. By night, the coral polyps capture floating particles of food, by day they themselves may fall prey to carnivorous fish or starfish. Around the clock, invertebrates graze on algae, small fish eat the invertebrates, and larger fish eat the small fish. It is a pattern that is mirrored throughout the world's oceans, from the mangrove swamps to the rocky shores, from the open water to the depths. Everywhere, animals eat and are eaten, in a self-perpetuating cycle of life.

bites at the spines does not usually live to encounter the fish a second time. Warning colours are therefore irrelevant. Indeed, these predatory fish are virtually impossible to see, their complex colour and texture making them look exactly like a rock or coral outgrowth encrusted by algae. Patiently vigilant, they wait motionless for hours until an unsuspecting small fish or other prey approaches within striking distance. In an instant, it is sucked into the

predator's jaws, and the fish returns to invisible immobility.

Lurking and pouncing is a common tactic on the reef which has an almost unlimited number of cracks, caves and tunnels from which to stage an ambush. Moray eels (*Gymnothorax*) stalk their prey through the dark recesses, driving them into the open and then pouncing, their formidable jaws agape. Another predator, the elongated trumpetfish (*Aulostomus*), has developed a means of mobile ambush using the cover of a large non-threatening species such as the parrotfish. Fitting its long slender body to the well-rounded contours of the parrotfish, the trumpetfish tags along unnoticed. When the pair approach some potential prey, the trumpetfish lunges out, breaking cover, to grab a meal.

With predation so rife, many of the smaller, unprotected animals spend their time permanently hidden within the coral. Worms, crustaceans and molluscs cower in holes and burrows. The female coral gall-crab (*Hapalocarcinus*) takes concealment to extremes: remaining stationary, she allows the coral to grow around her until she is totally imprisoned inside. Just one small opening is left to her sanctuary, large

HEADSTAND *Trumpetfish sometimes rest with their heads down among the coral.*

77-003-2